DRT HOB t4 02/04

A HISTORY OF
SCOTTISH
FOOTBALL
IN
100
OBJECTS

A HISTORY OF SCOTTISH FOOTBALL IN 100 OBJECTS

AN ALTERNATIVE FOOTBALL MUSEUM

ANDY BOLLEN

ARENA
SPORT

This edition first published in Great Britain in 2019 by

ARENA SPORT
An imprint of Birlinn Limited
West Newington House
10 Newington Road
Edinburgh
EH9 1QS

www.arenasportbooks.co.uk

ISBN: 9781909715738
eBook ISBN: 9781788851688

British Library Cataloguing-in-Publication Data
A catalogue record for this book is available on request from the British Library.

Designed and typeset by Polaris Publishing, Edinburgh
www.polarispublishing.com

Printed in Great Britain by CPI Books Ltd

CONTENTS

To Sharron

INTRODUCTION

Welcome to the Alternative Scottish Football Museum. We hope you enjoy your visit. Please take your time to look around the exhibits on display in each of our great halls, wings, nooks and quiet, more reflective rooms.

I'm Andy Bollen, the museum curator, and I'll be taking you on a guided tour through the eclectic history of Scottish football in 100 carefully selected objects that typify the game north of the border. Our exhibits range from Jimmy Johnstone's oar to Aggie the tea lady's trolley, Panini sticker albums and the unique taste of Bovril. Learn why Puskás and Socrates should have been Scottish, just how versatile a dubious meat pie can be, and explore a range of wonders old and new – from Arthur Montford's jacket to the phone-in, Buckfast, vanishing spray, Twitter, VAR technology and flares (pyrotechnics, not 1970s attire). These exhibits distil the beauty of the Scottish game, standing as testament to the collective hypocrisy and foolishness which links these people, places and items to the nation's favourite drug: football.

Any questions?

Wonderful. Let's begin. Please follow me this way . . .

MAIN HALL

MAVERICKS
&
CHARACTERS

Exhibit 1
Chic Charnley & the Flashing Blade

Welcome to the main hall of the museum and to our first exhibit.

Traffic cones have become a familiar motif in the cultural fabric of Scotland's biggest city, Glasgow.

There's the famous one, set at a jaunty angle, on top of the Duke of Wellington statue. City chiefs regard it as vandalism and high treason, but it is loved by the people and stands as part artistic statement, part humour, part healthy disregard for authority. The coned statue, which stands outside Glasgow's Museum of Modern Art, is now a city landmark in its own right.

Then there's the other traffic cone, involving the footballer, Chic Charnley. It, too, has its own place in Glasgow and, by extension, Scottish football folklore.

Charnley is among the last of a generation of cult heroes to ply his trade in the Scottish game. His career spanned more than twenty years, starting at St Mirren in 1982, and taking in spells at clubs such as Hamilton, Hibernian and Dundee, yet he is probably best remembered for his four spells with Partick

Thistle . . . and the seventeen red cards he amassed over his career.

Charnley was the classic football contradiction: the hot-headed rogue with a heart of gold; the bampot who could play; the prodigious, left-sided maverick who, when he stayed on the park, was (in Scotland at least) one of the modern greats.

It's fair to assume that Charnley will be glad he's out of a game that would be unrecognisable to him now. One full of academy players, strict diets, feeble tackling and softened by too much money, too soon. He came from the mean streets and played football for the love of the game, not money.

However, Charnley gains entry into the Alternative Scottish Football Museum not for this but, instead, for a clash he had with two locals who dared question his footballing ability.

In the 1990s, Scottish football was broke. Many clubs operated without training facilities or academies and would often train on any available public park they could find, placing their players at the mercy of local kids with seemingly nothing better to do than hit golf balls at them.

On one fateful occasion, after receiving abuse from a couple of locals while training in Ruchill Park with Partick Thistle, Charnley challenged his abusers to 'take it outside'. Since they were already outside, he rescheduled, inviting them to return after training for a square-go. As a dedicated, professional athlete, he would let nothing get in the way of his day job.

The challenged pair returned later, wielding a samurai sword and a dagger and accompanied by a dog that appeared to have been spawned by Satan himself. Charnley, unfazed, attacked them with the only weapon he had at his disposal – a traffic cone left behind after training. Like Jackie Chan taking down a room full of assassins with whatever props were available to him, Charnley went to work. The devil dog soon realised that it was up against a wilder creature than itself and quickly scarpered. Seeing the dog head for freedom affected the focus of its owners and they, too, made a break for it, though not before one left Chic with a scar on his hand from the attack. As the erudite *Observer* journalist, Kevin McKenna, would explain in his column in April 2010, 'Charnley had been raised in the neighbouring *arrondissement* of Possil where to survive the week was to have endured your own personal Passchendale.'

Of course, let's not forget, this was Charnley's workplace. How many people have staged a re-enactment of Akira Kurosawa's *Seven Samurai* in their office? The incident, as bizarre and ludicrously lampoonish as it sounds, established a place for Charnley forever in Scottish football lore – and thus his place as the first exhibit in this museum.

Charnley's default position was always to hit back and it was a trait that followed him throughout his tempestuous career. His trouble, though, wasn't only fighting numpties in Ruchill Park, or flare-ups with opposition players. His charge sheet includes the time he smacked his St Mirren manager, Alex Miller, with football boots, not forgetting his ignominious exit from Clydebank for punching his coach, Tony Gervaise. There was also a fracas in Love Street when he played for St Mirren against Dundee United and cracked Darren Jackson's jaw, which started an almighty riot in the tunnel and saw the opposing managers, Davie Hay and Jim McLean, come to blows.

Charnley's career took him to seventeen clubs (he's credited as playing for Cork City but didn't), which included four stints at Partick Thistle, two at St Mirren and what many consider his most successful two seasons: at Dundee in 1996/97, and then at Hibernian the following season.

The transfers point to an impatient personality, someone who needed to be handled in a certain way. He was a lightning rod for chaos and havoc and it's a wonder he managed stay in the game for as long as he did, drowning in systems and tactical strategies and strangled with over-coaching. He would thrive under managers who knew how to get the best out of him, managers like the inimitable John Lambie, who encouraged his direct style of play and allowed him the freedom to express himself.

Unlike most of today's young stars, Charnley only played a few times for his secondary school team and some Boys Guild football. He was too busy watching his childhood team, Celtic, both home and away, when he should have been playing. It wasn't until an uncle noticed his talent and pushed him to train that he narrowed his focus and joined Possil Villa and, later, the junior side, Rutherglen Glencairn.

James Callaghan Charnley was a delightful player but his unstable behaviour often overshadowed his will to entertain. To the purist, he was a walking liability; to the fans, he was a wizard who clearly understood he wasn't too far-removed from the punter paying at the gate. Perhaps his desire to entertain stemmed from an understanding that he'd not long left the terraces himself.

His greatest personal achievement occurred when he turned out for Celtic after then manager Lou Macari invited him to play in a testimonial match for Manchester United forward Mark Hughes. The call came while he was in the pub, midway through a mammoth session. He hung up the phone and decided to travel down to Manchester with pals, change into his suit and get dropped off at the team hotel with his boots in a plastic bag.

Charnley later claimed it was too much for him when, throughout the warm-up at Old Trafford, the Celtic fans sung his name. He was so moved by finally achieving a lifelong dream of pulling on the famous 'hoops' that all he did was cry. In one photograph from the match, Charnley is caught smiling as he skips away from United legend Eric Cantona, no shrinking violet himself. Charnley had deliberately kept his legs open to invite Cantona to nutmeg him, then quickly closed them and run off with the ball.

Charnley was one of the best players on the park that day. He set up two goals and did enough to earn a contract but Lou Macari, who would soon be sacked by the Parkhead hierarchy, took the fact Charnley holidayed with his Thistle teammates instead of accepting a three-week tour with Celtic in Canada as a snub and blocked a permanent move.

In April 2018, discussing the death of his mentor and friend, John Lambie, on Radio Scotland's *Sportsound* show, Charnley gave his version of events. He stated Macari had spoken to an unnamed former legend at the club who advised against his signing. Like football tends to do, time moved on quickly and the moment passed. However, it's a scenario many neutrals would've enjoyed.

Now working as a taxi driver, Chic Charnley is still seldom out of the news. He recently ferried a group of Rangers supporters whose bus had broken down to their game for free. They might be rival supporters but they were genuine football people needing to get to see their team. News also emerged of a woman who Charnley talked out of taking her life.

A maverick, a one-off and a true football man, Chic Charnley was, and remains, one of Scottish sport's most fascinating enigmas.

Exhibit 2
Cult Heroes

Elevation to 'cult status' varies from team to team.

In a traditional footballing sense, the hero is usually regarded as 'an honest big player', with 'loads of heart', who is 'solid in the tackle', 'gives his all' and, preferably, is 'one of our own', having actually supported the club as a boy.

Such players are usually loved because they display regular elements of psychosis and brutal levels of dedication, which endear them to the support. They play with a 'no nonsense' approach, are commanding in the air and are physically dominant. It's not a requirement but they usually have a broken nose and have lost their front teeth in battle. They're often unfashionable and, no matter the opposition, always throw themselves in the line of fire.

They're *that* guy.

In the 1970s, the legendary Manchester United player and Scotland internationalist, Jim Holton, married my mother's cousin, Nessie McLaughlin. This promoted him instantly, as befits the warped outlook of a football-mad kid, to my uncle. Holton was the performance of the cult hero at international level. Powerful, unrelenting and committed. He even had his own terrace song, a reworking of the eponymous number from *Jesus Christ Superstar*: 'Six foot two / Eyes of blue / Big Jim Holton's after you.' Incidentally, 'Uncle Jim' was six foot one and had brown eyes.

As for other club cult heroes, sometimes players who are otherwise awful become weirdly iconic in return for something as simple as scoring a single sublime goal. In 2002, the much-maligned Dutch centre-half Bert Konterman scored a 30-yard thunderbolt for Rangers against Celtic at Hampden in the CIS League Cup semi-final, laying waste to Celtic's treble hopes in the process. Rangers also had 'Big' Tam Forsyth, or 'Jaws' as he was known. They also had the 'Tin Man', Ted McMinn.

At Celtic you'd think Bobo Balde would be a perfect candidate for cult hero status, but he blotted his copybook towards the end of his eight-year spell at Parkhead by choosing to run down his lucrative, £28,000-a-week contract from the fringes of the first team. Jóhannes Eðvaldsson and, in his two seasons he spent at the club, Thomas Gravesen would fit Celtic cult status. Then there's 'Mad' Martin Hardie, a *bona fide* Partick Thistle icon. And, of course, it would be remiss to overlook the aforementioned Chic Charnley.

Airdrieonians goalkeeper John Martin was always good for a 'red top' photo op. So too Stevie Gray and Justin Fashanu, who, despite only making a handful of appearances for 'The Diamonds', nevertheless became a cult hero. Albion Rovers had Vic Kasule and Ray Franchetti. Motherwell had Brian Martin. St Johnstone had Roddy Grant. Hibs had George Best. Aberdeen had Doug Rougvie. Dundee United had Hamish McAlpine.

Scottish football has had many cult heroes, but they shouldn't be confused with 'fans' favourites'. Paul Sturrock's fifteen-year love affair with Dundee United is a good example of where the distinction must be made. A loyal servant? Yes. A prolific goalscorer? Absolutely. A hero amongst the terraces? Unquestionably. But categorically not a cult hero in my mind, despite many polls saying otherwise. Claudio Caniggia was a fans' favourite during his short spell at Dundee, as were Franck Sauzee at Hibs and Jose Quitongo at Hearts – but none are cult heroes, in my opinion.

Players rarely stay at the same club long enough to establish their cult status. The cult hero would deck an opponent with a left hook, or go in goal if all the subs had been used up and the team needed a 'keeper. The cult hero would breach the club's code of conduct by ignoring a drinking curfew forty-eight hours before a game. He'd get pulled over zooming around Edinburgh's Old Town, going the wrong way down a one-way-street with Dwight Yorke and loads of lassies in the back . . . a typical night out for Russell Latapy during his time at Hibs!

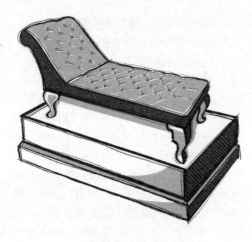

Exhibit 3
Flawed Genius

'Flawed genius'. A hideously overused expression yet, like most clichés, it endures as there is, generally, a huge dollop of truth contained within it.

I'm sure every country has its fair share of flawed geniuses but, in Scotland, there seems to be something in our DNA which produces more than the global average. We love the flawed genius so much, we even imported some to our game. George Best and Paul Gascoigne immediately come to mind.

More recently, Hibernian may have had Garry O'Connor, Derek Riordan and Anthony Stokes but they were wee laddies compared to George Best and his 1979/80 season at Hibs. At first, the public was dismissive of the mercurial Northern Irishman's move to Edinburgh. This was Best in his 'Fat Elvis' period, a jaded star on both the wane and the wine. And yet he was handsomely rewarded for his trouble. Best reportedly received £2,000 a week from Hibs at a time when some of his teammates were on £120. Still, the investment paid off immediately, with 20,000 fans cramming into Easter Road to witness his home debut against Partick Thistle. At this juncture, it might be helpful to imagine the classic Irving Berlin number 'Let's Face the Music and Dance'. At the start, the song advises 'There may be trouble ahead'. So it came to pass with Best and Hibs. On the eve of a cup tie against Ayr United, rescheduled for a Sunday because it clashed with a Scotland-France rugby international, the Hibs team decamped to the North British Hotel in Edinburgh. After the rugby, Best met up with French captain Jean-Pierre Rives and Debbie Harry of Blondie. At eleven o'clock the following morning, the party was just starting to wind down. Hibs won 2-0, no thanks to Best, who missed the game. It was an incident typical of his time in Scotland, which lasted just 325 days, during which he played twenty-two times for the Hibees and scored three goals.

Gascoigne lasted longer at Rangers – a whole four seasons, in fact – but his life off the field (and sometimes on it) was every bit as eventful. He scored thirty-nine goals in 103 games for Rangers but made as many appearances on the front pages of newspapers as their back.

Neither Best nor Gazza was Scottish but they clearly enjoyed the hospitality and genuine warmth shown towards them when they played here.

Jim Baxter is probably our homegrown version of George Best. Lavishly talented, regularly controversial and perhaps a little too well acquainted with the bevvy. Jimmy Johnstone's career may have stalled if it hadn't been for Jock Stein's relentless attempts to keep him out of the pub. Then there were those like George Connelly of Celtic, an enormous talent but fragile and fraught with it. These were players who weren't cut out for the job they appeared to excel in.

But none comes close to the flawed genius of Hughie Gallacher.

Born in Bellshill in 1903, Gallacher played 129 times for Airdrie, scoring 100 goals. As one of the cornerstones of the team's Scottish Cup win in 1924, he caught the eye of Newcastle. After making the move to Tyneside, he soon became a firm favourite in the north-east of England, scoring 143 times in 174 appearances and captaining the club to its most recent league title in 1927. His drinking, though. It was the stuff of legend. Reportedly fond of a drink *before* a game, never mind after, Gallacher was eventually offloaded by Newcastle to Chelsea. During his four seasons with the 'Blues', he was arrested for fighting Fulham fans and fell out with the board over wages. The fact he managed to bang in eighty-one goals in 144 appearances was almost a footnote to his time there.

Gallacher was said to be the same man off the park as he was on it: fearless, ferocious and quick to anger. Imagine a composite of Diego Maradona, Liam Gallagher and Garrincha – a World Cup winner with Brazil and serial womaniser who succumbed to liver disease while in an alcoholic coma, leaving fourteen children behind – and you're halfway to Hughie Gallacher.

Gallacher left Chelsea for Derby but spiralling debts and a costly divorce left him bankrupt. His transfer fee was given directly to the courts.

He represented Scotland twenty times scoring twenty-four goals and was one of the acclaimed 'Wembley Wizards', playing in the side that beat England 5–1 in 1928.

After bouncing around the lower leagues, he retired from football in the late 1930s and settled back in the north-east. At one point, he tried his hand as a sports journalist before settling on a new life as a labourer. When his second wife died, he started drinking heavily again and was involved in a domestic incident, an argument with one of his children. Gallacher overreacted, throwing an ashtray at his son, Mattie. The boy ran out of the house to look for his older brother, Hughie Jnr, and a neighbour called the police. Gallacher was arrested for assault and ordered to appear in court.

Gallacher continued to drink heavily and, suffering from what would today undoubtedly be diagnosed as depression, he struggled to forgive himself for hurting his own son. At the age of fifty-four, he went to Low Fell in Gateshead, to a spot known locally as 'Dead Man's Crossing', where he threw himself in front of an oncoming train.

Mercifully, society's attitudes towards mental health, alcoholism, gambling and other addictions have since changed dramatically and for the better. Today, there are better structures and systems in place to provide treatment and support.

Being a 'flawed genius' is a heavy burden to bear – but in an ever-awakening society, it thankfully no longer needs to be carried alone.

Exhibit 4
Moffat v Souness

For twenty-seven years, Aggie Moffat was St Johnstone's tea lady before, at the age of sixty-two, she hung up her apron in 2007.

The way many people show unstinting loyalty and unbridled devotion to a club is one of the peculiarly charming aspects of football. Unlike Aggie, however, most manage to stay out of the spotlight.

Aggie started out by washing the strips at the Perth club's old Muirton Park home in 1980, while her late husband, Bob, made sandwiches. Such invaluable members of staff aren't there for the money or the glory, yet they give more – considerably more – than many of the handsomely rewarded staff.

Aggie soon took on catering duties and, over the course of her career, looked after a string of managers and hundreds of players. She seemed to do everything: the laundry, the tea, the cleaning, you name it. According to local legend, she also made a mean pot of soup.

In the outlandish and often infantile arena of professional

football, Aggie staunchly insisted on politeness and old-fashioned manners. She didn't like players getting above themselves and kept the big heads in place while, at the same time, keeping a maternal eye on many of the younger players, often taking them under her wing.

Most football clubs have many similarly invaluable staff behind the scenes who don't take any nonsense. Managers, coaches and directors love them. They possess hearts of gold, are loyal and are cheap to employ. They are the pillars behind the scenes and everyone knows it's important to look after them and treat them with respect.

So it was that Aggie rose to national prominence in 1991 when she had a spat with the then Rangers manager, Graeme Souness.

Many of the players Souness came up against in his twenty-one-year career, lived in fear of his ferocious reputation – but Aggie Moffat proved a formidable adversary.

It was 26 February 1991 and Rangers were heading toward a third Scottish League title when Souness' men dropped points to the mid-table 'Saints'. Souness was livid with his side's performance and, in his post-match outburst, let rip, smashing a pot of tea against the dressing room wall. When Aggie learned of this, she confronted Souness in the corridor, facing up to one of the most uncompromising players the country has ever produced. She hailed from a time when you took pride in your belongings, your own space, and it didn't matter how big you thought you were; you behaved appropriately or suffered the consequences.

Naturally, the tabloids lapped it up when they learned that Souness had been brought to task by a tea lady. The story became one of class warfare and, just for good measure, it unfolded right in front of St Johnstone's owner, Geoff Brown, who found himself in the role of peacemaker. 'Leave it, Graeme,' he could be heard to implore. 'It's not worth it!'

Like most major heavyweight clashes, the two would have a rematch. The second contretemps was caused by dirty boots in the dressing room. Souness would later claim the petty arguments with a tea lady were the tipping point, the straw which broke the camel's back and convinced him to leave Rangers and take up the offer of the manager's job at Liverpool.

On the one hand, you had Souness claiming he had grown sick of the parochial ways of Scottish football. On the other, you had certain elements of the press pointing the finger at Aggie Moffat for driving Souness from his high-profile job at Rangers. In reality, the architect of the move was Souness's agent, who couldn't drive his client to Anfield quickly enough.

Aggie quickly learned how the media worked and, as if imbued by the spirit of Muhammad Ali, she began to shoot from the hip. 'He's just a plonker,' she opined. 'He always will be. I never liked the man and I never will. If he had come back next season I would have finished it. His nose would have been splattered all over his face. That's the only thing I regret not happening. That I didnae finish it. I should have broken his big nose.'

Aggie Moffat will always be remembered for her run-ins with Souness, yet that doesn't tell anything like the full story of a devoted football club employee who didn't seek the limelight, worked hard, and whose husband and family were everything to her.

Muirton Park and, later, McDiarmid Park were her workplaces and she was immensely proud and protective of them. Everybody who crossed their doors was expected to behave. It was that simple.

News of her death broke during the writing of this book. The outpouring of tributes, especially from those she looked after, were overwhelming and emotional. I considered removing this exhibit, before deciding that it perfectly summed up what makes Scottish football so special – how something as trivial as a fall-out can be elevated so quickly into a dramatic national story.

Aggie died on 14 April 2017 at the age of seventy-two. She is, and long will be, both dearly missed and fondly remembered.

Exhibit 5
Gazza's Magic Flute

In truth, any football museum wishing to cover sectarianism deserves to be met with incredulity. It's not an easy topic to deal with but it would be remiss to ignore it. And so this alternative museum includes a flute to remember the time that Paul Gascoigne mimicked playing 'The Sash' – a famous Northern Irish loyalist song, forever intertwined, in Scotland at least, with sectarianism – during an Old Firm clash in 1998.

The moment is forever remembered both for its idiocy and the scandal it prompted.

This being Scotland, the media stoked the fires, bringing the story into the mainstream and catching the interest of folk not normally interested in football. Folk like politicians, who quickly jumped on board, turning the story into a wider societal issue. Before we knew it, Gazza stood accused in the court of public opinion of being the lightning rod of everything Orange.

The mercurial Englishman, it was widely agreed, was guilty of little more than bad judgement and being what your nan might have called 'a bit of a stirrer'. The more serious questions should have been asked of those around him who knew better than to goad him into it. In truth, you also have to question the mentality and motivations of those who get upset by a man pretending to play an invisible flute. I may be wide of the mark here but I truly think most football fans, with any degree of common sense, thought Gazza was an idiot, not a raging bigot.

The SFA's Jim Farry described it as 'unprofessional and inflammatory'. He made it sound like Gazza should have practiced his scales and his imaginary flute-fingering before bringing his party piece to the pitch.

I wasn't upset by Gazza's invisible flute playing but, as soon as I saw it, I knew he'd get slaughtered. There's a blatant double-standard there, of course. It's not uncommon for a player to be subjected to vile abuse from the stands for ninety minutes yet, when they retaliate with 'something inflammatory', they're accused of starting a riot. For the record, no riots followed Gazza's moment of madness

To me, the whole episode was more '*Monty Python*' than anything more sinister. He was being daft and trying to provoke a reaction from fans on both sides. Gazza was the type of player who would have jumped into the Clyde if it got him a laugh.

I'm perfectly willing to go out on a limb and say Gazza didn't know about the Battle of the Boyne and 1690 when he did this. Of course, when he did it again later in his Rangers career, playing an invisible flute whilst warming up in front of Celtic fans, it proved what many had long assumed: that his brains were solely confined to his feet.

The incident cost Gazza £40,000 – two weeks' wages. An expensive lesson.

Exhibit 6
The hatchet man & the art of tackling

The 'hatchet man' has become something of a lost figure in Scottish football. A man forgotten in the mists of time. He was a different breed of player and should not, under any circumstances, be confused with a team's 'hard man'. The hard man can be five foot nothing and more like a wee, narky, Al Capone; the mental guy who loves a fight and often deliberately goes looking for one as soon as the ref blows his whistle. The hatchet man, on the other hand, was (past tense here) usually a cult hero centre-half or holding midfielder: ferocious, hard as nails and the type of guy who, after hanging up his boots, would become a God-fearing prison officer. The hatchet man was always acutely aware of his job. He revelled in knowing exactly how to intimidate his opponent. He was focussed, singular, calculated. He knew how to ruthlessly win the ball and then, if the ref allowed play to continue while his opponent floundered on the turf in agony, find the silky creative midfield playmaker.

His weapon of choice – the imperfectly timed and viciously executed tackle – is a dying art and widely frowned upon these days, yet in the era of Ralgex, the magic sponge (with more bacteria than a decaying fox) and a halftime ciggie, it was an intrinsic part of the game. In the glory, gory days of blood and snotters, the two-footed lunge was the norm; the crunching, late, over-the-top tackle, a rite of passage. Three factors have combined to bring the art of tackling to the edge of extinction: foreign managers, referees, and literally hundreds of television cameras capturing every moment of brutal savagery.

Awarding the dubious honour of 'football's most notorious hatchet man' is surely dependent on your age. For my generation in Scotland, it would have to be Gregor Stevens. He played for many clubs in the 1970s and 1980s, including Motherwell, Leicester City and Rangers. He brought a mix of scything brute force and psychotic pragmatism to his game. Stevens will always be tarred with what some people might consider a distinct lack of natural talent and it was probably frustration at this that made him dirty as a player – yet he was able to carve out a long football career in between red cards, suspensions and fines because managers such as Jock Wallace saw the value of having an 'enforcer' on the field. They understood they couldn't have silk without steel.

Graeme Souness could be brutal and, as he approached the end of his career, he had earned the right to play on the edge at times.

Older fans will fondly remember John Blackley at Hibs and Dave Mackay at Hearts. Celtic's Roy Aitken never took any prisoners, was 100% committed, hard, but also fair. Cammy Fraser played in a struggling Rangers side before the Souness revolution. Terry Hurlock briefly joined Souness from Millwall for £375,000, played thirty-five games, was booked twelve times and sent off once, but his robust contributions are still fondly remembered by the Ibrox faithful. Dundee United had Davie Bowman and Aberdeen had Doug Rougvie.

Scotland can occasionally have its moments of violence but the scarcity makes it more enjoyable when the odd brawl flares up. For some strange reason, even during the darkest days, players would knock the living daylights out of each other on the park yet be best mates off it. Players like Bertie Auld and John Greig were hard because it was the only way they could survive. So, as we look back to the era of the hatchet man, maybe we should celebrate the fact that the players from both sides were able to share a drink together afterwards, leaving their competitive thuggery out on the field – just as we now leave them in the past.

Exhibit 7
Jinky's Rowing Voyage

It barely seems plausible that somebody with such wonderful balance, skill, low centre of gravity and a mind capable of intricate movement and trickery could be so hopeless on a boat. And yet when Celtic's Jimmy Johnstone was cast adrift in a rowing boat, his seamanship wasn't helped by the fact that he was without any oars – and was completely plastered!

Can you imagine such capers today? Messi, Neymar or Ronaldo, adrift off the coast of Largs on a boat? This, though, was a different time, a time when footballers lived in, and remained part of, the community. Even those who moved to leafier parts of town stayed in touch with school friends, remained connected to the community and kept their feet on the ground. These were the halcyon days of Scottish football, when coaching manuals and badges were set aside and managers considered players getting pissed together as 'team building'.

Arguably one of the best footballers this country has ever produced, 'Jinky' Johnstone is fondly remembered for this comical incident which happened while staying at Largs with the international team. It almost came with the territory that the impish maestro, an exuberant whirling dervish on the pitch, full of trickery and mischief, was also the clown prince off it.

It was late on a Tuesday evening in 1974. Scotland had just beaten Wales, and were weeks away from heading to West Germany for the World Cup. The manager, Willie Ormond, allowed his players to partake in a few drinks, knowing they would sweat it out in training before the final Home Internationals match against England that Saturday. It was around five in the morning when the players were thrown out of the pub and were walking along the seafront back to their hotel. As many a poet, writer and playwright will attest, the sea wields an intoxicating strength, reminding us of our insignificance before its vast power. It lures us with a magnetic pull and being on the lash until the early hours of the morning helped entice the players toward the water . . .

When inebriated, an anomalous logic takes hold. One which makes the idea of rowing out to sea seem like a perfect way to clear the head. Easily cajoled, Jinky jumped aboard a small rowing boat and was shoved off by his pals. He stood up and started singing, unaware that the boat was caught in the tide and was now setting sail for the horizon. Davie Hay and Erich Schaedler were the first to notice things were going awry. They manfully decided to go out and save the day. However, both of the boats they chose started leaking. Denis Law recalls seeing Jimmy's boat getting smaller and smaller as it faded into the distance. In the end, the coastguard was called and the stricken winger's rescue made headlines as the national team built up to the traditional end of season match against England.

Johnstone woke up in the hotel the next morning and started piecing together events of the previous evening. When he managed to make it down for a late, late breakfast, around midday, Law started singing, 'What shall we do with a drunken sailor'. The manager wasn't happy and Jinky was cast adrift yet again – this time to face the baying press pack, who wouldn't buy the excuse that he'd decided to go fishing. The way the press painted the picture, it was almost as if he had been heading for the Atlantic bound for Nova Scotia. The reality was that he was on the Firth of Clyde. It would have taken the skill of Columbus and Magellan to navigate by Millport and down around Arran, by Campbeltown and then Islay, before setting sale across the Atlantic. They made a pariah of him.

It would be inaccurate to assume that generation was forever drinking. In Johnstone's case, especially under Jock Stein at Celtic, he was expected to be supremely fit. Remember, Stein had moulded and trained a team fit enough to out-run, out-pass, out-jump and out-fight a much-fancied Inter Milan in the searing heat of Lisbon in the 1967 European Cup final. Rangers' players also won the Cup Winners' Cup in 1972 in the baking heat of Barcelona. Not to glorify the archaic notion of 'running it off', these players could get hammered and still perform for club and country at an elite level. Modern medical teams and fitness coaches understand that alcohol is bad for you but it is also undeniable that, when players bonded like they did in the 1960s and 1970s over drinking sessions, they reached more finals and qualified for more competitions than the current generation of athletes.

It says something about the love and respect for Jimmy Johnstone, or maybe about the Scottish psyche, that despite being at Celtic from 1961 to 1975, winning the European Cup, nine successive league titles, four Scottish Cup and five League Cup titles, scoring 130 goals in 515 appearances, finishing runner-up in a further European Cup final in 1970, the infamy of the Largs boat incident endures. Johnstone was far from perfect and, in some ways, this made him even profoundly beloved.

The common man related to him, perhaps seeing something of themselves in his frailties. They could envisage being as daft when drunk and behaving in as disorderly and boisterous a way. Only a few could dream of being able to play football like him.

Disappointed by the media's broadly hostile reaction to his rowing expedition, Jinky produced one of his best performances for Scotland that weekend, giving England's Emlyn Hughes a torrid time. At the end of their 2–0 win, the players did a lap of honour – and Jinky duly threw two fingers up at the press box.

The esteemed journalist, Hugh McIlvanney, summed the whole incident up perfectly: 'It was probably quite characteristic of Jimmy that he went through all that nonsense on the Ayrshire coast then proceeded to perform like an inspired demon against England at Hampden'.

Players like Jimmy Johnstone remind us of a time when footballers weren't robots and drilled monkeys – they were men of the people; imperfect, normal men who conquered the improbable. They made mistakes, they achieved greatness and, most magically, they walked among us.

Exhibit 8
James McFadden and the Missed Flight

The happiness James McFadden bestowed upon the nation is, frankly, difficult to quantify. He brought sunshine and hope to minds lost in the dark psychosis of Scottish football's hurt locker. He was an exceptional footballer who also brought an emotional authenticity, which connected to the hearts and minds of an increasingly disenfranchised Tartan Army. Here was someone who showed an early capacity for lager bampotry, a tendency to lose it with a late tackle and the knack for scoring an opportunistic wonder goal.

McFadden's game was built upon incisiveness and intelligence. His gallus swagger was coupled with a precocious impatience for those who weren't on the same wavelength. He also had an eye for a pass and an innate habit of 'knowing where the goal was' and yet, in terms of pace and movement, he had about as much mobility as the Duke of Wellington's statue.

There were many moments in his forty-eight international caps and fifteen goals where McFadden showed his class. In the first leg of a play-off for the 2004 European Championships against the Netherlands in November 2003, he scored the only goal in a 1–0 victory. And who could forget that wonderful night in September 2007 when his effort from thirty-five yards out flew into the net and propelled Scotland to victory over the 2006 World Cup runners-up?

Headlines the next day proclaimed it to be 'the shot that echoed around the world'. There were also dramatic goals against Lithuania and Ukraine in the same year.

Every time Scotland won a free-kick within thirty-five yards of the opposition's goal, there was an air of legitimate expectation around the stadium. When 'Faddy' was at his peak, free-kicks were as good as penalties. He was that good. He was a match-winner, plain and simple.

McFadden was also part of the Scotland side that went into the final game of the 2008 European Championships campaign with all to play for. Standing in their way? The reigning world champions, Italy. In the end, the Scots lost narrowly, going down 2-1 thanks to an injury time winner that stemmed from a free-kick that never should have been awarded.

McFadden had endeared himself to the Tartan Army from the outset after 'missing a flight' in Hong Kong following his international debut under the maligned Berti Vogts. 'Missing a flight', for what it's worth, is a euphemism for a youngster being let off the leash, a long way from home. Initially, it was reported he had slept in. It was later suggested he had gone AWOL. In the end, it was agreed he was on the ubiquitous boozy night out with teammates and 'got lost'. The long and the short of it is: he missed the flight.

As far as managers or SFA blazers are concerned, 'missing a flight' is a monumental error. However, if you have a bit of footballing élan and are also a demon in the swally stakes, you're loved by the fans. 'Missing a flight' ensures lifelong membership into the booze-bag hall of fame.

The latter stage of McFadden's career was blighted by a cruciate knee ligament injury that deprived him the opportunity of unleashing his true potential at the highest level, on a platform it deserved. McFadden was the personification of the silky player with a lightning fast creative mind but who was, in terms of physical pace, as slow as a week in the jail. He was a player who had the toolkit to become world-class. In truth, he should've become one of the finest footballers the country has ever produced but a combination of bad luck, bad timing and, arguably, bad decision-making curbed what should've been a golden career.

After a short spell at Sunderland – his third English side – McFadden appeared happy and settled as a player-coach and assistant manager at the club where it all began for him, Motherwell. He was keeping fit, training with the youth team and made sporadic appearances to cover for the Motherwell first team when the squad was thin on the ground. He became a free agent after leaving the Fir Park side and, after training with his Everton teammate and then Queen of the South manager, Gary Naysmith, was offered a short contract with the 'Doonhamers'. When Alex McLeish became Scotland manager in March 2018, he named McFadden as one of assistant coaches.

More recently, he has been a regular pundit on BBC Radio Scotland football shows and has proven to be a natural conversationalist with a sharp and eloquent voice. As long as international football exists, there will always be a place at any radio station in Scotland for James McFadden to come in and have a chat. Unlike his self-belief on the park, off the park, he is modest about his achievements and claims if he had played one game for Scotland it would've been enough. To play forty-eight? A dream come true.

James McFadden was a mercurial talent with the ability to

leave fans spellbound. He was two caps short of the SFA Scottish Hall of Fame, so his inclusion to the alternative museum is a 'thank you' from the fans for his efforts – and, of course, for that one night in Paris.

Exhibit 9
Willie Johnston's Prescription

Football can be ruthlessly vindictive.

Willie Johnston travelled to the World Cup in Argentina in 1978 playing the best football of his career for West Bromwich Albion. Weeks later, he returned like a pantomime Pablo Escobar, his reputation in tatters after failing a drugs test at the tournament.

He will be forever entwined into the fabric of Scottish football history, harshly judged by those who would say there's no smoke without fire, and that an innocent mistake is a mistake nonetheless. The Scottish psyche can be malicious at times, delighting in witnessing people enduring misfortune. It often seems that we love to see someone in the public eye getting caught out and revel in watching their life unravel.

In 1757, the esteemed Scottish philosopher David Hume wrote *Four Dissertations*, within which he neatly summed up this way of thinking: 'It seems an unaccountable pleasure, which the spectators of a well-written tragedy receive from sorrow, terror, anxiety, and other passions, that are in themselves disagreeable and uneasy. The more they are touched and affected, the more are they delighted with the spectacle; and as soon as the uneasy passions cease to operate, the piece is at an end.'

However, in Johnston's case, it wasn't fiction, has never really stopped and has endured like a cloud hanging over him.

Johnston, despite being one the quickest and most skilful left wingers of his era, will always be remembered for failing that test, which the UK media elevated into a soap opera. He took his medicine, manfully accepting what came his way, although, in truth, he had no alternative, thanks to a weak and ineffective SFA, which hung him out to dry. The association's secretary, Ernie Walker, was brief and damning: 'You're being sent home. You will never play for Scotland again.' Johnston demanded an appeal, which was refused, as was the chance to phone his wife. He was told to pack his bags, was smuggled out of the hotel to avoid the press, and was driven 700 kilometres to Buenos Aires airport.

In their opening match in Argentina, Scotland performed dismally against Peru, losing 3–1. After the match, Archie Gemmill was unable to pass a urine sample and Johnston was randomly selected. He did his business and forgot about it. Days later, he would become one of the most controversial men in world sport when his sample tested positive for fencamfamine, a drug found in over-the-counter hay fever medicine, Reactivan. Johnston had been suffering from hay fever and a cold and so took two Reactivan, which contained a small trace of the banned stimulant. Hardly the stuff of Lance Armstrong or Ben Johnson, yet he was treated much the same.

An observer witnessing his reception at Heathrow would have been forgiven for thinking a raging coke-head like Tony Montana from Scarface was about to pace through the arrivals hall. He was escorted through the airport by three burly policemen, while newspaper photographers and news cameramen fought to snatch a glimpse of him. The reaction and outrage from a rabid Scottish press pack was ferocious as they rushed to judgement. Since he was a big name at West Brom, and because the English media had nothing to report given England's failure to qualify for the competition in Argentina, they attacked him, too.

Watching re-runs of Willie Johnston play in the 1972 European Cup Winners' Cup for Rangers, one thing you could never accuse him of needing more of was artificial stimulus. What a performance he put in. You could see why running up and down sand dunes at Gullane helped the Rangers' side as they overran and overpowered Dynamo Moscow at the Nou Camp, with Johnston slotting home two beauties. Across two spells at Rangers, he scored 125 goals in 393 games. If anything, his game improved at West Brom, earning him an invitation back into the international fold under Ally MacLeod.

Johnston's intemperate reputation followed him throughout his career. A remarkably shy and mild-mannered man off the park, he transformed when he crossed the white line. I love players with this attitude, those with an all-encompassing will to win, those who go to war to win. This mind-set should be instilled in our young players from an early age. Skill, pace and touch are nothing without determination and a will to win. Johnston was constantly kicked and snapped at because opponents knew he would retaliate. On most occasions, he would be reacting to near leg-breaking challenges.

His time at Rangers could best be described as explosive. As a seventeen-year-old, Johnston starred in his side's 1964/65 Scottish League Cup win. He was promised a £500 win bonus from manager Scot Symon, but only received £50. The boss thought too much money, too soon, would turn his head. Johnston was, not unreasonably, upset by this.

It became easy for the authorities to penalise him. Johnston was once fined £40 by his own manager for sitting on the ball and 'bringing shame to the club' during a Scottish League Cup final win over Celtic in 1970/71. In another game, against Partick Thistle, he decked a player – Alex Forsyth – who had spent most of the match kicking him up and down the touchline. Johnston was subsequently banned for forty-two games. His disciplinary record eventually became so bad that Rangers felt they had no option but to off-load him to West Brom in December 1972, the £138,000 they received breaking the transfer record between Scottish and English clubs. There, he became something of a club legend for his maverick ways, once playfully kicking a referee up the arse, another time grabbing a swig of lager from a fan before taking a corner. Over the course of two matches, he even successfully negotiated the purchase of a greenhouse from a supporter on the touchline while waiting to take a corner.

In many ways, his previous misdemeanours, combined with the SFA having never being overly fond of him, allowed the authorities to hang him out to dry and, in so doing, divert attention away from Scotland's abysmal performance at the '78 World Cup. Johnston's teammate, Don Masson, later admitted he took the same hay fever medication. One wonders how he might have been treated had he been selected for the test.

Amid the horribleness of the situation, there was one brief moment of levity. When he arrived at Heathrow, Johnston's club manager, Ron Atkinson, was at the centre of the scrum to protect his player. Atkinson promised to get Johnston through the storm and told the player he had already secured a contract... with Boots the chemist. He was subsequently transferred to Vancouver Whitecaps, where he won the 1979 Soccer Bowl... and is fondly remembered for starting a twenty-man brawl in a game against New York Cosmos. You can take the boy out of Fife . . .

Johnston eventually returned home for another stint at Rangers before joining Hearts. He continued to be controversial at both clubs, stamping on Aberdeen player John McMaster's head while at Ibrox, and headbutting Celtic's Davie Provan while wearing maroon.

For all the darker aspects of Johnston's career, it should be remembered that he was often fending for himself in an era of brutal physicality. There were also moments of light and wonder when he could jolt the crowd with the electricity of his performances. Hopefully, history will remember him more for his moments of magic, impishness and iron will to win, than for failing to read the ingredients on an over-the-counter hay fever packet.

Exhibit 10
Frank McAvennie

Frank McAvennie's accidental journey into football reads like something out of a boys' own story.

Today, the game has changed beyond recognition and it would be near impossible for him to make it in professional football. The notion of a player who simply played for fun, hated training, preferred to watch football than play on a Saturday and was spotted by chance, rarely, if ever, happens beyond the pages of a comic book.

The working-class boy living the dream, who goes on to play for the team he supports, then scores twice in the cup final of the club's centenary season? A script-writer couldn't do it any better.

Frank McAvennie was a magnificent striker who created a chaotic legacy that would overshadow his wonderful playing career. He would become better known for his decline into drugs and criminality which saw him briefly spend time in prison but not before he had cemented his reputation as one of the game's bona fide characters.

The story begins one cold Saturday in 1979, after a Celtic game had been called off and Frank bumped into some friends in Glasgow. They played for a local amateur side in Kirkintilloch, called the 200 Club. They asked him to come along and play. A number of scouts were there to check out another player but Macca completely stole the show and was subsequently offered a contract with two junior sides and trials for a number of senior clubs. In a trial for Partick Thistle, he came on as sub only to then be himself substituted. According to the Jags' manager, Bertie Auld, he didn't have a future as a footballer. In a trial for St Mirren, however, he proved Auld wrong and was immediately offered a contract.

That set in motion an extraordinary career. At twenty years of age, he was a compartively late starter but quickly made up for lost time as he set out on a journey which would change his life forever. After five seasons, one-hundred and thirty-five appearances and almost fifty goals for the Saints, McAvennie knew it was time to move on. He appeared destined to seal a dream move to Celtic only for then manager Davie Hay to sign Mo Johnston. McAvennie, instead, moved to West Ham and played in a side that almost won the First Division. He eventually signed for Celtic in 1987, the first of two stints at the club in a career that took him back to West Ham, on to Aston Villa and back to Celtic again. Somewhat surprisingly, despite his prolific strike-rate at club-level, McAvennie only won five caps for Scotland, scoring once.

During his second stint at Celtic, manager Billy McNeill worked out an agreement that allowed Frank to fly to London straight after the game on a Saturday, as long as he promised to return for training on Monday morning. The early-bird flights from Heathrow to Glasgow were notorious for being late and delayed, so McNeill had started to fine McAvennie when he didn't turn up on time. McAvennie, in turn, became frustrated with the fines and spoke to a pal who claimed he knew someone who could get him from Glasgow Airport to the club's Barrowfield training ground, on the other side of the city, in less than fifteen minutes. McAvennie met the man at the airport and, like something out of a James Bond movie, was covertly shuttled through the inner sanctum of the airport to a distant helipad. There, he met the Radio Clyde 'Eye in the Sky' helicopter traffic pilot who flew him to Barrowfield in ten minutes. McAvennie left his teammates and manager in hysterics as he jumped out of the chopper, narrowly making training on time for the first time in weeks. Talk about making an entrance.

McAvennie was no stranger to the inner workings of the judicial system, appearing in court on a number of occasion, most famously with Terry Butcher, Graham Roberts and Chris Woods after a minor stramash during a quiet 2–2 Old Firm match in 1987. In truth, referee Jim Duncan should have been in court instead of the players. His handling of the game was shocking.

As spectacular as this story is, McAvennie earns his place in the museum for another incident that sums up the madcap lunacy of his life, when was stopped by customs officials at Dover on his way to the Netherlands in 1996 with £200,000 in cash in his Land Rover. Magistrates ruled that the cash (£100,000 of which belonged to McAvennie) was intended for drugs trafficking. McAvennie claimed he had been 'duped' by unscrupulous business associates. His business partner told the court the cash was to buy a boat to salvage treasure from a sunken ship in the Atlantic. It's difficult to imagine McAvennie as some kind of treasure-hunting Jacques Cousteau, intrepidly exploring marine wildlife and searching sunken ships in a diver's suit. How he or the customs officials managed to keep a straight face at the far-fetched story is anybody's guess. The officials were having none of it. They impounded the money and Frank was left rooked.

I've always had a soft spot for Frank McAvennie. Not only did I write jokes for TV and radio about him but I followed his career closely after seeing him play for St Mirren against my hometown team, Airdrieonians, at Broomfield, in September 1981. McAvennie was a skinny red-head, lightning quick, more of an attacking midfielder than the out-and-out striker he became. With Airdrie 3–2 ahead, he scored twice to steal a 4–3 win for the Saints.

My first Scotland game was a World Cup play-off against Australia in November 1985. McAvennie scored his only goal for his country as Scotland won 2–0, with Davie Cooper getting the other, in a nervy night at Hampden.

Macca's diving suit finds its place in our museum for the ridiculousness of the story alone. He has endured glorious highs and excruciating lows, from his glory days at St Mirren, West Ham and Celtic, to being surrounded by hangers-on and making bad business investments. Later, in 2000, McAvennie went on trial in Newcastle Crown Court, during which time he was held in remand in Durham jail. The charge was conspiracy to supply £110,000 worth of ecstasy and amphetamines. He faced the prospect of ten years in prison but the jury acquitted him. He has confronted and beaten drug addiction, fought depression, taken the blows and come through the other side with some much-needed calm settling on him in later life.

He is the proverbial 'one-off', a loveable rogue who lived life the way he played football: by instinct.

Exhibit 11
Jim McLean v John Barnes

Scottish football had never seen anything like it. There we were, watching the afternoon's results roll in on the BBC vidiprinter, with the routine post-match interviews being carried out, when, on this particular Saturday in October 2000, all hell broke loose.

SCENE: Tannadice Stadium, Dundee. John Barnes, the BBC Radio Scotland reporter, is interviewing Jim McLean, the Dundee United chairman, who is speaking to the press in place of first team coach, Alex Smith. McLean is angry and frustrated (no change there) but moreso than usual following a humiliating home defeat at hands the of Hearts.

BARNES: How long do you give Alex Smith to get it right on the park?

McLEAN: D'you think I'm going to answer a stupid question like that?

BARNES: I'm only asking it.

McLEAN: Well, I told you earlier I wouldnae be f*****g answering it . . . and make sure that's cut.

[*McLean walks away*]

McLEAN [*off camera*]: I'll tell you something . . . [*FX: BOOOOOOOF*] . . . Don't ever offer me that again.

The effect '*BOOOOOOOF*' is, of course, the onomatopoeic sound of a humdinger of a punch. The item Jim McLean didn't want offered again was the microphone that Barnes had put in front of him.

McLean was reportedly aggrieved before he even met Barnes, believing it should have been Smith's responsibility to account for his team's dismal performance. McLean knew that stonewalling the press wouldn't help. Fans were becoming frustrated following a bad run of results and were starting to point the finger of blame in his direction. Refrains of that dreaded ode to the hapless director had made its way onto the United fans' songsheets: 'Sack the Board'. Few three-word songs have so devastating an impact. Like most Scottish football fans, the Dundee United 'faithful' had incredibly short memories and were turning on one of the club's greats. After the defeat against Hearts had left them marooned at the bottom of the league, the fans wanted blood – and McLean was the perfect scapegoat

Perhaps feeling that he was charged with putting out too many fires, his frustration spilled over at Barnes' expense.

McLean was notorious for demanding perfection from his teams and made a career out of relentlessly pushing and driving everyone he worked with.

His sides were always fast, fit, and tactically set out to play a counter-attacking and pressing game. It worked relative wonders. Back-to-back League Cup victories in 1979 and 1980 would be capped by Dundee United winning the Premier League in season 1982/83, not to mention impressive European performances against Barcelona, Anderlecht, Werder Bremen, Monaco, Borussia Mönchengladbach and PSV Eindhoven. In 1983, they reached the semi-finals of the European Cup and were unlucky not to make the final after controversially going out 3–2 to eventual runners-up Roma. Three years later, United reached the UEFA Cup final but were beaten 2–1, over two legs, by Gothenburg. The fans had become spoiled by success and, frustrated by the change in their fortunes, they turned on the architect of those glory days.

In the aftermath of the stramash with Barnes, McLean immediately recognised he'd crossed the line and resigned as chairman, managing director and club director. In a statement, he said: 'I very much regret what has happened and have offered my sincere apologies to John Barnes. I am particularly sorry that it was John of all people who was involved. From what I know of him, he is an honest, hard-working lad, who was only trying to do his job, as I was trying to do mine. Anyone who knows me, however, will know the passion I have for Dundee United and for football and I deeply regret that I allowed those feelings to cloud my judgment, albeit for one brief moment. In these circumstances, I have resigned as chairman, managing director and board member of Dundee United Football Club. I firmly believe that this is the right decision for Dundee United and Jim McLean.'

Scottish football fans – and Scots in a broader sense – can be quick to react and slow to forgive and forget. Mud sticks. When Jim McLean is spoken about now, it tends not to be for his success but for this outburst. It is a shame that a remarkable managerial career is blemished so.

FERENC
PUSKÁS
1927-2006
Drumchapel

Exhibit 12
Puskás in Drumchapel

Hungarian superstar Ferenc Puskás could easily have passed for Scottish.

He wasn't shaped like a footballer, yet he had a natural, muscular, athleticism that allowed for explosive bursts of brilliance. He had the robust physicality of a steel worker: stocky, broad, and barrel-chested.

As well as being shaped like a Scot, he drank, sang, ate, partied and, as it turned out, shagged like one, too. He is forever etched in the hearts and minds of a generation of fans as a glorious goal-scorer in arguably one of the most talked-about club games in the history of football, which, by quirk of fate, took place in Glasgow.

Some footballers are inextricably linked to a place, time and football city. The European Cup final of 1960 saw Real Madrid thrash Eintracht Frankfurt 7–3 at Hampden. Puskás scored four times in front of 130,000 fans. As well as being a glorious marksman for Real Madrid, the Scottish audience loved him for his role as part of a famous Hungary side who, in 1953, not only beat England 6–3 at Wembley but shamed an over-confident England side into rethinking the game both technically and tactically.

Puskás was the star of the wonderful Hungarian 'Golden Squad' of the early 1950s. Their tactics largely reinvented the game, not only with their fluidity, touch, speed, fitness and flexibility, but with their use of a deep lying centre-forward who would occasionally drift back into midfield. This style was a forerunner of what would become known as 'total football'.

Puskás had a left foot which dazzled, enthralled and bewildered, part cannonball power, part sublime deft and grace. This, combined with his remarkable football intelligence and an uncanny ability to read the game, saw him nicknamed the 'galloping major', bolstering his reputation as one of the game's legends.

In many subsequent interviews, he described how he was moved by the love the fans in Hampden showed towards Real Madrid and how the roar drove his side on. He also sensed from the cheers at the end of the game that the crowd were knowledgeable and full of appreciation for the way Real Madrid had played. Alfredo Di Stéfano may have scored a hat-trick in the game but it was his Hungarian teammate who stole the show.

His impact and achievements in Scotland are marked by a plaque in the official museum at Hampden. Like many of those players from that era, he connected with the fans and, as someone who, to coin a euphemism, 'enjoyed a night out', it was little wonder. When Real Madrid visited Glasgow in 1963 to play Rangers in the European Cup, Puskás was quick to seek out Jim Baxter after the game. Knowing Baxter's reputation, he suggested they go out together for a drink.

They soon ended up in one of Baxter's usual haunts, the St Enoch's Hotel. While partaking of some pints, they were invited to a party in Drumchapel. Not wanting to appear rude, they accepted. There has always been some dubiety about where the party took place and a lack of clarity and consistency as to the course of events but it was said that, during this legendary party, Puskás got amorous with a local lass in a tenement kitchen.

The story would be later verified by Jim Baxter, who said: 'I've always thought there should be a plaque in Drumchapel which would state, 'The great footballer Puskás scored here'.' If there's a plaque in the Hampden museum commemorating players' exploits on the field, maybe there should be something similar (a 'nookie plaque', perhaps) to forever acknowledge their off-field exploits? Drumchapel would be proud.

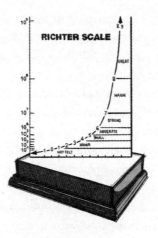

RICHTER SCALE

Exhibit 13
Mo Johnston

On 10 July 1989, one of the most controversial signings in Scottish football history took place.

The transfer was truly seismic. Many signings have come from left field, causing the odd shock, but none have caused the mania, pandemonium and bedlam that followed Maurice Johnston signing for Rangers.

To give the transfer some kind of modern context, it would be a bit like Lionel Messi swapping Barcelona for Real Madrid. At the time, it was assumed that, after two seasons at Nantes, Mo Johnston's return to Scotland would see him re-join for his boyhood team, Celtic. But then the news filtered through that he was reneging on a return of 'prodigal son' proportions and was, instead, crossing the city to play for the Bhoys' bitter rivals. It was, for a multitude of reasons, as unlikely a transfer as could have been imagined.

The newspapers, particularly the red tops, descended into meltdown. In the first place, it was extraordinary the transfer remained a secret. In today's fast-moving, social media age, with a voracious twenty-four-hour news feed, it wouldn't have remained a scoop but, in 1989, it did – and it caught every football fan on the hop.

When journalists were summoned to Ibrox for a Graeme Souness press conference, in which the Rangers boss would unveil a high-profile Catholic signing, the hacks showed up in a nonchalant mood. Their contacts had given them all the same name: Sheffield Wednesday's Republic of Ireland midfielder, John Sheridan.

So, imagine the disbelief when Johnston walked in.

Just two months earlier, Johnston, wearing a Celtic top, had been paraded in front of the media as the returning hero, having signed for Celtic from Nantes for a then Scottish club record fee of £1.2 million.

He was emotional and unequivocal about leaving for France under a cloud in 1987. 'I didn't want to leave Celtic then and I don't intend to now,' he said. 'There was some rubbish about me wanting to join Manchester United but it never entered my head to play for any other club. In fact, there is no other British club I could play for apart from Celtic.'

To Celtic fans, Johnston was already a legend, who had starred in a fantastic David Hay side. Here was a lifelong Celtic fan, who had scored fifty-two goals in a hundred games in green and white. He scored twice in a victory over St Mirren which, thanks to Hearts capitulating against Dundee, meant Celtic won the league at Love Street, in 1986. In fact, one of Johnston's goals is regarded among the finest team goals Celtic have ever scored. So, his move to Rangers, after having proclaimed his love for Celtic, was regarded as the ultimate duplicity. As far as Celtic supporters were concerned, Johnston had betrayed them, not only by jumping ship, but by choosing to sign for the enemy.

The transfer of the century riled both sides. Celtic fans were embarrassed, Rangers fans embittered, saying, '*Anyone* but him.' The press and TV fell about in a frenzy. No-one had seen anything like it. Souness and David Murray had stolen Johnston away from Celtic, making him the club's first high-profile Catholic signing. It was a statement of intent. Rangers were forging ahead and many more Catholic signings would follow. Before Mo Johnston joined Rangers, there was a general unspoken policy of not signing players who belonged to the Catholic faith. Everyone knew Rangers had signed Catholic players over the years – Don Kitchenbrand, Hugh O'Neil and John Spencer to name three – but it was rarely highlighted while they were playing. You would only find out years later, when it was mentioned in passing, in their memoir, in hushed tones.

Some Rangers supporters, particularly the hardcore fans, they resented the signing of Johnston. To them, this was the end of a tradition. They were angry. Scarves were burned and season tickets ripped up for news cameras. It wasn't the fact Mo Johnston was Catholic; it was that he was the type of Celtic player the Rangers faithful didn't like. He was 'Celtic daft', famous for rubbing Rangers fans' noses in it when he scored against them.

Eventually, when the goals started to go in at Ibrox, they came round, realising they'd got one up on Celtic, proving their side were miles ahead financially and confirming what everyone knew about the Celtic board: that they were tight as a gnat's chuff when it came to parting with money.

Reports vary over how badly the deal was handled. At the time, it was roundly blamed on Celtic's board for procrastinating and failing to meet tax payments on the transfer deal. FIFA sided with Celtic, stating the paperwork they received was, in effect, a pre-contract and therefore legally binding. They later fined Johnston three thousand pounds for reneging on the deal. Johnston's agent, Bill McMurdo, always at his querulous best, claimed the main problem with Celtic's handling of the transfer was their refusal to speak directly with him. McMurdo was a persona non grata at Parkhead.

Johnston's actions humiliated Celtic. The club believed it wasn't about consigning the religious divide to the past, as Murray and Souness claimed, but that it was simple one-upmanship. Decades years later, the scars still ran deep. Billy McNeill, the Celtic manager at the time of the transfer, told *The Sun* newspaper in July 2009, 'I implored Jack McGinn and the rest of the board to pay Nantes the balance of the transfer, another £700,000. This would have flashed a message around the world that Celtic were not a club to be messed with. I told Jack McGinn there was no way we could afford to let Maurice Johnston walk away from us. I couldn't care less if he didn't play for Celtic. Being in charge of the situation was all that mattered to me. But Johnston ended up being free to do what he wanted – and Celtic were made to look extremely foolish.'

This transfer was a JFK moment, one which still induces post-traumatic stress and shock for fans of the game. The *Glasgow Herald* summed it up perfectly: '£1.5m signing makes football history at the stroke of a pen.'

Johnston signing for Rangers obliterated the unspoken policy of not signing high-profile Catholic footballers and, for the club and society, despite the upset it may have caused, it was a staggeringly important watershed moment.

Exhibit 14
Rab C Sócrates

Sócrates, like Ferenc Puskás, should've been an adopted
Scotsman. Unlike Puskás, however, Sócrates didn't look like a
Scotsman. He was more of a Greek God: 6ft 4in tall, 12½ stone,
strong and quick. He resembled a 400m hurdler or a basketball
player – a lithe, natural athlete. He also had the coolest name in
football.

Sócrates briefly shared our Scottish pain of perpetual defeat
and anguish when he had his dreams crushed at the World
Cup. For him, it was 1982, when he was part of arguably the
best Brazilian side not to win the famous trophy. Despite this
ultimate failure in Spain, Sócrates was a hero to a generation
of football fans for the way he played, with an artistry and style
which exuded an air of unrelenting class. As well as being an
imperious midfielder, he was also outspoken and brave. He
would write messages on his iconic headband, such as 'Yes to
Love. No to Terror' in protest against the US bombing of Libya,
or 'No Violence' and 'Justice'. He was a phenomenal player but

also thought differently from many of his contemporaries. He knew, as a high-profile Brazilian footballer, that he wielded huge influence on the world stage and he tried to use it for good.

This is Scotland, though. If you ask Scots about Sócrates, the first thing you'll hear is, 'Oh, Sócrates. He smoked forty-a-day.' You get the same reaction with Dutch superstar Johan Cruyff. The fact they smoked like chimneys yet still managed to scale such dizzy heights is what truly captures the Scottish imagination. They would jokingly be acclaimed as role models or inspirational lifestyle coaches.

When we were playing football, in much the same way as you'd try to copy Kenny Dalglish shielding the ball before turning away to score from an impossible position, or Glenn Hoddle perfectly connecting with a volley, we would try to emulate Sócrates' free-flowing creativity. He could also take a hell of a penalty. He would take two steps and, *bang*, rattle the ball into the net. It isn't an unusual technique now but it was then – it was all about the massive run-up for everyone else – and we would all attempt to copy him. Such nonchalance. Two steps, goal.

Scotland faced Brazil in the World Cup in 1982, and despite being smashed 4–1, actually played extremely well. Watching the game from behind the sofa, full of fear like most Scots, we couldn't believe how easily Scotland were skelping Brazil in the first half. In the thirty-second minute, it seemed over for the plucky Brazilians when David Narey blasted Scotland into the lead. Yes, it was a toe-poke – but the Brazilians consider it a skill, being able to get a toe on the ball with power and accuracy. They even have a name for it: 'bico'. This, though, wasn't any Brazil side. This was the football aristocracy, with stars of world football like Eder, Sócrates, Falcao and Zico. And like an undefeated heavyweight champion, that unexpected left-hook in the first round awoke the prize-fighter in them. Angered by Narey's bico, they proceeded to swat Scotland away with some of the most sublime football the World Cup has ever seen.

It was unusual for Brazil to turn on the afterburners so early in the competition, especially in the opening week, when the big teams were still finding their rhythm. The post-match reports were full of the usual clichés but not unreasonably: 'football lesson', 'masterclass' and so on.

Sócrates not only smoked forty-a-day but was a proud nationalist and fond of a drink. His biggest vice, however, was women and his four marriages ably demonstrate this.

In 1982, Sócrates captained Corinthians to the Brazilian title. He had convinced the club and his teammates that success would only come if they remained united and he proceeded to turn the side into a workers' co-operative. Everything was done by a vote, including team selection, even staying at home, when possible, before big games instead of heading to hotels. Shirts were clean of the capitalist scourge of sponsorship and they played with the word 'Democracy' on their backs or sometimes a reminder of a day of an important vote. In 1984, Sócrates addressed a pro-democracy rally of over half a million people. 'It was the most perfect moment I ever had,' he would later say. 'The best thing football gave me was a chance to get to know human beings. I got to meet people who suffered and those on the other side of society that had everything.'

One of the reasons Sócrates is inducted into the alternative Scottish football museum is because of his Rab C. Nesbitt headband.

There's also this. After the Scotland game in 1982, was asked to give a urine sample. After running around for ninety minutes in eighty-degree heat, he was a tad dehydrated. When he suggested he needed a drink, a fridge was opened and it was full of beer, wine and Champagne. It took hours before he broke the seal.

It would be wonderful to imagine that Sócrates the footballer, with his brilliant mind, would settle down to a long and satisfying life. If he was Scottish, you'd have imagined him having his own newspaper column, living in Glasgow's West End and making guest appearances on football phone-ins. But Sócrates Brasileiro Sampaio de Sousa Vieira de Oliveira was a bit too intelligent for such banality.

He spent an unsuccessful season in Italy, at Fiorentina, before retiring from the game whilst still in his early thirties. He continued to rebel in the years afterwards – against authority mainly, but also often against domestic responsibility. He tried painting and poetry to divert his brilliant mind but, mostly, he drank and smoked and pondered. Every day, he pondered.

When he died in December 2010, aged just fifty-seven, a tribute paid to him by the former Italian footballer Paolo Rossi resonated with me. Rossi scored a hat-trick in the 3-2 win in 1982 which ended the Brazilians' challenge prematurely.

'It's a piece of our history that's broken off and gone away. Sócrates seemed like a player from another era. You couldn't place him in any category – on the pitch and even more so off it. Everyone knew about his degree in medicine and he had a lot of cultural and social interests as well. He was unique from every point of view.'

All heroes are flawed, yet they are still our heroes. Although he is now gone, Sócrates deserves to live forever. Individuals like him are too rare and too beautiful to ever be forgotten.

Exhibit 15
Battle of Bothwell Bridge (2000)

The Battle of Bothwell Bridge took place, surprisingly enough, at Bothwell Bridge, on 22 June 1679. It was fought between soldiers of the crown and militant Presbyterian Covenanters. It shouldn't be confused with the Battle of Bothwell Bridge in August 2000.

I should admit I've always been fond of the Ferguson brothers, Derek and Barry. My grandparents' house, on Mill Road, in Hamilton, looked on to the huge playing fields where Barry started playing at Mill United. A boys' club was launched there in 1977 and the quality of their football was always way above average, well organised and enjoyable to watch. As well as Barry, they brought through former Celtic, Hearts and Scotland midfielder Paul Hartley.

This particular battle occurred in the aftermath of Rangers' 6-2 defeat at the hands of Celtic in which Barry had been sent off. Following the game, Barry met Derek and two other pals for their weekly card game at Bothwell Bridge Hotel. A short time later, a group of Celtic fans arrived in jubilant mood and proceeded to wind up Barry, who was dressed in his club suit, shirt and tie. Barry, who had reportedly already consumed a fair amount of alcohol by this stage, complained to the staff that the fans hurling abuse at his table shouldn't be allowed to wear their green Celtic polo shirts as club colours were banned in the hotel. The fans were made put their coats on but the battle lines had been drawn and they continued to hurl abuse his way.

Eventually, Barry decided enough was enough. He jumped in a taxi, went home, changed into his Rangers tracksuit and returned to continue the session. When the Celtic fans complained about Ferguson's clear provocation, all hell broke loose. Kind of.

Asked by the management to change out of his Rangers trackie, Barry unleashed his inner bampot. 'I am a professional footballer,' he protested. 'These are my working clothes.'

Both parties were asked to leave and, once outside, a brawl broke out. Some claimed older brother Derek – himself a former Rangers player – whipped off his belt and got in about the opponents. Barry, meanwhile, was reportedly headbutted. By the time the police finally appeared, most of those involved had scarpered.

When the press heard of the story, it was reported that a full-scale battle had erupted on the streets. The papers focused on Barry and Derek, battered and bruised. Barry had been left with a gash from the headbutt and had to have three stitches. Derek was allegedly hit on the head with a Buckfast bottle. Those seriously injured were taken to separate hospitals: the Rangers casualties to Hairymyres Hospital in East Kilbride; and the Celtic victims to Monklands Hospital in Airdrie.

When police later pressed Barry for a statement, he was apparently vague about the details of what took place: he was attacked by around ten Celtic fans while in the street looking for a taxi; he didn't know how he had ended up with the gash in his head; he didn't want to press charges.

The papers reported of a 'drink-fuelled skirmish' and a 'battle royal'. As no-one involved made a complaint, as is the Scottish way, the finer details remained subject to conjecture.

GALLERY ONE

TACTICS,
THE GAME
& THE DUFFERS

Exhibit 16
The Coaching Badge

Geographically, Scotland is little more than a tiny outcrop on the side of Europe. And yet, for a time, the football world flocked to the north Ayrshire town of Largs, on the Firth of Clyde, to learn how to brutalise the beautiful game.

In years gone by, before the coaching manual took hold and football was rebranded with a modern academic touch, the question on every club owner or director's lips was: 'Can you manage this bunch of misfits, save us from relegation, galvanise the dressing room and create a winning mentality which will filter through the club?'

Now they ask, 'Do you have your badges?'

The culture has improved but there was a time in football when former professionals, after a long career and their last game on a Saturday, would be unveiled as manager on the Monday. There was no set-up for top names in Scottish football to start their coaching career educating the under-10s at the club they formerly starred for. It was assumed that if you'd played the game at international level and in European competition, you would be able to cobble together a team, copy the illustrious managers you worked under and restore an ailing club to its former glory. There wasn't any focus on the teaching side of things, like working on skills and technique.

However, over in the Netherlands, the opposite is true. The Dutch expect their coaches to begin at a club's under-10s and work extensively in the youth system until they are ready for a top job, irrespective of how illustrious and decorated a career they might have had. They do everything in a 4–3–3 system and focus on philosophy, clearly defining each player's role. What's more, the big stars don't think it's beneath them to roll up their sleeves and start coaching the kids. They understand it's another skill they need to develop. They know they need to get experience under their belts and learn how to communicate their message before they get anywhere near a club's first team.

In Scotland, meanwhile, they've started taking guys off the telly who are competent analysts and sound as if they know what they're talking about, believing that is enough to make them decent coaches. Let's call it 'the Neil McCann approach'. McCann left Sky Sports to manage Dundee on an interim basis, in April 2017, and steered the club away from relegation, which was no mean feat. After they failed to appoint Jack Ross, McCann was given the position permanently. A horrendous start to the following season – one win in eight games – meant his tenure was over barely before it began. He was sacked on 16 October 2017. It feels like a typical story in Scottish coaching and management.

Across the rest of the football world, fans and desperate directors have always loved football managers who once played the game at the highest level. Largs, however, made big names out of many managers who hadn't. They may have started out as video analysts or translators and shown some proficiency at organising a Christmas night out, but their true journey into management began when their employers suggested they head to a windy, wet place in Scotland called Largs to 'get their badges'.

The Largs coaching course allowed football geeks, for almost the first time, to become football managers – and first-rate ones too. Initially, some fans were cynical. They didn't like guys who hadn't played the game having any say with their team and for that very reason. But it soon became clear that a generation of coaching and managerial talent was graduating from Largs to begin a bright, new intellectual future in the game.

David Moyes, Andre Vilas-Boas, Jose Mourinho, Fabio Capello and Arrigo Sacchi are among the famous alumni who learned from Andy Roxburgh, the former Scotland national coach and one-time UEFA technical director. Roxburgh, along with Craig Brown, Walter Smith, Archie Knox, Jim Fleeting and Sir Alex Ferguson, would roll into town for a bit of a laugh and a few drinks while sharing stories and discussing footballing philosophies. More could be learned on a night out in the pub than a week coaching.

When these big names started to endorse players earning their coaching badges, Scotland quickly became recognised as a world leader in football coaching. Having played the game, these managers knew a football career was short and, as soon as they saw one of their own players showing any aptitude toward teaching and coaching, they would send them to Largs to get their badges.

Roxburgh, Brown and Frank Coulson were key figures in establishing and developing the centre's coaching programmes. Anyone looking to become a coach was encouraged to take the three-year courses for 'B' and 'A' licences. In fact, Brown's father, Hugh, set up the first coaching education course in the 1960s and Alex Ferguson, along with Jim McLean, would learn from listening to men like Eddie Turnbull and Willie Ormond.

Knowledge was continually passed down from one generation to the next. A simple concept – but brilliant nonetheless.

There are, of course, negatives in any system and initiative. In the case of Largs, football has become fixated with badges and training. It's too rigid a system. This means that the cavalier maverick or the exciting football star seldom has the chance to excel in management because they don't fit within the system.

When you look at those involved at Largs, they share one particular strand of footballing D.N.A.: ruthless pragmatism, a definite and distinct desire to break down play to avoid losing rather than setting out to win. This is the same line of succession that eventually saw the SFA employing a manager like Craig Levein. Instead, I say we get the best out of our retired players by starting them with the kids' teams at top clubs and national youth sides and allow them rein to impart their style and football philosophy until it becomes an intrinsic part of our culture. It would surely restore some of the magic and joy to the game – which is what we all fell in love with in the first place, not systems, percentage plays and parking the bus.

Exhibit 17
Duffer Signings

The surreal world of Scottish football could best be compared to a special soup made of a hearty filling and held together by a magical laughing stock. This exhibit is dedicated to the misplaced fortunes and ridiculous signings of complete duffers, those who found the weight of the shirt too heavy and failed to shine despite huge promise. In this exhibit, we have stuck primarily to those with the most cash to spend: Celtic and Rangers.

In November 2000, Rangers chairman David Murray appeared to have money to burn – and nobody thought to ask where it came from. He flew to Chelsea and, in a dismissive act of hubris, broke the Scottish transfer record by paying £12 million for an out-of-favour Tore Andre Flo. Despite, at times, looking like he was cast in the wrong movie, Flo still managed to score twenty-nine goals in fifty-three games for the Ibrox side. He was costly, probably around five or six million over the asking price . . . but he wasn't a total duffer.

Celtic, on the other hand, signed Rafael Scheidt for £5

million from Gremio, despite repeated warnings from Brazilian-based journalists and coaches regarding the player's ability. Celtic ignored their advice. The Scottish press and the Glasgow club seemed blinded by the light. Indeed, it was widely reported at the time he was signed on the basis of a 'best of' VHS, and no scouting missions.

As Celtic fans eagerly awaited their Brazilian superstar, they were instead presented with someone doing an imitation of a footballer. He was like an accident-prone brickie. In short, he was a calamitous signing. If you were a Scottish football manager looking to sign a player called Scheidt, wouldn't it occur to you to check him out before unleashing him (and his name) on your domestic game? Surely the risk of nominative determinism is just too great? But Celtic had thought this through (sort of) – he would be known as 'Rafael', which made him seem like the height of Brazilian sophistication. They would have been better off calling him Excremento. Scheidt isn't alone in a game full of ridiculously named players. Here's a five-a-side team of former classics: Paraguayan full back Francisco Arce, Brazilian centre-half, Argel Fucks, from the MLS and Montreal, defender Rod Fanni, Dynamo Dresden's striker Ralf Minge and FC Kaiserlautern striker, Stefan Kuntz. Yes, just to confirm today's line up: Arce, Fucks, Fanni, Minge and Kuntz.

In the end, he only lasted a few games before being punted back home, thanks to the intervention of the Home Office. A diligent employee (and Celtic fan) was cross-checking paperwork only to find that Rafael was no longer eligible for a work permit in the UK. Consequently, Scheidt was hastily loaned to Corinthians before being flushed back to Atlético Mineiro.

However, as Scheidt as the debacle was, he did play more games than Daniel Prodan. The Romanian, who tragically passed away at the age of forty-four in 2016, made his way into Rangers folklore for costing £2.2 million and never playing a game for the first team. The most surreal part of this particular saga was how easily he was given the all-clear after a quick check of his significantly falsified and clearly inaccurate medical records. Closer inspection of his X-rays may have revealed Prodan had a knee made of cloths pegs, Airfix Spitfire spare parts and plasticine.

Most of the modern ails levelled at Celtic, at least in the last five to six years, pointed to their approach to recruitment, or what the club liked to call 'projects'. The idea was to find decent players and sell them on for a big profit. This has proved largely successful, but for every Virgil van Dijk, there was a Morten Rasmussen or Mo Bangura; for every Victor Wanyama, they would sign gems like Derk Boerrigter from Ajax for £3 million. Yes, £3 million! The bold Derk arrived in Glasgow with a huge reputation but, instead, seemed to have an inner GPS system programmed to the treatment room. In his first game against Ross County, he hobbled off and never recovered. He scored one goal in 500 minutes. In the end, it was one of the club's better pieces of business when they wrote off his contract and slung him out.

Joey Barton was also a substantial duffer (despite being a free transfer, which gives him some leeway). Amazingly, he didn't seem to know what he'd let himself in for when he signed for Rangers in 2016. He strutted in, making proclamations left, right and centre about Celtic and the rest of Scottish football . . . but left with his tail squarely between his legs after just five league games and three League Cup ties.

Honourable mentions must go to Stephane Guivarc'h, Nuno Capucho and Francis Jeffers while, for Celtic, Du Wei, Stéphane Henchoz and Marvin Compper hardly set the heather alight and join the dubious band of duffers. God, there has been a lot of them.

Exhibit 18
Goalkeepers

Sometimes, in the gibbering mind of the nervous pundit, goalkeepers are referred to as 'a protected species'. This makes them sound like Forfar Bridies or Arbroath Smokies. Perhaps their six-yard box should be awarded Protected Geographical Status.

Goalkeepers are a mollycoddled, untouchable lot. As soon as an opposition player makes a challenge, they go down and the referee gives a free-kick. It seems like every decision goes their way. If an outfield player did the same elsewhere on the park, they would be red-carded for violent conduct or play-acting and, on some occasions, even expelled permanently from the game. Yet goalkeepers are seemingly judged to a different standard.

When they come out for a cross and the opposition striker hardly makes contact, they go down and the ref brings on medical experts and physios as if they are the anointed ones. They also have a habit of sticking their knee or foot in a kung fu kick when they clutch the ball, in a crowded box. If they did this on the street, they would be charged with assault. It's as though referees turn a blind eye to allow them to go hell for leather with their fists and knees.

Why are they allowed such freedom to behave like this? There must be an overarching reason for it. Scottish goalies, historically, have always been either daft or rubbish, sometimes both, so there's pity shown towards them.

We've had a number of great goalies – David Harvey, Andy Goram, Craig Gordon, Jim Leighton and Allan McGregor all spring to mind. Yet some have been comically bad. Take Frank Haffey, for example. The Glasgow man found his way into football folklore when England beat Scotland 9–3 at Wembley in 1961. Haffey was so mortified by the result he emigrated to Australia and reinvented himself as a cabaret singer. Perhaps it was because we had so many exalted outfield players at that time that we didn't need to worry too much about the goalie – but, soon enough, the whole team became as bad as eleven Haffeys.

Intrepid football historians have been keen to locate the source of this madcap Scottish goalie gene. Most evidence, unfairly it should be said, pointed to a chap who played for Aberdeen and Scotland in the 1950s, named Fred Martin. Martin joined Aberdeen in 1946 as an inside forward but loved jumping in goals so much he ended up becoming the goalie – and an accomplished one, too. Well, sometimes. He was the first goalkeeper to represent Scotland at a World Cup, in Switzerland in 1954. He made nearly 300 senior appearances for Aberdeen during the fifties and won the league in 1955.

As well as moments of brilliance, however, he was also prone to the odd catastrophe. He reached peak calamity in 1954/55 when, over three successive Scotland appearances, he conceded eighteen goals. In the 1954 World Cup, he conceded seven against Uruguay. When Scotland faced Hungary at Hampden, he lost four. And when we made the trip south to face England at Wembley, he let in seven.

Martin and Haffey are by no means the only Scottish goalies to suffer Wembley woe. Stuart Kennedy, for example, managed to concede five against the Auld Enemy in 1975.

Similarly, the lasting image of Alan Rough is of him being wrong-footed by Zico's free kick in Seville in the 1982 World Cup. Goalkeepers seldom have their terrific saves highlighted; only their calamitous errors. Rough played fifty-three times for his country and did most of it while still earning forty quid a week at Thistle.

I understand goalkeepers used to be treated brutally but I feel that the situation has done a one-hundred and eighty-degree shift now whereby they're over-protected. Anytime there's a collision, the keepers get awarded the free-kick; yet when the keeper is the aggressor, concessions are almost always made.

There's a strange laxity granted to goalkeepers from ex-players who are now pundits, which commentators and viewers have grown to accept. They have adopted a narrative which exempts the goalkeeper, referring to them as being 'a breed apart', 'nuts', 'a bit crazy', 'the joker in the pack'. The keeper is treated in a football team the way a drummer is in a band. They are continuously referred to as if they live in a separate world with other goalkeepers like some sort of goalkeepers' union. With this in mind, is it any wonder referees treat them with greater leniency than their out-field teammates? How else are they expected to react to someone stupid enough to stand in front of a ball that's rocketing toward their nether regions?

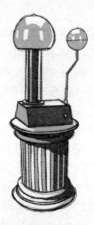

Exhibit 19
Giant Killers & Shockers

There have been many cup upsets and giant-killing moments in Scottish football but only two results which have truly reverberated across the fault lines and tectonic plates of our game.

On 28 January 1967, the reigning Scottish Cup holders Rangers were humbled by Berwick Rangers, going down 1–0 to a Sammy Reid goal in a game that has entered folklore. As the 13,365 who attended subsequently attested, it was a truly remarkable and unforgettable match. The huge gulf in quality between the sides was stark – Berwick's part-timers up against the fully pro superstars. Rangers had nine internationals in their starting line-up. The same year, they reached the final of the European Cup Winners' Cup, only to go down to a 1–0 defeat at the hands of Bayern Munich.

For Berwick supporters, the game epitomised the romance of the cup, but for Rangers it was a nightmare, a dire and catastrophic result that would haunt the club for decades to come.

Rangers must have felt as though the football gods were conspiring against them. In classic cup tie fashion, they were pounding Berwick, had three corners and three clear chances that were missed in the opening minutes of the game. In the first half hour, Rangers had forced ten corners without finding the Berwick net. In the thirty-fourth minute, Reid opened the scoring. A few minutes later, George Christie missed a gilt-edged opportunity to make it two for the Wee Rangers.

By now, Berwick were growing in confidence and had more chances in the second half. Jock Wallace was coach and goalkeeper of Berwick Rangers at the time. Willie Johnston was stretchered off after breaking his ankle when Wallace collided with him. Berwick saw the game out for a momentous victory. *The Scotsman* proclaimed it to be 'the most ludicrous, the weirdest, the most astonishing result ever returned in Scottish football'.

It was reported that Rangers' club captain, John Greig, demonstrated his class by sportingly shaking the hand of every Berwick player after the game. He would later describe it as 'probably the worst result in the history of our club'. Few would argue. The club would again have the odd shocker, like the 1–0 defeat to Hamilton Academical in January 1987, when Adrian Sprott grabbed the winner at Ibrox. Again, Rangers were installed as favourites to win the competition. In the league, they were thirty-three points ahead of John Lambie's Accies.

Still, nothing would come close to the enormity of the shockwaves which reverberated around Scottish football following the Berwick Rangers defeat. Scottish football is prone to getting a bit Old Testament when it goes wrong. In Leviticus, a goat is summoned and ritually burdened with the sins of others. The scapegoat is then cast adrift, into the desert, away from the club. Those let go in this case were Rangers' strikers Jim Forrest and George McLean. Both were shown the door within weeks: Forrest to Preston North End, McLean to Dundee. If there was an upside to the Berwick loss, the offloading of these two players prompted the introduction of two youngsters who would make a major contribution to the game. Alex Ferguson was signed from Dunfermline, whilst Sandy Jardine was given his chance from the reserves. Both players would ultimately have stands named after them – Jardine's at Ibrox, Ferguson's at Manchester United's Old Trafford ground.

The other giant-killing which jumps off the page is Inverness Caledonian Thistle's third round Scottish Cup trouncing of Celtic on 8 February 2000. Unlike the Berwick Rangers game, this came at a time when Celtic were in turmoil. Manager John Barnes had not only lost the dressing room, he was stranded, lost at sea and out of his depth. His side were ten points behind Rangers in the league. Barry Wilson set the calamity in motion with a brilliant header from a Sheerin cross only for Mark Burchill to restore parity almost immediately. When Caley's Bobby Mann won a header from a corner, it deflected off a hapless Lubomír Moravčík into the net. When Barry Wilson was brought down by Regi Blinker inside the area, Paul Sheerin scored the penalty. Inverness won 3–1.

The scapegoat on this occasion was Barnes. He was sacked the following day. Again, context is important. Inverness, at the time, were First Division part-timers. The biggest shock of the night was that they had almost 4,000 fans travel down to witness the victory. They must have sensed something special was brewing.

Celtic would also suffer a painful exit in the Scottish Cup in January 2006 with a 2–1 defeat at the hands of Clyde. This was Manchester United legend Roy Keane's debut for his boyhood heroes, whilst Chinese defender Du Wei was so bad that at half-time he was replaced by Adam Virgo. What is often overlooked is Clyde had two goals disallowed and Artur Boruc saved a penalty, as well as making a splendid save from a deflected shot from Clyde's Steve Masterton. It was 2-1 going on much more. Du Wei would soon disappear from Scottish football. Again, not the same level of shock as the Inverness Caley result but this was a Celtic side who, as well as Keane, included Shunsuke Nakamura, Neil Lennon, Shaun Maloney and John Hartson. There have been many cup shockers for Scotland's top flight but they only seem truly remarkable when they involve the Glasgow giants.

Exhibit 20
The High Press

In our house, the high press was a cupboard where freshly washed and ironed bed linen and towels were placed. It usually had a huge hot water tank which would keep the assorted sheets and towels warm when it slowly lumbered into action around bath time. Now, it's used as an irritating football term for what we used to call 'getting stuck in', 'retaliating first', or 'giving it some welly'.

Some trendy media guy probably came up with it, or perhaps some average ex-pro journeyman, who'd read a few books and considered himself brainy.

Coaching jargon is seldom sumptuous or nuanced, and is often slapped out in a cold, scientific way. Obese parents squeal about the high press from the touchlines, while drunken fans do likewise at the pub TV.

Barcelona, at their peak, found extraordinary success under Pep Guardiola, who was fast becoming football's answer to Julius Caesar, conquering the game and spreading the high press across Europe.

In Dortmund, Jürgen Klopp enjoyed success with 'Gegenpressing'. This is basically the same as the high press, and means immediate ball recovery. Lose the ball, put pressure on, get it back. In order for it to work, you need enough players close to the ball to press and pressurise the opposition into losing possession while hoping the opposition player doesn't slam a long defence-splitting pass into the space behind you, where you're most vulnerable.

Despite Guardiola and Klopp finding success with the system, it is generally agreed that the first coach to introduce the high press was Victor Maslov whilst managing Dynamo Kiev in the 1960s. It's unclear if it was called the high press then but his concept of restriction, limiting space and time on the ball, and pressing in packs in dangerous areas high up the pitch, caught the eye.

Austrian coaching legend, Ernst Happell, led Feyenoord to European Cup glory in 1970 with the pressing game, against a complacent, lacklustre Celtic side. Dutch coach Rinus Michels took the high press on to the international stage and, with it, led the Netherlands to the final of the 1974 World Cup. Here, Johan Cruyff would adopt his mentor's tactics, hunting the ball down in packs, shutting down any passing angles for the opposition and preventing attacks before they started. Cruyff incorporated this approach when he took charge of Barcelona in 1988 and Guardiola – who became a fulcrum of Cruyff's Barca side – would do likewise when he made his own transition into management.

The trouble starts when we try to play it in Scotland. Football intellectual property is relatively shallow and prone to shamelessly copying of any team that has found success. Fine in theory but when it filters down through our coaches and we mess it up trying to implement it at the likes of Ross County, St Mirren and East Fife, it ends up looking like something of a fool's errand. The system usually falls apart when pressing teams are caught on the counter, or when the goalie tries to play out from the back and dribble past strikers, only to lose possession and leave his goal wide open.

Brendan Rodgers won back-to-back trebles at Celtic with his ruthlessly efficient use of the high press. His refusal to adopt a more defensive set-up in the Champions League against elite sides exposed his over-dependence on the system and, arguably, a flaw in his abilities as a manager. (This didn't put off Leicester City who lured the 'Celtic mad' Rodgers, months away from a historic treble treble. 'It was the project, not the money,' claimed Rodgers, before getting his big teeth into Leicester and declaring his love for the side, and money.)

Then you had Craig Levein who, as Scotland manager, showed his staggering tactical nous by playing the pressing game in reverse. He set-up for a Euro 2012 qualifying match with the Czech Republic by controversially deploying his side in a 4–6–0 formation. He prepared for a war of attrition and hoped to break the Czechs down by soaking up their pressure and frustrating them with a siege mentality.

Less pressing game, more a depressing game.

Exhibit 21
The Ten Men Myth

The red card is there to help referees govern the game. It can leave teams, fans, sometimes a whole nation, bewildered, confused and heartbroken, as some Estonian whistle-blower cocks up a decision to render your slim chance of qualifying for the World Cup impossible.

What annoys me most about the red card, whether it's warranted or the result of a scandalously incompetent decision, is the way we (and by 'we' I mean Scotland and Scottish football sides) accept it, moan and complain, instead of being proactive.

This has to change. In the words of Rob Tyner, late frontman of the legendary Detroit force of nature, MC5, *'I'm here to ask, brothers and sisters, are you ready to testify?'* I'm here to tell you, it needn't be this way.

We've all heard the lazy cliché that it's harder to play against ten men, yet there seems to be an element of truth to it. Why does it happen? Is it because the side were coasting before their man was sent off? Perhaps they've been slapped into reality and every player on the pitch is now giving 110 per cent, fully focused and stretching themselves, as a collective, to get a result? It could be that a sense of injustice gels the team together. Or perhaps a sense of complacency sets in to those playing with eleven?

The first coach I was aware of who actively prepared and trained for just such an outcome was José Mourinho.

Whenever one of his players was sent off, he had his teams re-organise themselves immediately into something close to a tight and rigid 3–3–3. For decades in Scotland, we resorted to the usual routine: sacrificing the striker up front and shoring up the defensive line by dropping deeper and hoping for the best. Why do we always do this? It's asking for trouble.

What most top coaches understand is the damage that can be done in the spaces, gaps and pockets between the opposition's defenders. If these gaps are blocked, it's difficult to get by. We should be mirroring the elite sides like Barcelona, Real Madrid, Juventus or Bayern Munich and do what they do. They rarely launch long balls from deep. Instead, they probe, stretch and move the ball until they find pockets of space through the middle.

There's an elastic fluidity and mathematic rigidity watching top teams down to ten men playing the correct way. It requires training, practice, repetition and drills. Instead of hoisting the white flag and complaining about injustice, imagine we had a plan that could be put into immediate action? Instead of conceding it's over when we go a man down, we should change our approach, seeing it as part of the game, something we've prepared and trained for.

Then there's the psychological side, when the players have to focus, fight and close down space – it becomes less about skill and more about effort, toil and work rate. We can do it, surely? It's not rocket science having a red card 'Plan B'. Fail to prepare, prepare to fail.

In order for the game to disintegrate and for our 3–3–3 formation to be effective, we need a serial offender referee who loves a bit of red card action; step forward the quiet assassin, Willie Collum. Scotland, per capita, probably produces the worst referees in the world. They aren't cheats but their decisions are often farcical.

If proof is required, let's take an incident from a Scottish Championship match between Partick Thistle and Morton at Firhill in September 2018.

Thistle striker Kris Doolan scored a clear goal in so much as it hit the back of the net, universally accepted as a sign the ball has crossed the line. As the Thistle players wheeled away in celebration, the ball fell to a furious Morton defender who thumped the ball away in sheer frustration. It left the field of play and crossed the touchline, close to the linesman. After some feverish flag-waving from the linesman, referee Barry Cook gave a throw-in.

The decision mystified both sets of players, the watching fans in the stadium and the billions of people who almost broke the internet thereafter. Truly, one of the most peculiar and embarrassing decisions ever seen in Scottish football.

Exhibit 22
Sand Dunes

Jock Wallace played in goal for Airdrie, West Brom, Berwick and Hereford. He was player/manager of Berwick when his side knocked Rangers out of the Scottish Cup in the first round in 1967. He then joined Hearts as their assistant manager before, in 1970, Willie Waddell brought him to Rangers as his coach. By the summer of 1972, Waddell had stepped aside and Wallace was promoted to team manager. A successful career, but perhaps what Wallace will be mostly fondly remembered for was his ruthless approach to pre-season training and the sand dunes of Gullane.

It's difficult to fathom but, at the time, there seemed to be a direct correlation between overweight players, full of Spanish lager after six weeks in the sun, and real, tangible success on the football field. It was a time when the players returned from holiday refreshed, reinvigorated and out of condition to take on an unorthodox training regime that somehow led to winning trebles and glory in Europe. At Gullane in East Lothian, the players were forced to sprint up and down sand dunes until they threw up, before being made to do it again until they had nothing left. Let's hear it for the halcyon days of brutality disguised as football training!

And yet it worked. Rangers won the championship in 1974/75 for the first time in eleven years, going on to win the treble twice in the following three seasons. I remember being terrified as a youth when I saw images in the *Daily Record* of these players writhing in agony, bent double, wrenching up what was left of their breakfast, before continuing with my Cornflakes. I would marvel at the abject horror these poor players were going through. It was Wallace who was the most famous proponent of the sand dune as a gym. For him, fitness was everything. A gruelling, lung-bursting, stomach-churning grappling with the dunes was akin to man-to-man combat with nature.

As I sat reading the paper, living in mortal fear for the players subjected to this training regime while moving on to my toast and coffee, I shuddered at the sheer cruelty. I became so concerned I even joined in. I tried running up and down the stairs in pit boots for five minutes. I didn't puke but tripped a few times before regaining my sanity and sitting down to watch *Robinson Crusoe* or *My White Horses* or *The Flashing Blade* – whatever children's TV fare would be on during the wet summer school holidays. Somewhere at the back of my mind, I expected to see the Rangers first team sprint by Crusoe as he followed his own footsteps.

Some of the players looked like they were training for the Foreign Legion. The teams who endured the pain in July saw the gains the following spring, when, as the season drew to a close, the opposition wilted. The stamina amassed from those pre-season sessions saw the same players grow stronger as the campaign wore on.

There was method behind Jock Wallace's demanding approach. Yes, he was a hard man who made demands but many of the players he trained and managed would go on to have long football careers thanks to his 'tough love'. A fitness fanatic, Wallace had served as a commando in the Malaysian jungle. Having players run up and down sand dunes at Gullane until they were sick, then making them do it again, not only helped their fitness, determination and fortitude – it fostered team unity.

There have been many former Rangers players in the vicinity of Gullane for a pro-am, some forty years later, who suffered flashbacks. Many have reported actually becoming dizzy and sick as their minds are taken back to the scene of the crime as the sadistic pre-season ritual came back to haunt them.

Like Jim McLean, Wallace was of a time when football was about masculinity and power. These were intelligent men, who looked for inspiration abroad and would marvel at the discipline meted out by the likes of Inter Milan's boss, Helenio Herrera. *il Mago*, as he was known, famously ordered two of his players to walk six miles back to their team base because they were twenty seconds late for the team bus. That kind of discipline got their juices flowing.

Wallace acquired his steeliness while serving in the army. He instilled discipline, fitness, team bonding, tactics, and a clear objective, a fighting spirit, drilled like a sergeant major. He returned to Motherwell from Leicester in 1982 then, after John Grieg's unsuccessful stint as a manager, he came back to Rangers but would only win the League Cup twice.

Wallace also had a kind side, too. While at Motherwell, it was reported he would slip cash into the pockets of players he knew had families and who were struggling, particularly around Christmas. At the same time, I'm sure if any of the players told him he was a 'softy', he'd have strangled them with his bare hands.

Exhibit 23
Sitters (The Iwelumo Wing)

The name of Chris Iwelumo will forever be intertwined with the ignominious honour of having missed the biggest sitter in Scottish football history.

You see great opportunities spurned every week of every year in Scottish football. Some are televised, some aren't, but there are a few which immediately spring to mind – chief amongst them, Iwelumo's.

It's 11 October 2008 and Iwelumo is making his international debut against Norway in a crucial World Cup qualifier at Hampden. Having lost their opening match away to Macedonia and scraped past Iceland in their second fixture, the Scots know they can't afford to cough up any ground to the Norwegians, one of their main qualification rivals. Head coach George Burley even openly stated that the World Cup dream would be over if the team didn't win. He started with James McFadden up front, leaving Iwelumo and Kris Boyd to warm the bench. By the fifty-fifth minute, with the game still goalless, he took off McFadden and midfielder James Morrison, replacing them with Darren Fletcher and Iwelumo.

For Boyd, it was the final insult and the Rangers striker declared after the game that he wouldn't play for Scotland again while Burley remained in charge. Boyd had earned a reputation for scoring scrappy 'goal-scorer goals' from in and around the six-yard box with lucky deflections off the knee, back-side, shin or ankle. He had both the knack of shaping himself to the correct angle to receive anything coming in on the half-chance, as well as terrific positional sense. This was precisely what was required from Iwelumo when Gary Naysmith sent in a low, probing cross. It wasn't to be. From just three yards out, with the goal at his mercy, he turned the cross wide of the post. For once, the clunky cliché of 'it seemed easier to score than miss' was fitting.

Iwelumo told the press afterwards he was gutted, while, as is the way with the modern professional, appearing ridiculously positive and upbeat. Scotland drew 0–0, didn't qualify and, over a year later, Burley was sacked after winning three of his fourteen games in charge. Iwelumo, meantime, would go on to make three further appearances in the dark blue of Scotland – never hitting the net.

Another missed 'sitter' that springs to mind is Peter van Vossen's effort – if you can even call it that – for Rangers against Celtic. It was a cold, dreary evening in the East End of Glasgow in November 1996. Rangers were one league title win away from emulating Celtic's record of nine-in-a-row. Their city rivals, however, were ahead of them in the league and had the chance to extend their advantage with a victory in this particular encounter.

It was a game that had almost everything. A fabulous winner for the Ibrox men courtesy of their Danish forward Brian Laudrup; two missed penalties, one for each side; and even a fox invading the pitch.

However, despite the game's significance in the wider context of the league that season and more generally, as well as all of the other drama that unfolded, it is best remembered for Dutch striker van Vossen's inexplicable miss late in the game. The man himself was anything but a duffer. He had played in an Ajax side that had won the European Cup and had played thirty-one times for his country, scoring nine goals. That only made this particular miss all the more shocking. With Celtic pressing for an equaliser, Rangers sprung a counter attack. Their German midfielder Jorg Albertz broke through, getting in behind a Celtic defence that tried – and miserably failed – to play the offside trap. One-on-one with Celtic's Stuart Marshall, Albertz wrong-footed the 'keeper before squaring the ball unselfishly for his teammate for van Vossen to tap-in. Instead, he skied it clean over the bar from only a few yards out. Unlike Iwelumo's, this sitter didn't have any bearing on the result but van Vossen was scarred.

The final sitter worth a mention is Billy Bremner's against Brazil in the World Cup in 1974 – a miss that, to this day, still summons nothing but heartache. Not only would it have taken Scotland through to the final stages of the World Cup for the first time but it would have given the national side their most famous victory.

A few yards out with the goal at his mercy, Bremner was unable to adjust his body quickly enough to get a shot away, the ball instead ricocheting and bouncing off his leg. It wasn't quite a tap-in but it was still painful to watch.

Truth be told, it still is.

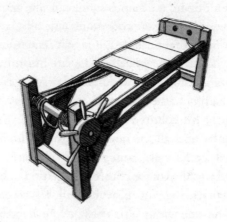

Exhibit 24
Strachan's Scotland Stretching Machine

Gordon Strachan is seldom without either rapier wit or a terrific turn of phrase.

Even when he is off duty, before microphones and phones are switched on at press conferences, he is full of perfect put-downs. When he is between jobs and not working as a head coach somewhere, his punditry is always articulate and astute. His line in banter is matched with a remarkably perceptive understanding of how the game is unfolding. He is fantastic at clarifying and zoning in on tactical variations. It's easy to understand why players like him.

So, after failing to quality for yet another World Cup after a 2–2 draw away to Slovenia in October 2017, it was a surprise to hear him explain why Scotland have made a habit of falling short. According to Strachan, the reason is simple: we, as a people, are too wee.

Strachan claimed the D.N.A. of the nation is what's holding us back. 'We have to work harder to get on the ball than bigger lads at six foot three,' he claimed. 'Genetically, we are behind. In the last campaign, we were the second smallest, behind Spain.'

Ah yes, Spain. The 2008 and 2012 European champions and 2010 World Cup winners. And what of other diminutive footballers? A lack of vertical supremacy has hardly held back the likes of Lionel Messi, or the great Diego Maradona before him. No giant himself, is Strachan really trying to suggest that he failed to hit the heights he could have – whether literally or figuratively – because of his own diminutive stature?

Of course, throughout the 2018 World Cup qualifying campaign, there were other mitigating factors for Scotland's non-qualification. Issues such as playing Kiernan Tierney, one of the finest left-backs of his generation, at right-back. Likewise, Strachan's failure to recognise that Leigh Griffiths was one of the most prolific marksmen in the country and in the form of his life. The manager ignored him, believing Chris Martin was the answer instead. Scotland also defended like a pub team at corners. Drawing at home to Lithuania, getting battered by Slovakia and poor concentration and composure against England had nothing to do with height.

For reasons known only to him, Strachan refused to select players who were on-form. Celtic's Callum McGregor and James Forrest, for example. McGregor couldn't get near the side, despite his excellent club performances and a clamour from the Scottish media for his inclusion. Meanwhile, Forrest – who was on the bench against Slovenia – had the game to destroy any defence. John McGinn, then at Hibs, now at Aston Villa, would run all day and was the type of player that the match in Ljubljana was crying out for. Most of Scotland seemed to recognise McGinn's performances were something special. But not Strachan. He appeared to resolutely believe that the English Championship was a better league than the Scottish Premiership, picking guys like Barry Bannan – all 5ft 6in of him – ahead of Forrest and

McGregor, despite the latter two having played Champions League campaigns. Strachan's selections served only to highlight another genetic trait common to Scots: stubbornness.

His last campaign was typical of Scotland. It started poorly, with a draw at home to Lithuania, and, by the time we got the campaign going, it was too late. Despite being unbeaten in the final six qualifiers, it wasn't enough. The team ran themselves into the ground and gave it everything but, in the end, were simply too wee. Apparently.

Exhibit 25
Think Tanks

When former SFA secretary Ernie Walker's death was announced in May 2016, the obituaries described a first-class gentleman and an excellent administrator. They also highlighted that, under his stewardship, Scotland made it to five major championships between 1974 and 1990.

Towards the end of his tenure, he openly voiced his concern that we, as a nation, were going backwards and, of course, he has been proven correct. We haven't been to a major tournament since the World Cup in France in 1998. Over the decades, our fortunes have worsened drastically. The teams of 1974 and 1978 were far better than the side of 1998, which, in turn, was light years ahead of the team of 2018.

Picture the scene.

It's a wet Monday morning in Hampden and the head-scratching has begun. There's been yet another football calamity resulting in calls for a root and branch rethink of Scottish Football. It was always in the aftermath of a disappointing campaign, amid the arguing and discussion, that the pundits would cry for improvement. In return, the blazers in charge of the game would commission a 'think tank'.

If it was a root and branch review of the game you wanted, Ernie Walker was your man. No-one carried out a review quite like the former SFA secretary. In his day, these rethinks were wide-ranging, in-depth and held considerable heft. This being Scottish football, their results were subsequently largely ignored. They were also carried out in a time when we were actually, with hindsight, quite capable of qualifying for major competitions.

Walker had the foresight to call on the advice of the legendary Dutch coach, Rinus Michels, a man who had started the Dutch football revolution in the 1970s, with the mercurial Johan Cruyff as his commander-in-chief. When asked to reflect on the Dutchman's death, in 2005, Walker told *The Scotsman*: 'He was probably the most respected coach in the world and his record was unimpeachable, from founding the marvellous Dutch system of coaching and playing, to his expertise in the development of young players. Every other manager and coach you could name looked up to Rinus.'

If you want to sum up Scottish football's parochial, bowling club mentality here's something to consider. In an effort to provide the technical and coaching expertise for his Independent Review Commission for Scottish football, Walker shrewdly reached out to Michels. When George Peat held the same office some years later, he reached out to Henry McLeish. The former First Minister for Scotland was tasked to call upon his glorious career as an East Fife defender and draw up a blueprint for a brighter Scottish footballing future.

McLeish had, up until then, shown a talent only for insulting his colleagues John Reid and Brian Wilson while live on mic. There was also the 'muddle, not a fiddle' line that forced his resignation in wake of a scandal over the letting of his constituency office. It was a big enough story to become a 'gate': 'Officegate'.

Being a politician, McLeish's Scottish Football Review reads like a commons policy document but is well laid out and, as commons policy documents go, is extremely interesting. It was slammed by default, of course, scorned for its bureaucratic tone and talk of 'strategy' and 'infrastructure'. The demand of £500 million to restructure and 'fix' Scottish football was its great undoing, proof to commentators that McLeish was a politician first and a football man second – if even that.

Still, it contained a lot of good recommendations, such as a streamlining of the three governing bodies, which did, in fact, happen. He wanted the SPL and a new SPL2 with ten teams, a winter break and a play-off system. He suggested the SPL start earlier in July, helping sides in the Champions League and Europa League qualification rounds. He wanted Divisions 1 and 2 regionalised, with a pyramid system and an overhaul of the SFA's nine standing committees. These would be replaced by two new partnerships: a professional and community board. McLeish's focus was to streamline, overhaul committees and open up the SFA.

Despite Walker's conviction and Michels having completely bought in to Scottish football, Walker's report was met with the same disinclination as McLeish's and quietly ignored. Ultimately, it would be down to the SFA to execute the findings. Walker and Michels did manage to get some aspects implemented, like getting kids started from an early age, at five or six, and a need for better facilities and indoor pitches. However, as always, there was something missing – a commitment and willingness by the members (clubs), to wholeheartedly engage and commit to these proposals.

Either way, reviews are always mercilessly pilloried. You're damned if you do and damned if you don't. So what about McLeish's review? The trouble with Scotland – 'those who played the game' and those 'within the game' – is that most are too insular to think big and dream. When idealists like Walker and McLeish make suggestions and propose something new, 'those within the game' and clubs with self-interest at heart have a default position, which is to pick it apart with the same old patronising line: 'What do they know about football?' It's full of self-serving chairmen who, despite their club's perilous positions, refuse to change. And of course, it's the speed of change which is the problem. There's a suspicion of and a resistance to interference from 'those outwith the game'. Reports and reviews take too long to filter down and clubs don't have an appetite for them. Football, after all, is 'a results driven business'.

Whether the ambition would be to follow the French academy model at Clairefontaine, or St George's in England, with a school of football excellence, no-one in Scotland would buy into it. The English FA have paid £105 million to build a state-of-the-art facility with thirteen outdoor pitches (one of which is a full-sized replica of Wembley), and a full size 3G pitch used by twenty-four national teams. Perhaps this has contributed to their improved recent performances, helping them reach the semi-finals of the 2018 World Cup, while we were still scratching our rear-ends at home.

The end-game has proven useless as no-one seems willing to accept and put into practice the ideas from either report which will affect change. No report or think tank is strong enough to shake Scottish football out of its petty and small-minded ways. The next think tank should be an investigation into the belligerent stance of those refusing to change. Only then will a national side reach a World Cup.

Henry McLeish reiterated his concerns in a 2018 story in *The Scotsman*, some eight years after the report. Scotland had failed to qualify for Russia, leading to the resignation of SFA chief executive, Stewart Regan. 'Turbulent times have revealed a game in need of radical reforms, aimed at transforming its governance and accelerating the modernisation of structures and relationships; giving fans their rightful place and developing more trust.' He remained concerned with the lack of ambition and the relationship between clubs and SFA, SPFL. 'Confidence and democracy within the game; building a bigger ambition; and changing the institutions, culture and the unequal distribution of power and money within the game are preventing progress and maintaining tensions between club and country and the SFA and the SPFL. The lack of any real democracy, effective governance or any serious reaching out beyond Hampden is, however, holding us back.'

The more things change, the more they stay the same.

Exhibit 26
Parking the Bus

To most of the human race, the bus is an everyday mode of transportation. To former Scotland manager Craig Levein, it was a tactical aspiration, a chance to revolutionise and transform the tactical approach, an attempt to capture the football zeitgeist. Forget technique and creativity; let's absorb and destroy. These were the cornerstones of the Scottish national team during the former Hearts defender's three years at the helm.

Levein is a talented coach. There's no question about that. But you got the impression he overanalysed football to the extent that his victim – in this case, the game itself – should be euthanised for its own good. A defensive strategy focusing on set plays is okay in a game against Brazil or Germany, but not when you're facing an opposition you should be able to beat. There's a point when coaches have to remove the shackles and allow players scope to express themselves and entertain the fans.

Levein watched Barcelona play in the Champions League against the plucky Russian side, Rubin Kazan. Instead of embracing the attacking élan of the Catalan giants, he was more intrigued by the Russians' 4–6–0 line-up. This 'we-will-not-get-humped-by-too-much' approach inspired his subsequent international policy.

Flamboyance and flare were substituted for honest graft and diligence. Skill and entertainment were benched for hard work and organisation. Opposition sides would visit Hampden to exploit the parked bus, nutmeg the wheels, pass under the chasse, bend it around the windscreen and into the top corner, whilst home fans would leave emotionally damaged after watching ten men defend, and lose.

Levein's appointment as Scotland coach was seen as an adventurous and forward-thinking move. He had enjoyed a broadly successful career, first at Cowdenbeath before Hearts and Scotland came calling, before it was curtailed prematurely by injury. That resulted in a young, highly-valued coach emerging onto the scene. The SFA needed a stronger, more disciplined man in charge following George Burley's dismal reign and they quickly settled on Levein, a man so committed to winning that he once punched a teammate, Graeme Hogg, during a game. The SFA liked the cut of his jib and seemed to believe he could instil fear and a winning mentality in the players.

They had good reason to expect big things from him. His managerial career had, up to that point, provided plenty of examples of tactical nuance with spells at Hearts, Leicester, Raith Rovers and Dundee United proving he had the character and resilience required to take on the Scotland job. However, his ten-pin bowling defensive structure led not so much towards a brave new world as down the garden path.

The single biggest issue with Levein's time in charge was that he had one hand, played it early and never got back in the game. He is clearly an insightful, clever guy and an effective coach. I know players who consider him to be the best coach they ever played under. In fact, one former professional memorably told me that, when he was listening to his new coach, he ignored him and thought instead of what advice Levein would have given.

His three years in charge of Scotland were hardly the worst: twenty-four games, ten wins, five draws and nine losses. However, he will always be remembered for his defensive formations. What really damaged him was that he dropped an in-form Kenny Miller in order to execute his defensive policy.

After leaving his role with Scotland, he became Director of Football at his beloved Hearts and then manager in August 2017 after the sacking of Ian Cathro.

In true footballing irony, when Rangers played Hearts in October 2017, at Murrayfield while Tynecastle's main stand was being constructed, it was Miller who scored twice to remind Levein that, even at thirty-seven, he could find the net. Equally, though, it's often forgotten that it was Levein's tactical acumen that stiffed Celtic's midfield in December 2017 and brought to an end the Parkhead men's sixty-nine game unbeaten domestic run. Looking back, he must reflect ruefully on the Czech Republic game which defined his international managerial career and consider the fine margins between success and failure.

GALLERY TWO

MEDIA, COMMUNICATION & TECHNOLOGY

Exhibit 27
Scotsport Arthur's Jacket & Stramash

For generations of football-mad Scots, Arthur Montford was Mr Sunday Afternoon.

He came from a time when coverage of the game was both scarce and sacred. This was before 'Super Sunday' and televised live games from around the globe. Back then, we lived for Montford's highlights packages. His coherent analysis and discussion always made the show immensely popular.

Even while watching in black and white, however, I sensed something of a psychedelic trip with Arthur Montford's jackets. The checks would undulate, shimmer and swirl as he moved – and sometimes even when he didn't. As much as anything, if I try to recall watching football on the TV as a kid, I see Arthur's oscillating jacket.

Scotsport and *Sportscene* were the lighthouse keepers, guiding us through stormy times, always present, through good and bad, reliable and true. As with most shows in Scotland who use the word 'sport', they mean football. STV's *Scotsport*, in particular, served us well. In fact, it was the world's longest running television sports show. In its latter years, the show was subject to some strange tweaks and odd spin-offs, due no doubt to bosses trying to adapt to a constantly changing broadcasting landscape.

Log-on to YouTube, listen to the original theme of *Scotsport* and allow your senses to wallow in sweet nostalgia. When the credits rolled and Arthur kicked off, it wasn't Cordon Bleu or fine dining TV we were getting. It was your mum's homemade soup, stovies and rhubarb crumble, straight from the garden. The show was delicious in its simplicity. *Scotsport* was what you came in to from the cold after playing football in the park on a rainy Sunday afternoon. It was the glorious witching hour before tea and bath time and getting ready to go back to school.

Many tried to copy Arthur's style but there was more to him than his Houndstooth jackets and outrageous shouts of 'what a stramash'. His ease and deftness of touch made commentating and presenting look easy. He'd been learning his trade for years, with a career path seemingly destined for the role which would eventually define him. Working for the *Glasgow Evening News*, *The Daily Record* and the *Evening Times*, his language was specific, emphatic and precise. BBC radio match reports were next, before he joined STV as a continuity announcer. He was practiced in the written word, the spoken word and timing. This made him a consummate professional and a brilliant host. He was at ease with the camera and the clock, bringing polite authority and a crucial journalistic background to the role. He commentated on more than 400 live games and broadcast more than 2,000 shows for *Scotsport* from 1957 until he retired in 1989.

During commentary at club matches, he had the remarkable knack of remaining balanced and not giving anything away but, during internationals, and despite his best attempts, he would often retreat back to being a fan. Impartiality was gone as he became personally involved in the game. Just another reason that he was so beloved. Two matches spring to mind: Scotland's World Cup qualifier against Czechoslovakia in 1973, when he shouted 'Watch your back, Billy!' when Billy Bremner was being chased down, and 'Watch your legs, Denis!', when Denis Law was under threat of being hacked.

The other was when Scotland played Wales in a crucial World Cup qualifier at Anfield in 1977. As Don Masson stepped up to take a penalty, Arthur captured the feelings of a nation perfectly: 'I can hardly watch.'

Instead of turning on him, like we would have had it been John Motson openly supporting England, we saluted him and warmed to him for being one of us.

Montford's career changed when STV opened studios at Glasgow's Theatre Royal in August 1957 and he was offered a job as a sports presenter. At first he wasn't particularly interested. 'I hadn't really thought much about it but when they said that my salary would jump from £14 a week to £20 a week, I became extremely interested and I was hired on the spot as the newscaster, sportscaster, continuity announcer and jack of all trades.'

He attributed his success and longevity to his journalist father's advice. 'My father told me that no matter how poor the game was, whether you were writing it, describing it on radio, or commentating on it, you must look for something worthwhile to talk about and not be negative. It was a thought that I always carried with me.'

Scotsport was as much about Arthur as Arthur was about *Scotsport*. It was only when he left the show that many fully realised just how accomplished a broadcaster he was.

He enjoyed his retirement, continuing to play golf – his second love – and writing for Scottish golf magazine *bunkered* well into his eighties, while continuing to support his first love: Greenock Morton Football Club. He died, at the age of eighty-five, in 2014.

Exhibit 28
Bob Crampsey

Bob Crampsey was always very highly regarded in our house.

He had written several books, was a headmaster in a local school, had a doctorate of journalism, knew how to construct a sentence and was *Brain of Britain* in 1965. Here was a bona fide intellectual, a renaissance man who could play piano, a historian who wrote books about cricket.

He gave STV's *Scotsport* credence and an air of academic substance. Until then, anything to do with football had been considered low brow and common. Crampsey's eloquence elevated the show to another sphere, paving the way for football to take its place as a subject for serious discussion.

He had an ability to bring even the most lifeless matches to life, throwing in, usually when bored, the odd literary metaphor or an obscure classical reference in his reports. A dour and boring goalless draw in Kirkcaldy would be compared to a dull battle from Homer's *Odyssey*, or a hack-fest at Morton to a scene from Shakespeare. He was an entertaining, peerless voice. Who else could get away with comparing a midfield maestro at Hibs to Euclid, or an on-form striker at Partick Thistle to Apollo, playing his golden lyre before harnessing his chariot of four horses and driving the sun across the sky?

Born on 8 July 1930, close to Hampden, Crampsey was a lifelong supporter of Queens Park. Throughout his broadcasting and journalistic career, he gained a reputation for meticulous research. However, it was his later stints on Radio Scotland – whom he joined in 1987 – I'm most fond of. He also had a popular column in the *Glasgow Evening Times* called Now You Know, which supplied the answers to the most obscure pub arguments about sports history for more than forty years.

Bob Crampsey could converse on almost anything, yet despite his intelligence, no matter the company he was in, he wouldn't show off. He wasn't afraid to laugh at himself and would joke about being the last journalist left from the days when pigeons carried match reports to newspaper offices. He would also leave colleagues in kinks with how useless he was with technology and would openly confess to being equally as bad at DIY.

A classic example of Crampsey's cutting wit could be seen (or heard) when he was discussing the legendary Dundee United figure, Jim McLean, on *Sportsound*. For context, McLean was fiery, judgemental, impatient and often blamed everyone else for his club's woes. If you could imagine a nuclear reactor with red lights flashing and alarms blazing, that was Jim in one of his quieter moments. Crampsey once described him perfectly when he said 'Jim is a joiner from Larkhall who thinks he's a carpenter from Nazareth.' Only Bob Crampsey could deliver this line and kill the discussion, stone dead.

In the 1970s, there was an award-winning Hovis commercial that was directed by Ridley Scott. The ad featured Dvořák's 'New World Symphony', the music wonderfully evoking Northern goodness. However, on BBC Radio Scotland's flagship football comedy show, *Off The Ball*, the same music was used to cue in the actors impersonating Bob Crampsey in the sketches. As a writer for the show, I wouldn't, no matter how tempted, make him the butt of a joke, preferring instead to let him take us off somewhere in history wherever his whim desired. Radio comedy is wonderful for taking the listener on a flight of fancy. So, accompanied by Dvořák, we would have Bob regale us with tales that ranged from Julius Caesar to Third Lanark's Cathkin Park, or Albion Rovers' cult hero Vic Kasule on his motorbike, like Evel Knievel, doing death-defying stunts over bread boards at Cliftonhill. We could literally take Bob anywhere in those sketches as long as we had him back in under sixty seconds, delivering a punchline that underlined a topical issue in Scottish football.

When his death was announced in July 2008, Richard Gordon, the BBC Scotland *Sportsound* anchor said: 'Bob had the sharpest mind of anyone I have ever known. He was a genius. It was such a joy working with him. If anything historical ever came up during a programme, Bob could describe not only the match in question, but name the referee and give the size of the crowd. He was a real football man.'

I think he would have been happy with that description.

Exhibit 29
Cliché

Nothing quite represents the existence of cliché in Scottish football quite like a banana skin. It is the overused, idiotic aphorism which rears its ugly head whenever a team faces a tricky away game against lower league opposition – the type of opposition that play in old grounds with rickety stands and corrugated roofs that are held together with barbed wire, where fans breathe down the necks of their more exalted adversaries and whisper sweet insults in their ears.

For the purpose of the museum, the banana skin is a reminder that Scottish football can regularly slap you in the face and cause no end of embarrassment. The phrase evolved, of course, from slapstick comedy. It is supposed to call to mind somebody unexpectedly falling from grace while nonchalantly going about life, thinking everything's fine. The term doesn't work for me. The fact clubs know it's a banana skin should surely dictate they will be aware of the danger and see the banana skin, therefore neutralising any potential danger? And yet . . .

In much the same way as they sport almost obligatory tattoos and hair weaves, footballers seem naturally inclined to speak in cliché. Most of it isn't really their fault; they pick up phrases from commentators and journalists and regurgitate them. They don't speak like normal people. If you were sacked from your job, would you say, 'I've been axed'? If you fell out with your colleagues, would you say you'd lost the communal area? If you were under pressure, would you say you were under the cosh? Of course not. But cliché has become the lexicon of footballers and football journalists everywhere, with clubs making a *swoop* for an *ace* striker who normally scores a *brace* each week. The officials who mete out disciplinary measures *rap* a player. An unexpected victory would mean the *underdog* might have managed to *stun* the opposition. And, of course, the match-winner always has a wonderful *engine* in *spades*.

When former footballers started to become pundits, they brought in an unhealthy fixation with clumsy metaphors. Fights breaking out were considered *handbags*. A player who clearly wasn't playing well might have been having difficulty *adjusting to the pace of the game*. The same way an office admin assistant might have difficulty adjusting to the pace of filing or picking up a phone.

The clever playmaker may have *missed an opportunity*, despite it falling to his *favoured* left foot. This implies he has at least three feet, two of which are his left feet. His *cultured* left foot may be into watching sub-titled movies, visiting museums and nights at the opera. What about his right foot? Is that a philistine?

Footballers rarely make a promise to 'carry out' something, preferring to make a *vow*. They *vow* to take revenge on their local rivals. Chances are normally wasted by the *hatful*. The star striker has an *off day* when he is profligate in front of goal. A manager in a precarious position hangs his jacket on a *shoogily peg*. Perhaps the job was a *poisoned chalice* – a bit dramatic this cliché but it's wheeled out regularly when a job seemed too good to be true.

The *plucky* boss normally faces the *axe* after a *catalogue of errors*, despite his team having a *vast array* of talent and a *galaxy of stars*. Managers are *armed* with a transfer *war chest* to prevent them falling into a *relegation dogfight*.

The smart managers always *take it one game at a time* and rely on their players to give *110%*. Due to the amount of goals he's *bagged*, the star striker is always *coveted* and is regularly the subject of *derisory* and *insulting* offers from other clubs. The unhappy star player might issue a *come and get me plea* or *down tools*. Some of the more intelligent coaches might accept *the form book has gone out the window* and, of course, *decisions tend to balance themselves out over a season*. They might concede they've *seen those decisions given* and his blue-eyed boy who has destroyed an opponent's career with a sickening, horrific assault masquerading as a tackle, *isn't normally that type of lad*.

Games are generally lost by *schoolboy* defending and, when fighting to stay in the league, a game becomes a *six pointer*. The playmaker typically has *genuine pace* and if *the shot he'd hit was on target, it would've been a goal*. The match is so important it's a *must-win-game*. When they take the lead and need the crucial three points, the same player wastes time by diving and winning a ridiculous free kick which should *see his side over the line*. When he does this, he is using his *experience to gain an advantage*. Wins *come in handy* as it's a *results-driven business*. When the player who *plays on the edge* is gently tickled in the box, he was *justified in going down*.

The players do their *talking on the pitch*. If they sign a new contract, they've *penned a deal* and, when they get tired, they've *lost their legs*. If they've played three games in a week, they *look leggy*. If a player's tall, he will have *a decent touch for a big man*. In the end, *it's a game of two halves* and *the lads did fantastic*. For the national side, well, there are *no easy games in international football*. Let's be honest, yes there are. Which brings us back to where we started, with banana skins. But if you don't win the easy games, it could lead to *calls for the coach's head* and blah, blah, blah . . .

To those who work in football, please save us all and start talking like normal human beings.

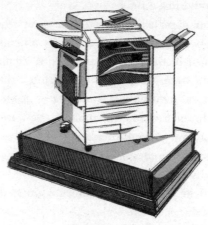

Exhibit 30
Fanzines

Fanzines should always have their place in any alternative football museum, in fact, they should be front and centre to any glance at the history of our game. Why? Well, there was a time when the narrative of football was controlled exclusively by newspapers, the clubs and national bodies. The fans' thoughts and opinions were unheard outside the terraces and pubs and given no vehicle for wider expression. But then along came the fanzine and everything changed.

Today, we are accustomed to Twitter, Facebook and Instagram, a vast array of fan sites, forums and sports news 24/7. Everyone is an expert. Fans at games become the sports-writing equivalent of Norman Mailer and Hunter S. Thomson. They have a platform, and a laptop, and assume they are the great white hope of modern football writing, the blogging saviours of the publishing world. Match reports can now be delivered from an iPhone. It is a golden age for self-expression but it took pioneers from a different generation to first give the fans a place where they could make their voices heard.

The original fanzines emerged in the 1930s with science fiction fans who wanted to share their love of the genre and raise its profile. As mainstream magazine and newspaper editors and critics ignored them, refusing to take the genre seriously, these fans created their own outlet. At the vanguard was *The Comet*, which was put together by the Science Correspondence Club in Chicago. There were other notable fanzine successes in the early 1960s, at the nascent end of the blues and soul scene, including the influential *Crawdaddy.*

The football incarnation was influenced by punk fanzines like *Sniffin' Glue*. Once the Xerox photocopier appeared on the scene, the game changed. Suddenly, mass production at low cost was a possibility for the first time. The fanzine saw amateurs writing and editing with as much passion and insight into the game as so-called professionals. This wasn't a director, manager or senior club official preaching on high in the programme notes. This was from the fans, to the fans.

More than anything, fanzines provide a brief glimpse of social history, a time capsule into the game. In fact, fanzines, especially when read today, give the truest glimpse into the grass roots and community of most football clubs. Clubs would produce official annuals but, as football is fast-moving and forever changing, these would age very quickly. Not so the fanzine, which appeared every week or two – always fresh, always up-to-date. Football fans identified with them because of the tangible, partisan passion the writers brought to their pieces. The fanzine, or at least the ones I remember best, would act as a dissenting voice. The original titles had a punk rock, DIY, homemade element and a post-punk attitude to their content and appearance: crudely created, smudged, photocopied, A4 in size, and full of rants and bad language. Fanzines would be done on a shoestring, hastily organised and, if you knew someone at the printers, produced on the cheap. Somebody would then cart a couple of boxes to the stadium, like a surreptitious Del Boy selling stolen watches while keeping an eye out for the law.

The most popular publications would, of course, come from the clubs with the biggest fan bases. Celtic had *Not the View* and Rangers published *Follow Follow*. But the beauty of fanzines was that it wasn't just the top clubs that got noticed. If it was informative, funny and well written, people would find out about the smaller publications, such as Hearts' memorable and entertaining *Always the Bridesmaid* and *No Idle Talk* or Airdrie's *Only the Lonely*, Motherwell's *Waiting for the Great Leap Forward* and Albion Rovers' *Over the Wall*. These fanzines would have an edge and, more often than not, rail against the official club line. They made the most significant impact when they existed on the fringes, like a militant trade union which liked cool music or a substitute teacher who liked The Fall and listened to John Peel.

Most fanzines were formed when the fans felt marginalised by their own club and, in a broader sense, by those running the game. They felt like no-one was listening to them. The publication would sell particularly well when clubs had unpopular owners. They prospered in times of radical change and uncertainty, such as moves to new stadia and the emergence of satellite broadcasting. They hit their peak in Scottish football around the mid-1980s and 1990s, when the game was being run by the likes of Ernie Walker and Jim Farry, who seemed to delight in belligerence, and club owners used words like 'customers' to describe supporters.

Fanzine editors quickly learned what worked. They realised with the right balance of quality writing, funny content, and legitimate 'edge', fans would buy into them. The fanzines were both DIY and local. They got it. Genuine fans, writing about football, for the love of the game, not profit.

I remember *The Absolute Game*. This existed from the mid-

1980s to September 2002. The fact it was an otherwise broad church about Scottish football which ignored the Old Firm was its unique selling point. It was like a Scottish version of the popular English fanzine, *When Saturday Comes*. The first fanzine I can remember physically seeing and trying to read was around 1984, in the school common room. Some teacher who was into Partick Thistle left it for us. It was called *Fitba Crazy*.

Remarkably, fanzines have been able to survive – albeit only just – in the fast-moving modern media age. Today's fan publications have embraced modern printing developments, Twitter, podcasts and some are even making money via advertising on their websites. Importantly, fans are still getting their messages out and are managing to maintain the same spikiness as ever. Perhaps it's because they appear so resolutely odd. But they continue to remain as pertinent and important as ever.

Exhibit 31
Football on TV

The humble remote control has probably done more damage to our game than we can begin to quantify. Games, when scarce, were a genuine treat. Today's fan, by comparison, has become spoiled with the constant stream of live games from a litany of leagues across the globe. Previously, you only had the Scottish Cup final, the European Cup final and the annual Scotland-England fixture. Changed days, indeed.

On any given Sunday, you can sit on the sofa from 11:30am and watch Dutch, Italian, Scottish, German and English football, before finishing off the day with a pair of Spanish games. Cameras are at most top-tier matches around the world. If you haven't had quite enough, or perhaps are mad with a fixed-odds coupon, you can continue your binge with 'soccer' from the MLS, followed by games from South America.

Bluntly, there's too much live football on TV. However, there's a wonderful upside to the mediocrity. If you have an inquisitive mind and a love for geography, these games can provide hours of fun. It's wonderful to watch football and pick up nuggets of information, learning, for example, that PSV Eindhoven was initially the Phillips works team and that the team has a number of nicknames, including *Boeren* (the farmers) and *lampen* (light bulbs). Then you come across teams like Roda JC Kerkrade, who sound like a 1970s porn director. Watching Serie A allows you to refresh your Italian geography and learn of new places, such as Crotone, which is a beautiful, historic port city that overlooks the Ionian Sea in Calabria.

I love German football. The crowds are enormous because of the 'fan first' ticket pricing policy. I also like to know where those giants of German football, such as Darmstadt 98, are based. The city of Darmstadt is in the state of Hesse. Did you know Darmstadt holds the title of 'City of Science'? Well, you would if you were bored rigid in west-central Scotland watching the wunderbar Bundesliga on TV while having access to Google.

Money from TV keeps the game going but at what price to the true fans? Games kick off at noon and fans are expected to travel sometimes four or five hours to make it in time. There should be some sort of quality control – less is more – but we have become so accustomed to it. We've moved on from a highlights package of a featured game on *Sportscene* or, when it was still broadcast, *Scotsport*, to expecting to see every game.

It all started when the BBC began experimenting with football in September 1937. They televised an Arsenal v Arsenal Reserves game. Arsenal was the nearest club to the Ally Pally, so they were local and accessible. The equipment was heavy and cumbersome so, for the next few years, the BBC didn't venture outside of London, preferring to film as locally as possible.

After a few tweaks, the Beeb was finally ready for the big one – a game between England and Scotland on 9 April 1938, from which they broadcast highlights. It wasn't until the FA Cup final between Preston North End and Huddersfield, in May of the same year, that the first full game would be broadcast live.

No-one could ever have foreseen television taking off the way it subsequently has. Back then, fewer than 100,000 people owned a TV set. The FA and SFA preferred it that way. They were reluctant to embrace TV, sensing it would hit their clubs at the turnstiles. How right they would be.

ITV was the first broadcast company to show real ambition and put their money on the table to televise twenty-six live league games in the 1960/61 season. This, though, led to arguments and fall-outs over player appearance demands and the deal subsequently fell through. ITV would show televised highlights in the 1962 season but only to its own regions. Eventually, the FA agreed a deal to show a highlights package on a Saturday night with the BBC for *Match of the Day* in 1964. By the time of the 1966 World Cup, football coverage on TV was improving, becoming more professional and starting to infiltrate many more homes.

By 1968, ITV launched *The Big Match* across the network, a highlights show broadcast on Sunday afternoons. In 1978, Michael Grade, while at London Weekend Television (LWT), won the exclusive rights to league football coverage for ITV. The BBC had to allow ITV the prime-time Saturday night slot in alternate seasons from 1980/81.

Scotland would continue to be served by both *Sportscene* and *Scotsport* showing highlights packages on Saturday evenings and Sunday afternoons. However, television coverage was changing and, in 1988, there was something of a watershed moment for football in the UK. Sky Sports made a bid of £48m for the rights to games in the English First Division, although it wasn't until 1991 that the FA unveiled its 'Blueprint for the Future of Football'. The following year, Sky managed to buy the rights for the new Premier League for £304m.

But what about Scotland? Sky bought the rights to our game in 1995. However, Scottish football and television haven't always been comfortable bedfellows. In 2002, Celtic and Rangers refused to get involved with a new proposed Scottish Premier League TV channel, leaving the other ten sides in a precarious position. The SPL Channel was the brainchild of the former SPL chief Roger Mitchells. Having rejected the proposal and with the existing Sky deal running out at the end of the season, the remaining clubs may have been left without a TV deal. In a joint statement, the Glasgow giants claimed the proposal was too risky.

Then, in 2008, Scottish football embarked on the Setanta debacle. Headlines at the time declared that Scottish football would celebrate a new £125 million deal for four years of coverage, doubling the current package. Most fans thought that sounded like nonsense – and most fans were correct. A year later, the Irish broadcaster revealed it was insolvent. The trouble was, many Scottish clubs had already started splashing the cash like lottery winners only to realise they had forgotten to buy a ticket. There would be no Setanta money coming in. As confusion reigned, a deal was eventually struck between ESPN and Sky for £65 million, nearly half the Setanta figure.

Scottish football is currently broadcast across five outlets – Sky, BT Sport, Premier Sports, BBC Scotland and BBC ALBA, although the BT deal is set to expire in mid-2020. Scottish football has been treated like the poor relation when it comes to TV money. When the previous deal was done, £18.75m was split between sixty live games. In Greece, they received £50m and, in Denmark, £46m from their respective TV deals. In October 2018, SPFL chief executive Neil Doncaster announced the overseas rights to Scottish football had been sold to beIN SPORTS for twenty-four countries, including those hotbeds of world football Palestine, South Sudan and Mauritania. In

November 2018, a new five-year deal was announced with Sky for £150m, a figure which sounds great but which is, in reality, dwarfed by the £1.71 BILLION the English Premier League receives in an average season.

Naturally, games between Man United and Man City or Liverpool and Chelsea are the gold standard but don't forget the Premiership, in season 2018/19, featured teams like Burnley and Huddersfield. Is a match between those two a more appealing prospect than one between Rangers and Aberdeen? Does Bournemouth-Watford hold greater appeal than an Edinburgh derby between rivals Hibernian and Hearts? Don't tell me a game between Cardiff and Wolves is that much more exciting than a fiery derby between St Johnstone and Dundee. Celtic and Rangers play a minimum of four games every season. The EPL's wage bill and transfer kitty make us look desperate as we scurry around begging for crumbs off the table. And with every game that is televised, fewer and fewer fans want to make the trip to watch their teams in person. Big games will always draw a crowd but if it's pouring with rain and blowing a gale at the end of January, are you going to brave the elements and lend your voice to your players' efforts and put some much-needed cash through the turnstiles, or are you going to stay inside in the warmth and enjoy the match from the comfort of your couch? Back in the 1930s, the powers-that-be at the FA and SFA correctly predicted the answer. As much as TV has given the game, it has also diluted it in profound away.

Exhibit 32
David Francey

The popularity of the transistor radio changed our relationship with football in the 1970s.

Previously, you had to be at a game to follow it most closely, but radio opened up a new world. Radio Clyde had Richard Park but BBC Radio Scotland had the one and only David Francey. What a voice. Listening back to some of his commentaries brings me out in goosebumps. As kids, if we were in the park playing football, someone would always show up with a pocket transistor radio so that we could tune in to the big games.

Side-offs up the park would include a wide and varied spectrum of ages. In between the shouting, the joking, the bad language, the slanging matches, there would be crazy moments of interplay and skilful flourishes – but throughout this, there would also be a shout, usually from the person in goal, to alert you to a corner or a penalty or a goal in the big game on radio. Our game would temporarily draw to a halt and we'd listen in, listening out for David Francey's distinctive timbre.

Francey was born in Glasgow in 1924 and started commentating for the BBC in 1964. He had an infectious enthusiasm which grabbed his audience. He delighted us with joyous expressions as he described the action unfolding with the professionalism of a broadcaster but the unbridled passion of a fan, marvelling at the football when it was bedazzling and going off on a glorious digression when it wasn't.

Francey had been a promising player but a cruciate knee ligament put paid to his football career. It is possible he still lived the dream, though, getting close to the action via his wonderful work as one of the BBC's finest commentators. And what a voice. They always say commentating and radio broadcasting are about painting pictures in the mind. What a wonderfully descriptive palette Francey had to call upon.

When I was growing in the 1970s, his voice was instantly recognisable when you were scrabbling along the dial. He brought a reassuring calm to the craziness of everyday life. He would eloquently explain what was happening on the pitch, thanks in no small part to his meticulous research. In the days before Sky Sports summarisers covering every game from every ground, Francey was the only source of any football action or news. Weirdly, the commentary didn't begin until towards the end of the first half, at 3:40 p.m. Francey would come on for the last five minutes of the first period and then the whole of the second half. When you heard his voice get louder, you knew something was happening.

I remember the first time I saw David Francey in the flesh. The mental image I had from his commentaries fitted the reality: a tall, dapper, silver-haired, handsome man. It was uncanny. It makes you wonder why he didn't move from radio to television. He could have been a famous face in every household like Archie Macpherson or Arthur Montford. The truth was that he loved radio too much to leave it – and it, in turn, loved him. His was the voice of football for a nation spoiled by success. He was there when Scottish football was actually thriving. He covered three European finals: Celtic in Lisbon in 1967, Rangers in Barcelona in 1972, and Aberdeen in Gothenburg in 1983. This was an era when our club and national sides habitually made it to major competitions and were a real force in the game. His BBC radio career spanned Jock Stein playing for and managing Celtic to European Cup victory to his death at St Ninian Park in Cardiff in September 1985. It encompassed Rangers from the Bill Struth era to the Souness Revolution.

Perhaps the biggest compliment paid to Francey was the huge number of people who didn't even like football but who would still tune in to listen to him. For them, the poorer the game, the more fun Francey had veering off on a surreal riff, only to re-focus when a chance emerged on the field.

Despite his huge popularity, he only ever worked on a freelance basis for the BBC (doing so for thirty-five years). His 'real jobs' included working for the Inland Revenue and in a managerial role for Scottish Gas and the Electricity Board. Among the many stories which circulated around the BBC Scotland offices following his death, at the age of eighty-seven in September 2011, one of the best concerned a David Francey imitation contest. A popular competition held in the BBC Club, one of his producers submitted a tape recording of the man himself – and he only managed to finished fourth.

Exhibit 33
Losing the Dressing Room

There's something quietly reassuring about an arrogant, conceited manager losing the dressing room. It is, after all, a rebellion, laden with the brutal echoes of the Roman senate as midfield linchpins Brutus and Cassius conspire to oust their leader.

What does 'losing the dressing room' actually mean? It generally applies when a manager is on a losing run and it looks as though the players have given up. It happens when players lose respect for the boss and refuse to listen to what he's trying to say. Is it the coach's tactics? The methodology? Spats with a club legend? Dropping players out of spite? Coaches lose the dressing room for a number of reasons.

It has long been a ploy for managers, especially those of an older vintage, to install a trusted player as captain to act as an ally and keep the other players in check. Someone who would suppress early signs of insurrection. The trouble starts, of course, when the trusted lieutenant is the first to turn.

Much as we try to veer from idiomatic expression, you won't

find a funnier or more appropriate cliché for the modern era as hearing a radio phone-in show discuss a manager losing the dressing room. Surely, back in the 'good old days', other players must have rebelled and downed tools, too?

Some, in fact, claim the problem started when football abolished the maximum wage. In 1961, they lifted a salary cap of £20 a week (£17 in the summer) and, as a result, players suddenly began to have real power.

Football's most high-profile coach, former Largs alumni José Mourinho, regularly has the accusation thrown at him. He famously lost the dressing room at Real Madrid, Chelsea and Manchester United. Each time, according to 'insiders' (usually dropped players), his troubles can be traced to his incessant demands for perfection and an obsession with success, all the while obstinately refusing to mature tactically. He found any player who refused to keep up with his exacting standards both infuriating and a hindrance. He also had a propensity to go straight to the waiting media after a defeat and publicly call out his dissenters. In December 2018, Mourinho was sacked by Manchester United, with the majority of the subsequent headlines focusing on his £24m pay-off. By the time you're reading this, he will probably be losing the dressing room in Milan or Rome.

Being a brilliant goal-scorer, having the vision to read the game or play a defence-splitting pass all pale into insignificance when compared with the capacity to smell blood. Some footballers have the ability to sense weakness like a vulture hovering over a dying gazelle. The instant a dressing room full of blood-thirsty predators senses a manager is vulnerable, they pounce. One of the biggest sins, in the players' minds, is when a manager hasn't played the game at a high enough level. Textbooks and tactics often mean nothing unless the person delivering the message has, once upon a time, also crossed the white line. In their minds, it's about gravitas and authenticity.

Another key factor to losing a dressing room is, à la Mourinho, the public naming and shaming of a player. That goes double if it's one of the team's star players. During Pedro Caixinha's brief stint as Rangers boss, for example, it wasn't long after he openly criticised and then banished Kenny Miller that he was handed his pink slip. Maintaining harmony in the dressing room is critical to getting the best out of any team.

Still, if a top coach like Carlo Ancelotti, who managed at Juventus, Chelsea and Real Madrid, is capable of losing the dressing room, it can happen to anyone. Ancelotti is no mug. Along with Bob Paisley at Liverpool and Zinedine Zidane at Real Madrid, he is one of only three managers to have won Europe's top club competition three times. Yet when Ancelotti replaced Pep Guardiola at Bayern Munich, things went pear-shaped (and fast) when he fell out with several senior players. His vast experience and track record of delivering success counted for nothing when that happened. There was no way back.

David Moyes (another Largs alumni) was also subject to a brutal downing of tools when he replaced Sir Alex Ferguson at Manchester United. His players even took losing the dressing room to another level, reportedly placing bets on when he would be fired.

Then there's André Villas-Boas, yet another Largs alumni, who won the treble in Portugal and was seen by Chelsea as the new José after Mourinho's first stint at Stamford Bridge ended 'by mutual consent' in September 2007. The trouble was, at thirty-three, hiring Villas-Boas was like sending in a babysitter who was younger than the spoiled rich kids under his command. The highly-paid stars sensed blood as soon as he arrived. After a bad run of results and a defeat to Everton, Villas-Boas cancelled a day off and hauled his squad in for a meeting. Senior players questioned his tactics in front of the club's owner and, ten days later, for a Champions League game, he dropped three of the biggest names in the team: Frank Lampard, Michael Essien and Ashley Cole. The manager gambled on who wielded the greatest power in the club – him or the players. He was sacked after just nine months in the job.

At Celtic, Ronny Deila bumbled through the final months of his tenure in 2016, consistently insisting that he hadn't lost the dressing room, when, in fact, he had quite clearly lost the dressing room. The players, it later emerged, had been unhappy with his training methods and tactics from the start. Failures in Europe did little to help his cause, yet fans largely took to the amiable Norwegian. So, too, did the Celtic chief executive Peter Lawwell, who respected Deila enough to make it look like the coach had made the decision to leave rather than admit he'd been told to jump before he was pushed.

Perhaps we're missing a trick. There are two simple reasons why the successful coaches, like Sir Alex Ferguson and Pep Guardiola, succeed. They seek assurances from the board that no player is paid more than the manager. Also, as soon as there's any show of dissent in the dressing room, they coldly jettison those involved. Ferguson hunted Keene and Beckham when they were becoming divisive in front of the team. After all, Ferguson, who won forty-nine trophies in his career, knew the value of his experience. In his 2015 book, *Leading* he wrote: 'When the Glazers and David Gill agreed to a big increase in Wayne Rooney's salary in 2010, they wanted to know how I felt. I didn't think it fair that Rooney should earn twice what I made and Joel Glazer immediately said, "I totally agree with you but what should we do?" It was simple. We just agreed that no player should be paid more than me. We agreed in less time than it takes to read the previous sentence.'

Exhibit 34
iPhone

Everybody has experienced it.

The stadium is full, fans are singing, the place awash with colour – but something isn't right. The whole experience isn't as exciting as it used to be. Something's changed. The stadium seems quieter, the applause more subdued. Why? Because 30,000 people in the crowd have their phones in the air recording a video. The smartphone has completely changed the match day experience – not only in the way we watch the game at home but in the atmosphere at the stadium, too.

We now live in an age when phone-obsessed fans are too busy looking at messages, posts, photos and videos to actually watch the game. These guys aren't football fans; they're tourists. And while we're on the subject, if I can't take a bottle of water into the stadium, why can this lot whip out their selfie sticks and wave their wands around the place with impunity? Surely that's a much more effective weapon than my plastic bottle?

That's to say nothing of Periscope and the like – apps that

allow people to live stream a game from the stand and, worse still, encourage viewers to interact in real time. If you think the game's enjoyable, you can tell the guy filming the game (not watching it live as such because he's also looking at it through his screen) how much you love the game with a heart emoji. You can leave a comment, too. Isn't technology wonderful?

The talk amongst supporters in the stands used to be about the big club sniffing around your thirty-goal-a-season superstar and whether they would be able to cut it at a higher level. Now, it's about software updates or making sure you've installed the latest version of iOS.

I would only permit the use of smartphones in football stadiums for fans to maybe cash out on a bet, check replays of important decisions, or to take emergency calls. Otherwise, switch them off and keep them in your pocket. Love the game in real time and embrace it with all your senses.

Exhibit 35
Outside Broadcasts

It's difficult to convey the frenzied excitement which would greet a phone call or, even better, an animated friend at the front door telling you the football cameras had come to town.

I remember the heart-thumping surge when I heard my local team, Airdrieonians, and their old stadium, Broomfield, was being wired for sound and vision by the BBC or STV outside broadcast vehicles and that the game would be on *Sportscene* or *Scotsport*.

A bunch of us would immediately go down to the centre of town and check out the vans and the cables and plugs and wires cascading over the walls and into the stadium. Maybe it's because kids have grown so accustomed to the idea of TV cameras, with Sky Sports, BT, *Match of the Day* and *Sportscene*, now filming most games, that this particular sense of wonder hasn't been carried forward by the current generation. Back in 1977/78, however, visits were few and far between and the concept of seeing a TV crew and cameras showing up at a provincial club was something of an event.

On one such occasion, a young Alex Ferguson brought his St Mirren side to play Airdrie. They were celebrating having won the First Division title. Airdrie applauded the St Mirren side onto the pitch. I also remember, as well as TV, that we saw radio reporters and loads of St Mirren fans. But the main event was that the *Sportscene* cameras were there. TV stardom beckoned. We had to play our cards right, keep it cool. My pal Paul Hawthorne and I were in the ground for 1pm, two hours before kick-off.

We watched Tommy Walker play keepie-uppie, his usual warm up, flipping the ball from shoulder to shoulder then controlling it stone-dead on his head. He was generally on the park before everyone else. Then Airdrie's version of George Best – at least with his beard – Mark Cowan sprinted up and down the sidelines at an alarming speed. Sometimes, you'd hope a ball would accidentally be passed toward the touchlines and a player would gesture for you to play it on to them. There would be a race to vault over and get a kick of a real match ball on an amazing surface.

As much as we wanted Airdrie to win, we knew St Mirren were the better team and more likely to score, so we stood behind the Airdrie goal. To make sure we would be easily spotted on TV, Paul and I had the cunning idea of turning our Parkas inside out. This meant the near fluorescent reddish-orange lining would stand out better. The trick worked. Later, as I was dozing off, the closing titles of *Kojak* woke me up, then it was the news, then it was *Sportscene*. And there we were, jumping and waving behind the goals as bright as day.

The result didn't matter. I think it finished 2–2 but I'm not sure. I'm not even sure I care. I know Mark Cowan scored a fantastic goal, cutting past three players from the wing then whizzing the ball into the opposite corner, past the St Mirren keeper. But what I remember most clearly is that Paul and I were on TV.

What also amazed me as a ten- or eleven-year-old was the amount of technical wizardry involved in broadcasting a game. More than anything, what always stays with me about the whole day was the tangible connection between my hometown, the community, a football ground, the TV cameras and the rest of Scotland. The only downside was that Archie Macpherson wasn't on commentary duty that day. Even then, it was a near-perfect, magical experience.

Exhibit 36
Public Address Systems

The matchday experience has undoubtedly been enhanced with the widespread use of the Tannoy system.

The term 'Tannoy', like the Hoover, is generally used colloquially in Scotland as the generic term for the stadium's public address system. It's actually an electronic sound amplification and distribution system… so there! The early public address systems were big and impractical. They also took forever to warm up. Imagine an Aberdeen defence with Doug Rougvie and Brian Irvine and you'll get the picture. This beast was called the Magnavox.

The stadium Tannoy was a quantum leap in communication. It wasn't long before their introduction that half-time scores were done with chalkboards or numbers on a slate, which corresponded to games in the match programme.

The Tannoy system was a major advancement. Sometimes the announcements themselves were more entertaining than the game. Fans loved to hear a shout-out to the owner of a certain car which required immediate attention as the lights had been left on. Other times, there would be police announcements for car owners who had blocked people in, followed by near complete silence as fans listened out to hear the colour, make and registration. The affronted owner would then sheepishly try to sneak out, often to a rendition of 'Cheerio, Cheerio, Cheerio'.

You would hear marriage proposals and then a nervous wait for a 'yes'. There would be urgent calls for men to leave immediately because their wives had gone into labour. There would be a booming message put out to the drunken dad of kids who'd wandered off, asking him to report to the police at the main stand immediately to collect the children he'd forgotten about, as if they were lost luggage.

I can clearly recall one particular game in 1980 when the result of the Grand National was announced over the Tannoy to the delight and cheers of those who had backed the winner, Ben Nevis.

The Tannoy eventually evolved into a public safety system for emergency announcements. These days, it's probably more associated with the booming of myriad weird and wonderful songs when a player scores. It's an integral part of the build-up and half-time entertainment, with powerful systems as loud as festival amplifiers. This has, in turn, inspired a ubiquitous catalogue of football anthems from the likes of Oasis, Kasabian, Kings of Leon, The Fratellis and White Stripes (but rarely Can, John Coltrane or Captain Beefheart). It also provides the opportunity for each club to blare out their official or adopted anthem as the players enter the pitch, rousing the fans and intimidating their opponents. These can vary from Wagner to The Tijuana Brass; from 1960s TV shows to cheesy hits from the same decade.

Many a Tannoy announcer has become famous for their quick wit and good timing. In one Aberdeen game against Legia

Warsaw, the Polish visitors fielded a player called Piz (pronounced 'Pesh'). When he was substituted, the Aberdeen announcer quipped, 'Personally, I didn't think he was bad.' Another of my favourites was the Motherwell announcer who declared, after his side dominated a game only to lose to a last-minute sucker punch, 'Scorer for Kilmarnock, number sixteen, D. Turpin.'

Going to football has changed beyond recognition. In an effort to become more 'showbiz', PA announcers now interact with the crowd. This first entered our game from Europe. Bayern Munich's announcer would use the stadium's deafening PA system to shout out the player's first name for the crowd to bellow the surname. This would happen when the teams were announced pre-match and any time a player scored. It was so popular, clubs all over the world quickly followed suit. Similar traditions are now as much a part of the matchday experience as a pie and a programme.

The PA system has been with us for a while now and let's hope it continues to keep us informed as well as entertained. We should collectively encourage our announcers to be more expressive and crack even more funnies. Sometimes their patter and interaction can be funnier than the game itself. With the continuous quantum leaps in technology, the PA could become a thing of the past, we might all be beeped into grounds via electronic gates using our phones and messaged the team line-ups, the scorers and any announcements. Let's hope not for now. Keep it loud.

Exhibit 37
Twitter

A few years ago, no one gave a hoot about a tweet. Now, Twitter is a central tenet to all marketing, branding, information, news and messaging for footballers and fans alike. Of course, it's insanely egotistical and as dull as a wet Sunday but, for some, knowing what their favourite player thinks, has for dinner or has to say about the latest episode of *Love Island* is an essential part of the day. In many ways, Twitter was tailor-made for the short attention span of the 100 million or so users who drool over it every day.

Scottish football has taken to and embraced Twitter. At last, something we excel at. There have been tweets which wreaked havoc and, as our press would say, 'sent Twitter into meltdown'. Some tweets have even been funny and allow us to see that some of our players have natural wit and can be both self-deprecating and grounded. Anthony Stokes tweeting from Inverness, for example, highlighted his frustration at being dropped from the Celtic squad when he posted, 'Buzzing to be brought all the way up to Inverness with the team to sit in the stands today, lovely weather for it too'. The message showed some cheek and sarcasm but it also broke the convention about 'keeping it in the dressing room'. Despite later apologising, the tweet ultimately pre-empted a loan move to Hibernian and confirmed two things: Stokes wasn't afraid of his manager, Ronny Deila; and Twitter had made the policy of 'what happens in the dressing room stays in the dressing room' harder to administer than ever before.

Inverness Caledonian Thistle had fun at the expense of Celtic fans following one of the most blatant decisions in Scottish football history. In a cup semi-final against the Glasgow side, the Inverness side's centre-half Josh Meekings quite clearly handled the ball in the box, yet a penalty wasn't given. Alongside a photo of Leigh Griffiths shooting and Meekings handling it, Caley's tweet read, 'Celtic fans booing the ref but in fairness that is a cracking save.'

Those who use it effectively are funny and engaging and some are actually better on Twitter than they were as players. Former Celtic, Motherwell, St Johnstone, Kilmarnock and Jagiellonia Bialystok forward, Cillian Sheridan – he of the loud Christmas jumpers – tweeted the following about a Barcelona starting XI: 'Looking through that Barca line-up, I don't think in our lifetime we'll see such a talented and gifted bunch of tax dodgers.'

It's easy to see why football clubs and players have taken so easily to it. It's short, sharp and full of banter. It's also a chance to show off on a public forum. It's about social proofing. Messi does it at Barcelona, Pogba does it at Man United, and the characters in the dressing room at Cowdenbeath and Peterhead do it because everyone else is.

Twitter also gives fans the opportunity to think locally and act globally. Let's hope big business doesn't take the fun and sublime ridiculousness out of it because this is where the real gold lies.

It would be remiss to speak about Scottish football and

Twitter and not mention Joey Barton's short spell at Rangers. Barton was quick to grasp Twitter's effectiveness. He was the first player recognised for his articulacy on social media as much as his football ability. Barton was skilful in debunking his past, reinventing himself as a renaissance man, the man football fans thought sounded brainy. Twitter was the perfect outlet for the smart player. Barton was apt to telling his four million followers everything, particularly when he had another book ready for publication. Publishers love a player with a huge Twitter following. Joey obliged, at one point proving how much of an everyman he'd become by appearing on BBC1's *Question Time*. By then, he was living off his reputation on Twitter instead of the football field.

Barton came to Rangers as a saviour and left after a dressing room fracas. He tweeted that Scott Brown wasn't at his level and that he was in Scotland to win the league. After a 5–1 defeat to Celtic, Barton allegedly let rip at his teammates and the management. After what's known in football as 'a full and frank discussion', during which 'some words used did overstep the mark', Barton was signed off with stress and his twenty-grand-a-week contract was later terminated. He lasted eight games. In truth, he wasn't the worst player. Rangers' Swiss international Philip Senderos, who was signed around the same time as Barton, looked like he was tweeting while Celtic took corners. At one point in that same mauling, he managed to misjudge the bounce of a ball and gave away a free-kick which saw him red-carded and mercifully put out of his misery. He was a total #bombscare.

In the US, football coaches, as early in the process as 2012, were monitoring Twitter for recruitment. They were particularly interested in a player's behaviour, how he lived, how he communicated, and so on. The biggest sports stars can now secure endorsements based largely around their presence on

Twitter, Facebook and Instagram. What commercial director wouldn't see the value of players with millions of willing followers / prospective customers?

Of course, it isn't perfect. Some clubs have difficulty grasping the finer points of the social media platform. Dundee United took to Twitter to transfer list their goalkeeper, Cammy Bell, like they were trying to sell a second-hand sofa. Thus followed a hilarious barrage of offers. We also must be careful with this new power. Twitter is a wonderful platform for engagement, fun and banter but we need to be cognizant of its pitfalls. Berwick Rangers felt that they had no option but to fire their social media administrator after a tweet from the club account went viral during a 1–1 draw with Cowdenbeath in March 2019, which read: 'Ugly scenes in the dugout as Cowdenbeath's manager has just told Johnny Harvey to "take his face for a s****" #BRFC.' The writer might have got away with it if he'd apologised and shown some remorse, but he actively refused to delete the tweet and it was only taken down when control of the account was wrested away from him.

The lesson, as Spiderman's uncle Ben once told him, is that with great power comes great responsibility.

Exhibit 38
Adjutant v Alex Cameron

Alex Cameron was one of the finest and most respected sports journalists of his generation. He was unafraid to take aim at whoever annoyed him and was more than able to hold his ground. He kept his powder dry for two targets in particular: the SFA blazers and Alex Ferguson.

He is, though, perhaps best remembered for an incident that took place outside Hampden in 1977. Scotland were playing Czechoslovakia in a crucial World Cup qualifying game. We used to play crucial World Cup qualifying games in the 1970s. For context, it bears repeating that, at this time, football matches televised live were a special treat. The build-up to crucial international games was exciting, with football magic in the air. So, being upstaged by a horse and caught on camera would always be quite funny, but the fact it was live made it all the more memorable.

The hilarious incident occurred during Cameron's pre-match piece to camera when he was knocked akimbo by a police horse called Adjutant. Clearly, the filly was no fan of his work. Cameron was waiting for the Scotland team bus to arrive in the hope of grabbing a star player or the coach for a quick word when Adjutant bowled him sideways. Alex manfully dealt with it, keeping his balance and whatever dignity he may have had left. No mounted policemen controlling the crowds would stop him from getting his story. Except Adjutant then placed his behind right in front of the camera. Alex struggled to get into shot and, when the man in the saddle finally figured out what was going on and led Adjutant away, the horse had one last laugh when it knocked the microphone out of Alex's hand.

At the time, the laugh was on Cameron. From his many appearances and rants on TV and radio, as well as his *Candid Cameron* column, the general public thought of him as quite an abrasive figure. Of course, this was before they realised how good he was at his job. He's only in here, and it is with a smile, because he was famously upstaged by a horse's backside.

Starting out at the now defunct *Stirling Journal*, Cameron headed to Scottish Newspaper Services in Glasgow, then spent sixteen years at the *Daily Mail's* Edinburgh desk. He moved again, in 1968, to the *Daily Record*, where he stayed until his retirement in 2000. He covered many top sporting occasions: seven Olympic Games, seven World Cups, eight Commonwealth Games. Cameron's reputation always loomed large. At the 1972 Olympics in Munich, he was first on the scene – claiming he was a Russian ambassador in order to gain access – to report live from the compound where Israeli athletes had been kidnapped by Black September terrorists. He would do almost anything to get the story.

He also reported from many world title boxing bouts. He was old-school, meticulous and worked harder than most to get his many scoops. He also expected those around him to perform and work with the same enthusiasm as he did. 'Chiefy', as he was known, knew his stuff and was unrelenting in his work. He especially enjoyed sparking debate with his opinion pieces in his *Daily Record* column. He was also a regular face on STV's *Scotsport* and a familiar voice on radio.

In keeping with his love of athletics, Cameron used to highlight Scots who achieved greatness. He was on the scene in Moscow, in 1980, when Alan Wells became the Olympic 100m swimming champion. In 1991, he was in Tokyo, covering the World Athletics Championships and Liz McColgan's 10,000m gold. As for his many favourite football games, Cameron would list Jim Baxter's demolitions of England at Wembley in 1963 and 1967, along with Real Madrid's 1960 European Cup final at Hampden, amongst his favourites. As if to show there were no hard feelings, he would also include the Adjutant game, Scotland's famous victory over the Czech Republic in 1977.

He always joked that he'd have been rich if he owned the copyright to the Adjutant clip given the number of times it was shown across the world. Ironically, his column was a word play on the popular show of the time, *Candid Camera*, which replayed the clip endlessly over the years. And so it is fitting that sugar lumps for Adjutant go on display in the Alternative Football Museum to remember the other star of the show who should also have benefitted from such widespread fame and affection.

Exhibit 39
Wi-Fi

Modern-day football arenas are now fitted with high-density Wi-Fi as standard. But is this a good thing? This isn't a restaurant, shopping centre or coffee shop; it's a football stadium. If you'd prefer to be on your iPhone, stay in the house.

I grant you that there are a number of features that are quite attractive about bringing technology to the matchday experience. Who can argue with a facility that guides fans safely to and from the stadium? What's wrong with wanting to go online to check scores or team line-ups in other matches, or getting opinions and replays of contentious decisions? Why wouldn't you want to take a photograph of the game, share it and receive the love of your friends and followers on Twitter, Facebook or Instagram? And what if you wanted to place a bet... and then have the option of cashing out?

Fans at 'soccer' games in the US have their matchday experience enhanced with wi-fi under their seat. They log-in, download an app and, in return for a few personal details, can order a beer, pizza and buckets of chicken. They then simply pay by tapping their card when the poor stadium attendant comes running to their seat with food and refreshments.

In many ways this all sounds great. But for purists, the advent of Wi-Fi and the availability of high-density coverage is no force for good. They believe it detracts from the fundamental simplicity – and beauty – of the matchday experience. In fact, in the Philips Stadion in 2014, fans of PSV Eindhoven unfurled a banner instructing Wi-Fi to go and fornicate itself. What the protesters were probably complaining about was the fear that fans might not be giving their full attention and support to the team. In general, I agree with them. You see thousands of fans taking photos at corners and free kicks and penalties when they should be ready to go mental if their team score.

Then you have the issue of handing over your personal details to download an app to use the club's 'free' Wi-Fi. What sort of idiot wants to give away their data that freely? Intelligence agencies from Russia treat hacking our Wi-Fi like a tricky cryptic crossword. They could hack in and check out what you've been buying from Amazon as a player gets ready to take a throw in. They might even outbid you on a priceless piece of vinyl on eBay. Handing over personal details is crazy talk.

The introduction of Wi-Fi has brought so many positives to the game, mostly based around the narcissism of the modern fan. High density Wi-Fi solutions have been found to keep everyone connected. It's the only way clubs can appeal to their millennial consumers. But social media and smartphones have obliterated the traditional routine and habits of the football fan. Perhaps the museum should accept this is the future and embrace it, but Scottish football likes tradition and struggles to embrace change – and so, therefore, should this museum. This technological stuff is too exciting and cutting edge for curmudgeons like us. So no, put your phones and tablets away and just look at the bloody exhibits.

Exhibit 40
Scotsport Jumps the Shark

There's a scene in *Annie Hall*, Woody Allen's 1977 gem, which, incidentally, beat *Star Wars* to the Oscar for best movie, when Annie (Diane Keaton) is talking about California. She says to Alvy Singer (Allen), 'It's so clean out here.' Alvy responds by saying, 'That's because they don't throw their garbage away, they turn it into television shows.'

Which brings us to the demise of *Scotsport*.

Football is such a popular Scottish pastime that weekly football highlight shows aren't enough for its ravenous supporters and fanatics. The punters demand more, like phone-ins and spin-offs from the successful main strand. In this regard, *Scotsport* was beaten and battered to the point where, instead of being embellished, it was destroyed. Anyone familiar with Sidney Lumet's black comedy *Network* knows that TV loves a bloodletting and will do anything for a share of an audience. Even so, the producers of *Scotsport* should have faced charges for the sheer extent of the GBH they inflicted on their own show.

The demise of *Scotsport* was so excruciating it's up there with the most painful moments in Scottish football history. Moments like Aberdeen 1-5 Sigma Olomouc; Artmedia Bratislava 5-0 Celtic; and Rangers 1-4 Unirea Urziceni.

In the world of television, if a show is moved from its familiar slot, trouble surely follows. *Scotsport*, after many subtle changes over the years, was moved around and renamed more times than a killer guide dog. The first strand was professional and informative. From 1979-84, *Sport Extra* followed the Scottish news on Friday evenings, drawing attention to the coming weekend's games.

When the show was just called *Scotsport*, and covered football, it wasn't all disaster. In fact, credit to Jim White, who had proven his worth as *Scotland Today's* sports reporter – he had travelled to Mexico for the 1986 World Cup and a few years later was given the job as host of the show. In the 1990s, they also filmed live games. White left for Sky Sports in 1998.

From 1988 until 2000, we had *Scotsport Extra Time* – it changed its name to just *Extra Time* in 1994, which was mostly broadcast on Friday evenings, at 10.35pm until it moved to 12.30pm on a Saturday. It moved to Friday evenings for the start of the 1996/97 season, with less football and more features on rugby, golf, snooker and (hold me back) ice hockey. The format was slowly being eroded.

There was a brief return to form with Jim Delahunt at the helm in 1998. It retuned to a 6.00pm start, before moving back to its original 7.00pm slot. So it remained until May 1999, when it again moved to Saturday lunchtime, where it was accommodated until December 2000.

When STV held the rights to Scottish rugby, there was a rugby *Scotsport* show from 2001 to 2004. While they held the highlights rights for Scottish Premier League and First Division games, *Scotsport* was divided into *Scotsport First*, transmitted on a Sunday morning, and *Scotsport SPL*, broadcast on a Sunday afternoon.

Scheduling and fitting a brand into a successful slot is difficult, and once it's there it should be coveted but, instead, STV continued to mess with the formula. By the time we were introduced to the rebranded magazine package show, launched in 2004 and hosted by Delahunt, Sarah O'Flaherty ('Sarah O') and Julyan Sinclair, the show had been tweaked too far. It was unpopular and lasted just two years before the axe fell – although some of the fan interaction must have gone down well because another strand, a 'forum format', was briefly introduced with *Scotsport Fanzone* airing on a Thursday evening during the 2005/06 season.

Where did the magazine highlights format fall short? The producers had the idea of keeping it real and dragged what amounted to drunk guys, junkies, and anyone 'real' and glaiket-looking to stand in an imaginary terracing behind the presenters. We can only assume the hospitality was generous. If not, security guards were remiss in their duties and failed to check for carry-outs of Buckfast, Super Lager and smack.

Along with the 'fans' straight out of the Bampot Casting Model Agency, there were issues with its broadcast slot late on a Monday night . . . two days after the majority of the action had occurred. Even then, we were so mad for Scottish football we actually stayed up and watched it, if only to witness an audience that resembled Peter Howson's depiction of Dante's *Inferno* on acid. It was quite a departure from the original *Scotsport* to what amounted to *Scotsport Car Crash TV*. With Sarah O, who loved the camera, Julyan Sinclair, miscast and looking like a fish out of water, and the steady Jim Delahunt, looking around wondering what he'd done in a previous life to deserve this whilst trying to hold it all together, it was all-too-often tough to watch. One particular night, it got worse.

To most football fans, the show 'jumped the shark' (a term from an episode of *Happy Days* when the Fonz water-skis over a shark, now widely acknowledged as the point when a TV show can't get any worse) when journalist and pundit, Graham Speirs, closed the show by playing the piano. He wasn't to know he would be knowingly and wilfully contributing to the death of light entertainment sport with his rendition of the Elton John classic 'Your Song'. Not even Speirsy's corduroy jacket with its leather patches and his fine head of hair could save the day . . . and the show would soon be axed.

This sealed the show's fate. Grant Stott and Andy Walker tried to repair the damage with a brief spell at the helm but, in truth, the ball had long since burst. STV had tried everything with *Scotsport*, apart from *Scotsport in Space*, which could, actually, have worked. Anyone with any knowledge of physics knows space is a vacuum and devoid of particles, so you wouldn't be able to hear anything. Perfect.

Exhibit 41
The Phone-in

The radio phone-in gave every football crackpot and wannabe philosopher a wondrously elusive tool: a voice.

A confused one, mostly. Until the advent of the phone-in, the airwaves were almost exclusively marshalled by experienced broadcasters or seasoned journalists, capable of expressing themselves quickly, effectively and eloquently. Important factors, such as coherency, sticking to the point and not using bad language, were key. But when they launched the phone-in, talk radio changed significantly.

The shape, concept and tone haven't changed since they started the format in 1974. Generations of football fans have come and gone but their views remain entrenched. It takes a high-profile Scottish football death for a ceasefire to break out and rivals to come together. Even then, peace only lasts for a few days before normal service resumes.

We now all know what to expect when we tune into the football phone-in. A guy who claims (lies) that he rarely misses a game, home or away, calls in to tell us what he thought of today's match. A match, when the panel ask him to comment on it, he often happens to have missed.

The phone-in has become akin to therapy for the irate and angry football fan, a chance to vent their anger at both their own team and their biggest rivals. It is, essentially, football's equivalent of the Samaritans.

The original Scottish fan phone-in was Radio Clyde's *Scoreboard*. First aired in 1974, it was innovative, serving Glasgow and the West, reaching across the Central Belt. *Scoreboard* was an immediate success, gaining traction because of its perfect timing. In the same way record companies cashed in on vinyl with the emerging market and advance in sales of record players, the head of music and sport at Radio Clyde, Richard Park, sensed the portable transistor radio – the 'tranny' – was the future. Until then, fans couldn't take a radio to the game. If they did, they would need a removal van and Laurel and Hardy to help lug it up the stairs to get it inside the ground. Park had spent time in America and loved listening to the sport phone-ins there. He quickly realised there was a niche in the market for a similar show in Scotland, tailored for fans no matter where they were – at the match, at home, on the bus, in the car or the train. The theme music, 'Lap of Honour' by the London Stadium Orchestra, was soon blaring out from every radio in every car across the land. Incidentally, that music was also ITV's official 1974 World Cup theme.

The original show on Clyde had a clever mix of authoritative and heated debate, as well as punters calling in. Amongst the legendary voices on air, you would have the exuberance of Park; the eloquence and intelligence of Bob Crampsey; and the nasal tone of the razor-sharp James Sanderson, who, as they say in these parts, could start a rammy in an empty house.

As the show evolved, Paul Cooney, Gerry McNee and Hugh

Keevins would provide some journalistic insight, with ex-pros, including Derek Johnstone and Davie Provan, providing the players' point of view, giving the inside line, and discussing the varying fortunes of a new manager or big money signing. They understood the dynamic in the dressing room after a heavy defeat, or the elation of a crucial victory. They could speak about tactics and more technical issues unfolding across a hectic Saturday afternoon. By this point, the show was called *Superscoreboard*.

You don't tune in to football phone-ins expecting a germane, high-brow rewriting of the first drafts of history, nor Norman Mailer or Hugh McIlvanney levels of erudition. Rather, it's heated, passionate and angry, featuring livid guys from Easterhouse, who hate Celtic or Rangers or the *Daily Record* or *The Sun* or the referee or the member of the panel they disagreed with.

The radio phone-in earns its place in the alternative Scottish football museum for perfectly capturing the delight or dismay of the average Scottish fan. This platform allows them to 'squeeze the plook', as it were, and, as it turns out, they're pretty good at it.

It is a perfect companion to the game in a country that is completely obsessed by it. As long as there is football to speak about, there will be people at the other end of the line willing to spout their opinions. They may be mad, funny or even, on occasion, insightful. But, without fail, they will always be entertaining.

WING

CULTURE

Exhibit 42
Agents

The image of the football agent – the cigar-puffing, hard-nosed Colonel Parker type – is now largely consigned to a bygone era, though, in some ways, their methodology and approach to getting a deal closed hasn't changed much over the decades.

It's difficult to accurately pinpoint the moment when agents became the scourge of football fans, managers and coaches alike. It might have been when serious money began to infiltrate the game. As the agents' profiles were raised, whether through big money moves, wage demands or contract renegotiations, the relationship between football fans and these 'middle men' became fraught. It could be because an agent had done a deal to steal our top scorer away from our beloved team. But in all truth, what fit and healthy, twenty-two-year-old striker could shun the lure of the bright lights of London, Liverpool or Manchester and a move that would earn them five or ten times more per week?

Perhaps it's because football delights in claiming it is part of the entertainment industry. This has given agents carte blanche to treat footballers like showbiz entertainers – but few are *actually* box office. The fan on the street could accept it if they delivered every time, like those showbiz acts have to do every night to stay at the top of their profession – acts such as bands, stand-up comedians and big names in a West End musical – but footballers are moody and inconsistent.

Agents are subject to derision because they seem only to pop into the spotlight when your favourite player announces he is moving on. Maybe it's because they throw in a few grenades around contract negotiation time to stir things up, claiming their star player is unhappy and thinking of heading out the door. They leak a line or two to the press, starting speculation that not enough love (i.e. money) is being shown to the player. Sometimes, they seem to forget their client is playing in the SPL is not Elton John negotiating a 450-show residency in Las Vegas.

Then there's the simple fact they try to tell you they are doing everything they can in the best interests of their client when everybody is well aware they are on a huge commission. The transfer market is a massive cash-cow for them. Players staying put? Not so much.

Anyone involved in the creative industry – a writer, author, artist, actor – will tell you an agent is a necessary evil and it's now nearly impossible to get anywhere without their services. In football, the agent's role has changed considerably over the years. Some look after every detail of a footballer's life. They organise everything from endorsement deals to detailed itineraries. Then there are agents who facilitate deals, encouraging clubs to negotiate. Some also behave like scouts, acting in an advisory capacity for clubs. There are also agents who do all of the above.

Some football clubs employ agents to look after their younger players. I have to confess that I was surprised to find the vast majority of agents aren't all money-grabbing shysters and, instead, act like surrogate parents, doing what's best for their players, many of whom are from deprived areas, poorly educated, and have left school early with few of the life skills required to deal with the pressure that comes their way. Players can easily take the wrong path, especially with the huge wages thrown at them. It is up to more experienced, more savvy people, such as agents, to look after them. It's a short career, after all.

But that's not to say the industry is completely devoid of people with what some fans would call 'questionable' motives. Take Jacques Lichtenstein, for example. The representative of former Celtic defender Dedryck Boyata, he found himself – and his client – in the headlines in August 2018. Lichtenstein accused Celtic of breaking promises and refusing Boyata the chance of a £9m move to English Premier League new boys Fulham. When the transfer failed to materialise, the player allegedly threatened to down tools and go on strike. His timing was horrendous. Celtic faced a crucial Champions League qualifier against AEK Athens and, with suspensions and injuries leaving them threadbare in defence, Boyata was desperately needed. Suddenly, an injury he picked up in training a few days earlier left him unable to play. After Celtic's exit from the competition at the hands of the Greek side, the club's then manager Brendan Rodgers confirmed Boyata wasn't, in fact, injured but had instead refused to make himself available.

Celtic fans were hurt. The Belgian defender had hardly set the heather alight when he first arrived for £1.5m from Manchester City in 2015. It wasn't until Rodgers arrived that he started to settle and become a decent player. In short? He owed Celtic far better than to sit out a crucial game for the club for what amounted to little more than spite at not getting his own way.

Apart from fleeting moments of high drama such as the Boyata case – he eventually got his move at the end of the 2018/19 season, incidentally, moving on a free transfer to German side Hertha Berlin – Scottish football hasn't been too badly troubled by agents. According to the FA, in the year from February 2016 to January 2017, English clubs paid £220m in agents' fees. The Premier League contributed £174m of that and, alarmingly, the Championship a whopping £42.4m. Scotland, meanwhile, coughed up what equated to three ginger bottles and a record token for Woolworths. Long may it continue.

Exhibit 43
Aluminium Studs

The legendary crime writer Elmore Leonard once advised writers never to start with the weather. So it is with all due respect that I completely ignore him and start with the rain. In this particular scene, it's chucking it down. It's an intense match, in a packed ground, under floodlights. A player slides in for the perfect tackle, the aluminium studs glistening in the floodlights. Perfect.

You can't beat the surety of aluminium studs when playing on wet, medium-to-long grass. This being Northern Europe, it rains regularly, so the ground underneath is soft. In the days when Scottish players wore aluminium studs, we almost made it out of the group stages of the World Cup. Proper football men, with hairy chests, knew they were allowed a few brutal tackles in the opening ten minutes before the ref would have a word. In the days before football got over-protective, players were allowed to wear metal studs. Ten minutes running on concrete would sharpen them up nicely. A stud mark was a calling card; if you drew blood, even better.

But let's not get ahead of ourselves. It's time for a brief history lesson. The football boot itself has been around since the 1800s, yet what we consider to be the forerunner of the modern boot didn't start to take shape until the 1950s. In 1952, Adidas, under the guidance of co-founder Adi Dassler, patented the concept of screw-in studs on the sole and developed such a boot for the West German captain, Fritz Walter, called the 'Adidas Argentina'. He played in them in the 1954 World Cup, which the Germans won.

The 1954 final is known as 'The Miracle of Berne', because the West German side came back from two goals down to beat Hungary's 'Mighty Magyars', widely regarded as one of the best sides of all time. Before facing Puskás and Co., West German manager Sepp Herberger eloquently observed, 'The ball is round, a game lasts ninety minutes, and everything else is theory.'

After just eight minutes, Hungary were two to the good but Herberger stuck to his plan of stifling Puskás. The Hungarian superstar was struggling with an ankle injury and, in truth, shouldn't have even been on the pitch, so Herberger focussed on wearing down the Hungarian midfield. Their continuous probing and haranguing of the opposition engine room, combined with some resolute defending, eventually broke the Hungarian will and it was Walter, wearing his screw-in Adidas Argentinas, who lifted the Jules Rimet trophy in the torrential rain after one of the most exciting World Cup finals ever contested.

In February 1965, another German player, Uwe Seeler, tore his Achilles tendon. Adidas designed an orthopaedic boot with built-in cushioning to take pressure off the injured part of his foot, providing additional support to help speed up his recovery. This boot had aluminium studs and washers.

By 1974, Adidas had lighter boots and aluminium studs, and West Germany provided the rain. This was the first World Cup I can clearly remember watching on my grandparents' colour TV.

I recall waiting to watch games and there would be fire engines on the pitch trying to remove water. It was almost as if we were watching a news report from a flooded city. Horns were sounding, the nets were a square shape, pegged high to stanchions, and it just rained and rained and rained.

This World Cup was about wet weather and the pain of being a Scotland fan. Scotland, despite being unbeaten (one win, two draws), lost out qualifying from the group on goal-difference. I couldn't understand the injustice. Three teams in a group of four had four points.

West Germany, again wearing aluminium studs, won in the rain when they beat the glorious 'total football' playing Dutch side. This was their secret: long aluminium studs and powerful, light, waterproof Adidas boots. Most top players and sides played in Adidas. In fact, both sides in the final were sponsored by Adidas. However, Cruyff famously refused to wear either the boots or have an Adidas strip because he had an exclusive deal with Puma. He was such a superstar that the Dutch FA and the national side turned a blind eye and allowed him to play in another sponsor's shirt.

Most players and fans who came into football around the Beckham and Zidane era will forever love the Predator, Adidas's most successful boot. Then you had Brazilian Ronaldo sporting Nike Mercurials. And that's to say nothing of the classic design and comfort of the Adidas '74, '78 and '82 boot. However, I'd unscrew the plastic studs (or nylons) and replace them with aluminium. Whilst doing so, I'd repeat Sepp Herberger's mantra to myself: 'The ball is round, a game lasts ninety minutes, everything else is theory.' In other words, if you apply yourself, on any given day, anything can happen. But aluminium studs might just give you the edge you need.

Exhibit 44
Car Watchers

Apart from men (and the occasional woman) peeing in your garden, full scale riots between rival casuals and the odd window being smashed with a Buckfast bottle or brick, it always struck me as the height of exotica to live next to a football stadium.

This exhibit explores the psyche of those who happened to do so – and it might be one of those exhibits that only works in Glasgow. It's one of social banter, the cheeky wee ticket, full of the patter, and the junior sociopath plying his trade – the Glasgow kid who would kindly ask, 'Mister, can I watch yer motor?' I'm sure these kids must have existed in some form or other for centuries. In Victorian times, Charles Dickens would've incorporated them into a book with a narrative involving the Artful Dodger and Fagan. If the setting was more modern, their quiet menace could fit into a clichéd, generic Glasgow crime pot-boiler, full of blood oaths and omertà.

The beauty of the question is that it's actually a threat. The fact it comes from a twelve-year-old only makes sound more sinister. The sales pitch should've been reworded or explained thus: 'Mister, see if you don't let me watch yer motor, I will take the Stanley Knife you know I have hidden somewhere and slash your tyres. If you give me any grief, your car will, in a few hours, be on fire and sitting on bricks without wheels – and that's if you're lucky enough to even find it.'

All of this delivered in a low key, relaxed manner which prompted many people new to the area to make the mistake of leaving without agreeing. You felt sorry for those who didn't understand that if you didn't comply with the kid's request (demand), then your car was getting it.

These dubious young entrepreneurs divided up the areas around football stadiums. Every side street was checked and covered. The kids had their patch, their allotted turf. They were organised, marshalled and ferociously effective at exhorting money. If Police Scotland want to understand how kids can go from primary school and slip straight into a career of debt collection, racketeering or protection money, then this youth academy is the starting point.

These kids made a fortune from the initial payment – some loose change from every car owner – and more when the owners returned. If you looked closely enough, behind the nonchalance of the car-proud dad, uncle or designated driver, you could always see fear.

I remember one particular occasion when a couple of well-attired gangster types parked a big Jeep, which would've been *de rigueur* at the time, near our car. Most flash car drivers would have known to respect the kids. These guys did not. Instead, they pointed to a devil dog in the back seat. It, not they, would do the minding. When the two chaps returned, they found a confused-looking dog, staring at a car that was mounted on four bricks. The kids who stole the trendy alloy wheels would likely have sold them on before the end of the first half.

Why are they are included in the museum? Purely as a reminder that, while football might now be underpinned by a huge global corporate infrastructure, it still belongs to, and is part of, the community.

If we could only adopt these kids' mastery and cunning on the football field, I'm convinced we would be qualifying for major competitions and competing in the Champions League every year.

Exhibit 45
'Dirge of Scotland'

We're at Hampden. It's a huge international game. We're excited. The stadium is buzzing. No, it's *bouncing*. It is pounding and pulsating. Fifty-thousand people are all pumped up. The players stride down the tunnel on to the wonderfully manicured pitch, under the floodlights, as the noise is cranked up another notch. The teams line up – and then it happens . . . the national anthems start. And, with that, the excitement and energy disperse like a fart in the wind.

This alternative museum proposes that we send 'Flower of Scotland' packing. Homeward to think again, as it were. Let's opt for a newer, brighter, more uplifting song. 'Flower of Scotland' is a song about a glorious victory, at home, against a stronger English side, in 1314. Let's move on, though, and stop banging on about winning old fights. Enough is enough.

I always assumed the modern footballer would be prepared, ready and mentally attuned to a match situation. They would be focused on their role, who they are marking, and block out any external distractions, taking little notice of the pre-match formalities like the anthems. Surely singing a song makes no difference to how an elite athlete performs? But no, as it turns out, new research has confirmed that teams who sing their national anthem with greater gusto are more likely to win games.

Scottish people, at least those who are now middle-aged, were never encouraged to show off. Singing loudly was arrogant. If you were getting above your station, you would be brought right back down by those around you. As soon as you banged on about yourself, you would be extricated for your conceit. The idea of putting your arms around a teammate and squealing openly at the top of your lungs about your greatness hardly comes as second nature to Scots.

Another major flaw with 'Flower of Scotland', particularly in the modern era, is that we are often asking a team half comprised of Englishmen to sing a rousing version of a song that involves bludgeoning Englishmen.

French sides, with their chests puffed out, sing the triumphant 'La Marseillaise'. Portugal sing a brave, noble anthem. The Croatians place their hands on their heart and seem to undergo emotional turmoil during their anthem. The Brazilians sing along like mad, in tears, then the music stops so the fans can sing a section *acapella*. And then you have the Italians who sing a jaunty, upbeat rousing song.

Now, I don't know what these countries are actually singing about. No doubt, it will involve similar moments of uprising or historic benchmarks when their brave country won a battle.

Those days are passed now. Scotland is a cool nation and 'Flower of Scotland' doesn't best represent us any more. We've moved on from the 'See You Jimmy' image, a time when English people called us all 'Jock'. It's time to modernise the anthem. Don't forget, 'Flower of Scotland' isn't our official anthem; only our default sporting one.

Scotland has a vast array of talented musicians and songwriters who could do better. Freshen it up. I would commission The Proclaimers, Teenage Fanclub and Mogwai and lock them in a studio for a week to see what they can come up with.

Anything but the dirge we currently have. Please.

Exhibit 46
The Existential Side-Aff

There's an element of sporting socialism to a big side-aff (a pick-up game of football, self-governed and with as close to an equal number on each side as possible). It's a perfectly imperfect version of the 'Beautiful Game' bringing a group of like-minded people together. These games are rarely played on level, luscious football pitches, with markings and nets. Instead, they take place in the unglamorous setting of an abandoned school park, on a red ash 'pitch' or an unused car park, with the obligatory jumpers for goalposts.

The best games are those spontaneous gatherings when sometimes eighteen-a-side come together, both teams trying their best to apply a vague set of laws. Anyone who's available is invited to join in. Sometimes, random strangers or passers-by or even those just waiting on a bus join in without even asking; they appear from nowhere and play. That's okay. Everyone's welcome in a side-aff.

Where else would you share the same field with people

who would become emeritus professors, bosses in financial institutions, car mechanics, journalists, carpenters, headmasters, electricians, company directors, painters and decorators and men who never recovered from steel works or mining closures? Yet you'll find them here, playing a game based on principles drawn up centuries ago. Okay, it isn't eleven-a-side, but each team tries to maintain some degree of fair play and sportsmanship, even at this level.

Among the skilled players on show are the brooding, the charismatic, the skilled, the hard working, the maverick, the fighter, the hoofer, the thinker, the Bowie fan, the punk, the guy with the hair like Cruyff, with the boots and the looks ('all the gear but nae idea') and a local lad called Terry, the kind who 'likes a drink' the same way Kim Jong-un likes to test rockets. And there's a dog. There is *always* a dog.

All in agreement, since the score's 16–16 and everyone's been playing for the regulation three-and-a-half hours, the cry goes up: 'Next goal's the winner!'

This is a sport based on a system of thought, played out by daydreaming philosophers.

To play a side-aff is a life-affirming experience. It's a broad church, ranging in ages from boys of fourteen to men of fifty, no quarter asked or given. It's rough and tumble, hard but fair. This is the original school of hard knocks. A tackle might be over the top but if you don't shirk it, respect is recognised with a friendly pat on the head. The young guys don't know it at the time but they're learning huge lessons. Nothing is given easily in life; everything is down to you and what you put in. Success is achieved with camaraderie and team work.

Some players are accomplished, the best being the aforementioned Terry, who is lightning quick, and was once on the radar of most senior Scottish sides when he was a promising junior. He's a true maverick, rarely passing to a teammate, but is a sublime footballer nonetheless. His hero should have been Denis Law but was more likely George Best.

Terry doesn't play for the full three-and-a-half hour game. He prefers to come on for the glory in the last ten minutes, when he hears 'next goal's the winner'. He collects, controls and traps the ball, runs rings around his own team, not so much kicking the ball but caressing it instead, elegantly zipping past tackle after tackle, feinting here, defying gravity there, spinning and swerving by the opposition. Then he wallops the ball between the jumpers with a ferocity, accuracy and technique no-one can fully comprehend. To see Terry zoom past tackles, spilling not one drop of his open can of Super Lager, is like watching Bruce Lee take on the Keystone Cops.

But as good as Terry is, the game is about the collective. We play for each other. Not for glory. Terry knows that, too. You can tell by the way he keeps running down the hill, twirling his T-shirt in the air in jubilation, away to a party, celebrating his goal and his own existence. In those entertaining, thrilling moments, when Terry focused and played, he summed up the trouble with Scottish football. When we had players like him, we got to major championships – but managers these days can't handle such free spirits.

You walk home thinking life truly has meaning. The game, no matter how humble, is described as beautiful for a reason. We exist. We are alive. That is the beauty of a big side-aff.

Exhibit 47
Golf

There has always been a peculiar synergy between footballers and golf. It was generally considered acceptable, if not compulsory, that a footballer be a member of the best golf club in the region. It was a place for them to let off some steam on their days off and enjoy a couple of sherbets in the clubhouse afterwards with some of the lads.

Older managers were split over this particular hobby. Some loved it because it kept their players out of the pub, if only for a little while. To them, it was a better alternative to the snooker hall.

For the players themselves, it was perfect as it gave them something to do after they finished training at midday. They could be on the first tee twenty minutes later. To most, it was a serious hobby, and I dare say, this being Scotland, they would have a few bets placed and some gorgeous courses to play on.

But not every manager was a fan, and it wasn't the pesky modern-thinking foreign coaches either. There was a period

165

when it was frowned upon almost everywhere. Liverpool's Bob Paisley, who you'd think would be happy for his players to enjoy a brisk walk, was known to become uncharacteristically apoplectic when his players played golf. To him, walking miles and launching a metal stick at a wee ball buried in wild terrain made them prone to muscle pulls and tears. He would know. Paisley had planned on becoming a physio when his playing career finished. He had quietly started doing courses and was looking forward to becoming Liverpool's physio. Instead, somebody at the club noticed how much the players loved his training, listened to him and respected him. For Paisley, it was all about work rate, keeping the game simple and fast, and catching teams on the counter. Someone pointed out he would be better served as coach and he was promoted to reserve team manager.

Paisley likely inherited his suspicion of golf from his predecessor, Bill Shankly. He was less concerned about injuries, and more with the snobbery of golf club officialdom.

Many of Liverpool's Scottish stars – Kenny Dalglish, Graeme Souness and Alan Hansen particularly – were golf fanatics. Many of them, in fact, lived in Southport, regarded as 'England's Golf Coast' and home to many wonderful courses, such as Open Championship host venue, Royal Birkdale.

Officious jobsworths are the order of the day in Scotland, going all the way back to James II who was none too keen on allowing golf. His 1457 Act of Parliament introduced a full ban on the game. He wanted his subjects honing their archery and doing something worthwhile in the event of a war being declared. The Act stated: 'It is ordained and decreed that the lords and barons both spiritual and temporal should organise archery displays four times in the year. And that football and golf should be utterly condemned and stopped… And concerning football and golf, we ordain that those found playing these games be punished by the local barons and, failing them, by the King's officers.' Harsh words, indeed. Football hadn't yet been invented, incidentally. All sport not played on horseback was described as 'football' before 'association football' came into existence.

The advent of foreign coaches coincided with the introduction of double training sessions. That meant no afternoons off to hit the links. Big mistake. Maybe they should've introduced archery practice to help keep their eye in?

There were other strict disciplinarians, though, who actively encouraged golf. Sir Alex Ferguson and Walter Smith, for example, both loved the game and the camaraderie it fostered.

The aforementioned Alan Hansen nearly made a career out of golf, as it happens. He played golf for Scotland at youth level, representing the Scottish Boys' golf team, so it was a toss-up between that or football. When Hibs came calling, he rejected a professional contract with them because he wanted to continue playing competitive golf. You can imagine him as a laid-back golf pro, bemoaning the 'shocking' state of the greens, but he was also clever. A successful playing career (three European Cups, eight league titles and two FA Cups), preceded twenty-two years as a highly-paid pundit on *Match of the Day*. One day's work. That left six for golf.

Aside from causing the odd injury and players getting inebriated in the clubhouse, what else has golf done to damage Scottish football? Hours of walking in the countryside have no doubt sparked numerous conversations about wages, transfer deals and how players don't rate the latest manager. Safe to assume it wouldn't have been jokes about tricky lob shots, birdies, awkward lies and trying to get a hole-in-one. I think it's fair to say that most fans would wish that, instead of playing golf, the players worked on their set pieces, or went to the gym to find the extra five per cent that might take their club to

European glory or the national side to a major competition. Is that too much to ask?

Exhibit 48
The Lift-over

When football seemed close to perfection, when it was played with implausible ferocity and genuinely exciting pace and skill, when it was entertaining, when players had moustaches and the air smelt of fags, lager and Ralgex, the game was infinitely better. Yet there is also a delicious dollop of irony as, during this period from the mid-1970s, in the days before season books and electronic turnstiles, we regularly got to see the 'Beautiful Game', in its halcyon days, free of charge.

The process of illegal entry to a match was called a lift-over (known colloquially as 'a lift 'er'). This involved asking a grown-up who had taken you to the game, or sometimes even a complete stranger, if he would lift you over the gate. It was quite a thrill, getting in for free.

When you're nine, you don't think of the future ramifications. Like most people who steal something from a big supermarket chain or, in this case, a football club, we thought, 'They're not going to miss it, are they?' The trouble is, you didn't think of the thousands of others who were also being lifted over. The loss of revenue caused by children sneaking in to see games for free must have been astronomical over the years.

I received a lift-over to see George Best play for Hibs in a Scottish Cup semi-final against Celtic at Hampden in 1980. By this point in his career, Best was slightly overweight and quite slow, but he was still brilliant to watch. He could read the game, see a pass and waltz past opponents.

I had a similar experience seeing Johan Cruyff play in a 1982 European Cup tie at Celtic Park.

Nothing compared to watching Cruyff under the floodlights. To see the way he controlled the pace of the game, thinking like a chess player, starting moves from deep-lying positions and knowing where the move would end up was to watch a genius at work. There was a wonderful fluidity to his play. He was also constantly coaching and instructing others around him throughout the game. He was always three or four steps ahead of the game. Whereas Best and Diego Maradona were the stars of their teams, Cruyff, with his skill and tactical awareness, somehow made the team the star. The Dane, Soren Lerby, was another who stood out in that incredible Ajax team.

Seeing wonderful footballers via a lift-over was a rite of passage and, over the years, thousands of our best footballers presumably must have been inspired by their heroes in much the same way.

Of course, getting a lift-over eventually came to a natural end. When you're sixteen and six-foot-plus, it's time stop taking liberties. Now, it's simply not possible. Times change and some things will happen again. I'm just happy I got the chance to enjoy this rare, simple thrill.

Exhibit 49
The Magic Sponge

The magic sponge has baffled and confused some of medicine's greatest minds for decades.

What secret qualities hide within this miraculous mockit sponge, enabling it to cure so many ails? No matter how serious the injury, we became accustomed to seeing a fat trainer in a sheepskin coat and tight tracksuit bottoms running on to the park with a big bucket. On top of the filthy water slopping around inside it, floated the magic sponge. The dirtier it looked, the more effective the alchemy seemed.

Despite the fact you could buy a brand-new sponge for fifty pence, or a decent one from the pound shop for twice that, treasurers at football clubs across the land clearly felt that this was still too much to pay. The magic sponge was always brown and dirty.

In the 1970s, when such matters weren't too important, the man in charge of running on to perform miracles was always a coach with basic first aid competencies. These were the days before physios, club doctors and stadia with medical centres that look like the wing of a private hospital. In bygone days, the medical treatment might, to the casual junior doctor, appear basic, but the coach-turned-physio had a system. The injured area was grabbed and treatment based upon the volume of the squeal that elicited. As soon as the sponge was applied, if the player didn't immediately bounce back up, the treatment would intensify. If it was more serious, some expensive Deep Heat would reluctantly be applied to the injured area. If this had no effect and the player genuinely was suffering from a break or ruptured tendon, then a ten-year-old crepe bandage would be applied.

By rights, the magic sponge should have been upgraded to miracle status, placed in a shrine and turned into a place for religious pilgrimage. For unknown reasons, once it had been applied, players were known to jump up and set off zig-zagging down the wing. Perhaps the real reason for producing the magic sponge was to cheat the referee and run down the clock. The magic sponge was the oldest trick in the book and was about one thing: gamesmanship. It's now been replaced by a magical wonder spray.

Apart from the blood contamination in the event of a cut, the spreading of three million germs and the basic ridiculousness of the principle, it seemed to work. Medical experts have confirmed that the sponge, or at least the application of cold water, reduces the blood supply to the injured area and helps prevents swelling.

The legendary magic sponge has been in football since 1888 and has treated many a serious injury. Alas, players now have world-class physios who sprint onto the park like Olympic champions in an attempt to diagnose the latest critical ailment to afflict their star man. Of course, seldom is there anything wrong. Strangely, though, there now seem to be more injuries than ever. In the halcyon days of the magic sponge, there were fewer career-ending injuries. Maybe the men were tougher and could take a kicking. Some of football's hardest players would sooner die than miss a game as a result of a dead leg or knock. A dab of the magic sponge and a cry of, 'Get up and run it aff!' was all they needed in the good old days.

Exhibit 50
The Mining Holy Trinity Cliché

They are often lumped together in an over romanticised mining metaphor but The Holy Trinity of Scottish managers Jock Stein, Matt Busby and Bill Shankly were much more than that. Hewn from humble working-class roots in Burnbank, Bellshill and Glenbuck respectively ensured a tremendous work ethic. However, their real talent was an understanding of football's power to connect and unite people. This is what made them great leaders of men.

Of the three, Busby had the toughest upbringing, losing his father and three uncles in the First World War. By the General Strike of 1926, Busby, aged seventeen, would certainly be politicised. He watched the men of Orbiston and Bellshill starved back to work, forced to accept longer hours and lower pay. Eamon Dunphy, who was an apprentice under Busby at Manchester United and would eventually write his biography said: 'He had learned a lesson about trust and loyalty, about rhetoric and promise, about family and community but most profoundly, about power and powerlessness.'

Sir Matt Busby was considered an avuncular figure but was unafraid of the authorities when he needed to take them to task. He was unflinching in 1956, taking on the Football League management committee lead by the Nigel Farage of the day, the xenophobic Yorkshireman, Alan Hardaker. He didn't want English sides accepting an invite to play in the European Cup. Busby thought it was crucial to both his club and the evolution of football to accept and take on the European elite. Busby said, 'It always seemed to me the logical progression that the champions of England should pit their abilities against the best of Europe. You cannot make progress standing still. Looking back now, I can see that our resolve to enter into European competition was a significant milestone in the history of the game.'

If Stein, Shankly or Busby attended Eton, they would be Prime Ministers, politicians or captains of industry. We like to highlight their upbringing and background. As Scots, we revel in this mining-stock metaphor, as if it's a badge of honour. These were intelligent men though, driven to succeed. Their background and where they're from merely served to remind them, on a daily basis, of the humility of those they were there to entertain. It was the same miners, factory workers and ship builders who paid at the gates to watch the game they loved.

When asked in an interview in the *New Statesmen* about his and the working-class Scottish backgrounds of Stein, Busby and Shankly, Sir Alex Ferguson confirmed, 'I think we're back to the values we grew up with in the kind of places we came from. Hard work. Teamwork. Strong beliefs. Jock was an incredible guy. I was manager at Aberdeen when he asked me to be his assistant with Scotland as well, so I had eighteen months to see him close up. The two things I remember above all were his humility and his intelligence. He knew everything that was happening in Scottish football, everything. He knew about players I was looking at before I knew it myself.'

Stein was arguably the best tactician, willing to learn, change, adapt and try out new formations. He visited Inter Milan and met their coach, Helenio Herrera, in 1963 because he was regarded as one of the top coaches in Europe. He noticed Herrera had full control of team affairs, was impressed by his use of attacking full backs: commonplace now, but unusual then. When he came up against Herrera in the European Cup final in 1967, he was now facing a man acclaimed as the best coach in the world – certainly the highest paid one – and the winner of two European Cups. Herrera was famed for 'catenaccio', a steadfastly defensive approach. In Italian, catenaccio literally means 'door-bolt'. Stein adopted a 4–4–2 formation with advanced wingers, Jim Craig and Tommy Gemmell. In the final, Inter soaked up Celtic's early advances and hit them on the counter, winning a dubious penalty. Celtic had forty-five shots to Inter's three and ten corners in a game where Inter had none. The Glasgow side's eventual 2–1 defeat of Inter was widely viewed as a victory for attacking football.

Their upbringings would have taught them many lessons. A sense of duty, an appreciation of how lucky they were, honesty, integrity and trust. The team you supported and the songs you sang meant nothing when you were at the coalface. What mattered was the collective strength of those who stood shoulder to shoulder with you. As well as schooling them in the complexities of the human condition, it will have shaped them politically.

Shankly's village, Glenbuck, produced more than fifty professional footballers, eleven becoming internationals. Four of Shankly's brothers became professional footballers, seeing football as a way out of life in the pits. Shankly's passion and drive was hued by a sheer belief in socialism: 'The socialism I believe in, is everybody working for the same goal and everybody having a share in the rewards. That's how I see football, that's how I see life.' Shankly's socialist views, his determination, his fitness, even his personality appeared to be shaped by the village he grew up in. Then he would impart that on to the players and the fans. Shankly knew his way out and that was football. Though throughout his career he seemed driven by never being too far from the memories of his first job, in terrible, filthy, rat filled, cramped mines.

It undermines their achievements in football to keep lumping them in as heroic pit workers. Busby had an eye for a player – Charlton, Law and Best being fine examples – and encouraged a free-flowing entertaining, uncomplicated approach. Shankly, too, stuck to simple principles: drilling, repetition, continuous improvement, hard work, supporting the man in possession. He had the players believing they were world beaters.

All three Scottish managers had their teams fit and worked them hard, knowing all about back-breaking work, the tough, hard yards, and the slog. Celtic, Liverpool and Manchester United were successful because of their team's flamboyance and flair but this was underpinned by their work rate, fitness and stamina. Most crucially, the three understood that the fans and club worked as one. They couldn't function without each other. The managers also learned to look their fellow man in the eye and, in most cases, were able to bring out the best in him.

They certainly would've learned, in common with the mining industry, that football was brutal once you'd served your purpose, no matter how successful you'd been. Once you were done, it was over. There was no sentiment or loyalty. Stein and Shankly were treated badly, despite the success they delivered for Celtic and Liverpool. When Shankly was discarded by Liverpool, his obsession with the game meant he found it impossible to give it up and he would cut a tragic figure, hanging around the club he gave so much to. Eventually, they had to ban him from the training ground. Stein, meanwhile, was offered a job in charge of Celtic pools. Both should have been made honorary directors or general managers. It's something to consider when we look at the piece of coal, and dust off the clichés. Working in mines or being of a generation destroyed and ravaged by war, their background would have prepared them not to expect too much in return – and that's exactly what they got.

Speaking on Sir Matt Busby's retirement, Hugh McIlvanney wrote: 'It was utterly extraordinary that three great managers, Matt Busby, Jock Stein and Bill Shankly, came from the same area of Scotland, and it was, I think, very significant. These people absorbed the best of the true ethos of that working-class environment. There was a richness of spirit bred into people from mining areas. Stein said that he would never work with better men than he did when he was a miner. Shankly, the great warrior/poet of football, nevertheless retained that sense of what real men should do, the sense of dignity, the sense of pride. All of that was present in Matt.'

Jock Stein though, called it right on the subject of mining and football, when he famously said: 'If you've been down a pit, you're not going to worry too much about a wee kerfuffle in a football club.'

Exhibit 51
The Quagmire

It is no empty reminiscence to quietly reflect on the devastating damage footballers of the 1970s could do on a roughed-up field, the likes of which cows would turn their noses up at. Yet here were players whose skills were matched with bravery and strength in the face of oncoming defenders, who were assassins, disguised as brick outhouses.

Determined to entertain on these waterlogged and clumpy football pitches, they would jink to avoid saturated mud packs, meandering, if they were lucky, to the odd bit of playable pitch somewhere down the wing.

Perhaps this was why, when they were given a decent surface and got to strut their stuff on the perfectly manicured bowling green lawns of the Santiago Bernabéu in Madrid, or the Catalan citadel of the Camp Nou, they performed so well.

The surfaces we have today are perfect by comparison and are kept in pristine condition throughout the year. If there has been one major development in the game which should be applauded, it has to be the improvement of the pitches. When you watched sides playing in the 1970s, the playing surfaces were often so desperate that, when they ran down the tunnel, the players might as well have been checking their snorkels as much as their studs and shin pads.

Even the top sides of the day had terrible pitches. Dundee United's was routinely covered in sand, hence their nickname 'the Arabs'. Celtic's ground in 1970 was a sodden field and Aberdeen's, throughout both the 1970s and 1980s, was terrible. Motherwell should be applauded for the transformation of their surface which, a few years ago, was regarded as something of a patchwork mud heap. In fact, in 2010, they were fined £50,000 by the SPL due to the state of the Fir Park pitch. Surely a loan or a fund to help clubs improve their surfaces would be better than hitting them with a financial penalty…

It was a similar story in England. Due to the way football was broadcast in the 1960s and 1970s, it became customary to see games down south with dreadful pitches like Stamford Bridge, Derby's old Baseball Ground or Arsenal's old home, Highbury. There was a famous FA Cup moment when non-league Hereford beat Newcastle United in 1972 at Edgar Street. The BBC loves to show Ronnie Radford's thirty-yard shot which forced the game into extra time, but the eye is drawn to state of the mud bath of a pitch as much as it is to the strike.

That said, if I had a choice, I would prefer sodden fields to the new synthetic ones. It doesn't lend itself to silky football but players are required to have an exceptional level of fitness and, of course, when the parks are waterlogged, there's a serious amount of long ball hoof, which can be exciting. No-one debates the style or approach once the points are in the bag. But the main point is that football has always been played on grass and it should always be played on grass. The weather *should* affect a game and the tactics used over any given ninety minutes. The mental aspect of adapting to the conditions is as much a part of the magic of outdoor sport as the ability to do step-overs or nutmeg an opponent. Take the elements away and you lose something fundamental about the beauty of the game. See you later, 4G. Bring back grass.

Exhibit 52
The Smell of a Saturday Morning

I love the smell of Ralgex in the morning. It reminds me of Saturdays, boots polished, mind focused on the game ahead. If I had the money, or influence, I'd commission the trained noses at the world-famous Givaudan perfumery school near Paris to recreate the scent. If they were looking to create a robust, bright aftershave, they could do worse than think about Eau du Ralgex. It sure would nip but you'd smell like a cool footballer.

Ralgex – the magic muscle rub gel – evokes memories of pre-match excitement and nerves. It is as much the smell of a game of football as grass and mud and sweat. The prolonged scent that stayed with you until you'd showered and walked home and shoved your shirt in the wash – all part of the wonderful Saturday morning routine, finished off with a well-earned bacon roll and settling down to watch *Football Focus*.

Ralgex is also the dressing room prankster's number one ally. It's up there with nailing shoes to the floor, letting off a fire extinguisher and leaving a dead fish to rot inside a teammate's car. Who could argue against the comedy of smearing your arrogant striker's jockstrap with Ralgex to bring him down a peg or two? Sure, he might end up hospitalised but it's dressing room banter; the lads letting off steam.

The unhinged craziness aside, Ralgex is up there with the magic sponge in terms of its effectiveness in masking the pain of a leg break or cruciate medial ligament damage. The spray was normally applied by the previously mentioned magic sponge administrator – the fashion zealot, with a comb-over, in a sheepskin coat and trackie bottoms – when a player had been attacked in a common assault moonlighting as a tackle.

Even when I wasn't injured, I would spray some on or apply some of the cream as I felt it was the mark of a true footballer. Some players fake an injury to get out of a game. I used to pretend I had one so I could douse myself in Ralgex and wear a bandage out of little more than a melodramatic disposition.

For its services to serious injuries in the 1970s, Ralgex spray is in the museum. In those days, you rarely saw a player being stretchered off and, if you did, you knew that it had to be serious if the Ralgex couldn't fix it. In fact, I'm just off to spray some on now.

Exhibit 53
Rod Stewart Cup Draws

Scotland has always been fixated with the Scottish Cup, and little wonder.

It's the oldest club competition in the world and, when the trophy is wheeled out for a cup draw, it is exalted like the Holy Grail. Some Scottish Cup draws, though, have turned into drawn out melodramas, with more sweating brows than Sidney Lumet's tense courtroom drama, *12 Angry Men*.

What was the nadir? Without doubt, 22 January 2017, the day Rod Stewart visited Airdrie to watch Albion Rovers play Celtic in the Scottish Cup and, at full-time, perform the draw for the next round. A great idea for the TV audience but it's fair to assume, due to his performance, that Rod had made the most of corporate hospitality. Who would've thought a slightly inebriated rock star could have stumbled upon a way to breathe new life into making boring cup draws infinitely more entertaining and watchable? And bring in a worldwide audience to boot?

With the exception of a wee Westie dug chewing a Tunnock's Tea Cake, whilst downing some Irn Bru and shooting at the Krankies with an air rifle, there is nothing more Scottish than a live Scottish Cup draw. The excitement of the occasion alone is more than sufficient but when you throw one of Scotland's favourite pastimes into the mix – watching famous people making diddies of themselves – you have TV gold. We, as a nation, genuinely love it when people make fools of themselves live on TV or radio… and the more famous, the better.

Let's rewind for a second and focus on the concept of the draw itself. It's quite a simple process: balls containing wee bits of paper with team names on them are swirled in a glass bowl, then selected and opened before the name of the team is slowly revealed by fumbling fingers. It was once the more serious, older committee men, with cold, clean faces and grey hair who would perform the duty. The problem was that subterfuge eventually came into play, with some of the balls reportedly heated in advance so that the person making the draw could keep the big guns apart until the latter stages.

The solution? Balls with numbers on them and a list of teams with numbers beside them. Who would've thought it could be so easy?

The inclusion of the Scottish Cup draw in the museum, however, owes much to Rod's performance on that particular day in 2017. The draw was presided over by SFA president, Alan McRae, and former Hibs and St Mirren coach, Allan Stubbs. Their sobriety was in perfect contrast to Rod's peculiar behaviour.

For those who haven't seen the footage, Rod flamboyantly delved in to take each ball out, then pointed it at the camera with an over-the-top flourish. At one point, he distracted Alan Stubbs so much he called a six when it was nine. He then appeared to grab the SFA president's bum.

It was interesting, in the aftermath, to see how the newspapers described the peculiar drama. They called Rod 'over enthusiastic', implied that he 'had been enjoying hospitality', and described his behaviour as 'bizarre antics'. They were also annoyed at Rod for not shaking Alan McRae's hand. He actually wasn't looking, so technically it wasn't a refusal. Rod was too busy trying to sober up, check TV monitors and preen himself. There was clearly no malice involved.

I suggest that, from now on, we ply top celebs with booze and have them appear beside two others who are sober. Why not bring in live music? Any razzmatazz to counterbalance what is a normally dour affair. A full rebrand. Have top acts bid to play it. One song, draw a tie, second song another tie.

If Rod's promoters are sharp enough, they could even send him throughout the world on a Cup Draw World Tour.

Now, there's a thought . . .

Exhibit 54
Trialists

Whenever your team fielded a trialist, there were usually howls of derision. Trialists were always a gamble and playing them might cost your team a match. You'd look through the teamsheet and see this mysterious figure included – always listed as 'A. Trialist' or sometimes 'A. Newman' because they hadn't been registered. Clubs would be allowed to field one in an emergency, but they could very well be the director's pal's son who scores for fun down the park and the director's given the manager a nudge to take a chance on him. It was risky but there was also always an element of excitement and gossip when 'A. Trialist' was announced in the first team. Who was he? Was he decent? Was he famous?

In all likelihood, he was neither. How exceptional could these guys be if they couldn't get a game elsewhere? Maybe they played like Messi in training but were absolute garbage in games. Maybe they knew how to get a shine on the boss's car. Maybe they had compromising photographs of the director and manager at the Christmas night out. Who knew?

We were naïve and easily entertained but, more often than not, the poor trialist was underwhelming and we rarely saw them again.

I'm not acquainted with the regulations regarding the trialist system. There was always a lack of clear and unequivocal fact with regards to their use which also appeared to change depending on the competition. A lack of clarity also meant the rules were easily taken advantage of. Usually, smaller clubs could register a player as an emergency and play him as a trialist. This was far more beneficial for part-time sides but, in 2017, the League Cup rules changed. The competition's early summer stages were an ideal time for clubs to sign a player on a trial basis, while they weighed up whether or not they were worth a deal. Trialists, if they are signed now, have to remain with the club until the next transfer window.

In a pre-season friendly, in July 2017, Inverness Caledonian Thistle fielded five trialists against Forres Mechanics. The team was Esson, Raven, Trialist, Mckay, Warren, Trialist, Polworth, Draper, Trialist, Trialist, Trialist. Impressively, ICT and their quintet of trialists managed to engineer a 1–0 victory.

It would make it interesting if you could field four in each team, near the end of the season. What have you got to lose? Apart from sporting integrity, that is, but if you are mid-table and the league winners have already had three weeks of celebrations, why not?

Maybe we could offer the trialist places to players who came with huge credentials, players who were once tipped for stardom only to fade back into obscurity. They can still play. I'd get them back in and have them as my trialists to see if the they can make good on the promise they once showed.

Another thing. The name, 'A Trialist', is a trifle understated and boring. Why can't we include daft and made-up names? Imagine 'Groucho Marx' up front, 'Che Guevara' on the wing and, in goal, 'Princess Grace of Monaco'. It's football. It's a game. Let's have some fun with it.

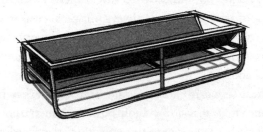

Exhibit 55
Urinals

For some, the idea of losing the tip of your member while peeing into a razor-sharp end of an empty beer can has long been more appealing than visiting the away ground's urinals. I say urinals; they're more like troughs for cattle.

Again, we return to the theory that when we had less, we had more. When we had grounds that were dumps, wrecks, fire hazards and a public health danger, we were far better at every level of the game. When we started to become family-friendly, became concerned about health and safety, brought in mascots, and allowed fun and frivolity – and had to install clean toilets with hot running water – that's when it all started going wrong. I have no idea why there's a correlation but there it is.

As a kid, I used to go and watch Airdrie and Albion Rovers play on consecutive weeks. Anything to see a live game of football. But I'd always make sure I'd been to the toilet before I left the house so I wouldn't have to go at the ground. After going to the loo once at a game, you learned very quickly to keep it in thereafter. God help you if you needed a number two at Broomfield. Cliftonhill wasn't much better.

I have two abiding memories of venturing to the toilets: one, when I did go for a quick visit, I always missed a goal; and two, it was always freezing – and by freezing, I mean *Baltic*. The toilet at the back of Broomfield was always sub-zero, even in summer. Airdrie's ground was the highest above sea level, and when you had to pay a visit, it felt like you had to acclimatise and prepare for the conditions.

Back then, toilets in most grounds were so bad they made the famous one in *Trainspotting* look posh. Those at the national stadium at Hampden, prior to its renovation, were hardly Hilton-esque either. Honourable mentions for horrific loos should also go to Morton's Cappielow, Clydebank's Kilbowie and St Mirren's old ground at Love Street. Most fans have their own nightmare toilet visit, usually at any ground but their own.

These days, most clubs are flush with success, and environmental services will close them down, especially if food's being served in the grounds as well. But maybe we should do a survey and ask fans if they would accept a return to dodgy loos if it meant another crack at European glory? I reckon I could probably put up with holding everything in for two hours in exchange for that.

Exhibit 56
The Vinyl Frontier

It would be a gross dereliction of duty if the museum didn't take a look at the epoch-changing, ground-breaking musical contribution the 'World Cup single' made to the nation. Time to take a journey through sound to the vinyl frontier...

Getting to the World Cup these days would almost be generation-defining but there was a time when it happened regularly. It also provided the nation with a back-catalogue of Scottish World Cup squad hits. Some were okay, most were average, and one or two truly diabolical. In many ways, they perfectly reflected the team's performance, with some brief moments of excitement but, in the end, ultimately disappointing.

Your favourite Scotland World Cup single is similar to your favourite Doctor Who – it depends on your age and who you grew up with. My favourite was 'Easy Easy' for the 1974 World Cup in West Germany. The hair, the look and the style were iconic and the song tuned in to the glam rock sound of the time. Rock guitar, handclaps and drums with a rousing beat. It was written by Bill Martin and Phil Coulter, who had collaborated on many hit singles. From the Bay City Rollers' famous 'Shang-a-Lang', to 'Puppet on a String', to 'Back Home' which was the English anthem for the 1970 World Cup in Mexico, they were a true song-writing dream team.

However, 'Easy Easy' ultimately disappeared as quickly as our tournament hopes. Despite going through the tournament unbeaten, we lost out on goal-difference and were sent home before the knock-out stages started.

It would be fair to say 1978 saw a crop of singles that matched the national side's performance in Argentina. I didn't enjoy Andy Cameron's 'Ally's Tartan Army' in 1978. I was particularly unimpressed with the couplet 'He's our Muhammad Ali / He's Alistair MacLeod'. If you listen carefully during the middle-eight, you can almost hear the ghosts of our great poets openly weeping.

Scotland didn't shake them up in Argentina in 1978 to win the World Cup. To this day, we are laughed at for the over-optimism shown by team boss Ally MacLeod, who made the fateful mistake of daring to dream. At the time, Scotland had excellent players. Kenny Dalglish had scored the winner in the European Cup final in 1978. His Liverpool teammates, Alan Hansen and Graeme Souness, also made the squad. Joe Jordan and Martin Buchan from Manchester United were in a side full of experience along with Asa Hartford and Willie Johnston. Our talent ran so deep that we could afford to keep the likes of Archie Gemmill and Lou Macari on the bench for our opening match.

Over the course of three games, the songs for 1978 evolved from a celebratory playlist into a soundtrack for disaster. Until then, Peru was most famous for being a deep, dark place where a young Paddington bear spent his formative years. Now, they had Teófilo Cubillas, the 'Peruvian Pele'. In our ill-fated opening match against them, Peru started slowly, Scotland scored first with a Bruce Rioch goal. Peru equalised before Scotland missed a penalty. Cubillas then scored two: the first, a free-kick from outside the penalty area; the second, a twenty-five-yard rocket with the outside of his right foot into the top corner. I remember watching this game and could see that we had underestimated them. They kept passing the ball in triangles, constantly finding their man. Scotland looked tired in the Cordoba heat.

MacLeod made five changes for the next game, a 1-1 draw with Iran. Scotland were terrible and this result, with hindsight, sealed their fate. By the time we finally woke up in Argentina and faced the Dutch, it was another case of 'close, but no cigar'. Somehow, we beat the competition's eventual runners-up 3–2.

Rod Stewart's 1978 offering, 'Ole Ola', was an upbeat song and captured the optimism of a side who, on their day, were capable of strutting their stuff. Ally MacLeod had promised to bring back medals. He failed. He went into a major competition not knowing his best eleven. He may have had too many big names to choose from.

It wasn't hubris that cost Scotland a place in the latter stages. It was a terrible lack of preparation. The SFA also failed abysmally in their organisation. One of the buses transporting the team to their hotel broke down. One of the hotels had no carpets and no water in the swimming pool, despite the SFA being convinced the base, Hotel Sierras, was an Argentine Gleneagles. The training facilities and hotel were sourced by Ernie Walker but both were like something straight out of a *Carry On* . . . movie.

Of course, it's possible you can be too pumped up. By the time Scotland left for Argentina, MacLeod had the nation as high as a kite. Thousands showed up to wave their heroes off on their World Cup odyssey. Then, of course, in characteristically Scottish fashion, it all caved in and the soufflé collapsed.

There's misty-eyed romanticism toward 'We Have a Dream', Scotland's song for the 1982 World Cup. It's an okay song.

Funny, with a nice sentiment and a rousing singalong chorus, it's really not bad. It's also the most successful Scotland World Cup single of all time, reaching as high as number five in the charts.

Del Amitri's 'Don't Come Home Too Soon' for the 1998 World Cup in France was a decent effort, mixing self-deprecation with understatement. But Scotland singles need bluster. A World Cup song should be an anthemia piece of pantomime. This was a rom-com song and would've probably been a huge smash if it accompanied a film starring Hugh Grant and Julia Roberts. But it's not a football anthem.

Maybe next time, if we ever get to a World Cup again, we'll get it right – and it will be the difference we've needed to finally make it to the latter stages. I don't know which one is more likely to happen: a great song or a great campaign. To date, we haven't had either.

Exhibit 57
Bad Taste in Boots

It would be fair to assume that any player who's willing to don a pair of orange boots isn't exactly lacking in confidence. This isn't the footwear of choice for a wall flower. You are hardly likely to find their wearer standing at the bar, on their own, writing poetry, listening to The Smiths, or acting like Pat Nevin, reading the *NME* and reminiscing about John Peel's 'Festive Fifty'. No, this type of footballer is devoid of depth, wallows in the culture of the lads and enjoys being both mental and thick.

Can you imagine a side that could think and wore only black boots? One that could complete a difficult cryptic crossword but could speak at length about dirty stuff too? One that liked their nookie chat but always underpinned it by relating it to Sigmund Freud? Imagine a Scottish side schooled in intellectual ostentation with more cultural references than a name-dropper's convention, a meeting of minds for the truly elitist. The chat on the team bus could be about Isadora Duncan, Gertrude Stein and even the crazy world of Arthur Rimbaud, the French poet who famously once defecated on a table. Instead of card schools, we would have cultural Top Trumps. An anecdote about Nabokov here, a gloriously nostalgic sensory memory attributed to Marcel Proust there, followed by a wonderful crow-barring of existentialism and Arthur Schopenhauer into a conversation about cheese.

Imagine a side drowning in good taste who could riff about Woody Allen movies, Samuel Beckett and the early work of Pablo Picasso. A fight on the park could be compared to a brawl between Gore Vidal and Norman Mailer. Imagine our new team of Noam Chomskys. I would try anything if it brought success now. Imagine Scottish football exploding into some far-fetched adventure which could take us to major tournaments, out of the group stages and allow something wonderful to happen? Imagine, for once, having the luck of the bigger sides, receiving a dodgy penalty and an offside goal and reaching the semis? Think about what it would do for the country? Thinkers wearing black boots.

Sir Alex Ferguson didn't allow his Manchester United youth players to wear luminous boots. He insisted they all wore black. Once they broke into the reserves and the first team, they could do as they wanted but he didn't want his young players wearing flashy colours out of fear they would be singled out if they had a bad game. His theory was, 'If you're going to draw attention to yourself, you better be good'. By the time Cristiano Ronaldo wore his tangerine boots at Old Trafford, he'd earned the right to do so and had the skill to carry them off.

When you consider the wider issues within football – issues such as financial irregularities, corruption, ridiculously high wages, racism, homophobia, misogyny and gambling – it is perfectly understandable that pondering the player's right to wear pink football boots with a teal flash might pale into insignificance. Football, in a broader sense, might be fumbling around for its moral compass but it doesn't mean coloured boots shouldn't annoy me – and for that reason they're here on display at the museum.

If you truly want to stand out from the crowd, don't have tattoos, a hair weave or play in coloured boots. There was a time when any self-respecting footballer worth their salt would have the standard black boots made by Adidas, maybe Puma if they were a maverick. No nonsense, comfortable, the same as every other player on the park. Then something happened. Something really weird happened. Now we have crackpots not only wearing luminous boots but the eejits are wearing odd boots too. If we went down to the local park for a game of football in odd boots as kids, we'd have got such a slagging (and possibly a kicking) that we would probably never have played the game again.

I would make it a prerequisite that every team play at least four players who have come through their youth system and make them all play in black boots. Forgive my curmudgeonly attitude. It could also be bitter experience or a refusal to accept that this is a massive branding and commercial exercise which goes hand-in-hand with a sport seemingly out of financial control. The newspapers and experts love it. It's boom time. Of course, those of a certain vintage understand that the word 'boom' is sure to be followed by 'bust'. And it will. The current spending on transfers and wages isn't sustainable. Clubs will go broke and fold.

These days, there are limited edition boots with a tiger design worn by a Japanese player. There are boots that look like an outbreak of psychedelic measles and chicken pox. There are boots that are like a cross between a New Order twelve-inch single cover and the interference you get on a computer when the screen goes wobbly. Bad taste thrives in the epicentre of the footballer's mind.

Today, we can blame it on loud, outrageous players who think they are trendsetters. In the 1970s, you would need to give a player a couple of grand in a brown paper bag to get them to wear something that stood out. The first players to wear even white football boots must have received pelters. Famously, German boot brand Hummel wanted to make inroads with the UK market and wasn't afraid to pay a player to wear its gear.

The first mention of the coloured boot in Scottish football, though difficult to accurately pinpoint, probably dates to the mid-1990s. Playing for St Johnstone, Attila Sekerlioglu was having such a nightmare against Dundee in his yellow boots that he changed them.

Reporting on the November 1996 match for the *Sunday Times*, Archie MacGregor wrote: 'It was perhaps a portent that the afternoon was going to be a rather grim affair, when St Johnstone's Attila Sekerlioglu decided to dispense with his notorious yellow boots.'

In other words, if you're going to prance around like Billy Connolly in big banana boots, you better play a blinder.

HALLWAY

HAIR,
TASH
& TATS

Exhibit 58
Comb-Over

The comb-over referenced here is the one used by balding men who grow their hair long and then sweep it over the bare part; not the version you might see on *Peaky Blinders*.

The balding comb-over could soon be a thing of the past. Getting a brand new head of hair during the summer break is as easy as buying and transplanting some blooming Begonias from the local garden centre… and probably cheaper. The trouble is, you've got to go to a decent hair transplant expert. You can't get a taxi into the Barras and find some tattoo artists trying to set up a stall called 'Wonder Weave'.

In the comb-over stakes, we absolutely play second-fiddle to our neighbours down south. If Sir Bobby Charlton was playing now, he'd have hair like Elvis. It beggars belief that players would put themselves through this instead of have it shorn. Charlton had a happy face, a bit like a friendly greengrocer. Yet he was so self-conscience about his hair that it became a major distraction for him. He was a brilliant footballer, who achieved so much.

He played 606 times for Manchester United, scoring 199 goals. He played for England 106 times, scoring 49 goals. He won countless awards, including the World Cup, European Cup, World Footballer of the Year and the Ballon d'Or. Yet what do we talk about? His hair.

He's not alone. Former Chelsea man John Dempsey wore one well. It was a bit like an Oscar Wilde comb-over that had been dragged through a hedge. There was another player called Ralph Coates at Tottenham Hotspur who had one in the 1960s and, of course, who could forget 'Big' Ron Atkinson's effort?

Now for the Scottish connection. When Dick Advocaat came to Scotland to manage Rangers in 1998, many expected he'd bring his classic Mick Miller-era look – long at the sides and the back, nothing on the top – with him. However, by then he'd seen the light and was either starting or in the process of fine weaving. Our former international gaffer, Craig Brown, was fond of combing his lovely natural blond hair across a sizeable chasm to cover his football brain.

Drew Jarvie, of Airdrie, Aberdeen and St Mirren fame, was a legend in our house because he played for Scotland three times while at Airdrie. He was also from 'up the road in Annathill'. He had a classic comb-over. He's one of those guys that looked like an old man on the pitch but, when you see him now, he looks better than when he played.

Of course, we have to save the best until last. Did you really think we were going to forget about Scotland's best footballing comb-over, property of the wonderful Archie MacPherson? Big Archie, in the halcyon days of *Sportscene*, will forever be etched into our collective psyches for doing erudite pieces to camera, in gale-force conditions, whilst his hair flapped around like Shredded Wheat. What a man!

Exhibit 59
Hairdos & Hair Don'ts

In a recent tweet, the former Celtic, Manchester United and Scotland star, Brian McClair, shared a fond memory of the late Tommy Burns.

McClair, in his dry, acerbic style, explained that, when Burns came into training every day, he would hold up his hands and pretend he was a lion, a reference to McClair's lustrous, majestic mane of a mullet.

Of course, McClair wasn't alone in sporting a mullet in the 1980s. Bono had one. Charlie Nicholas had one. We all had one – or, at least, a variation of it. It's difficult to work out why football has always acted as a lightning rod for a cornucopia of bad hairdos. Maybe it's because they – footballers – are exhibitionists, willing to express themselves and think that when they wear something outlandish, they are pushing the frontiers of fashion when, on most occasions, they just look ridiculous. Bad haircuts aren't unique to Scottish football, however. Bad taste is a universal affliction and the worst culprits were usually the super-powers of Germany and Brazil.

The Germans seem to have a real penchant for bad hair. For example, Rudi Voller, one of the stars of the German team that won the 1990 World Cup, sported a soft-perm/mullet combo that made him look less like a footballer and more like a porn star plumber.

In 2002, Ronaldo – the Brazilian – showed up at the World Cup with his head shaved, except for a triangular patch at the front. His compatriot Neymar has also fallen victim to some dreadful haircuts.

Then we have football's very own 'Sideshow Bob', David Luiz, a man who is singularly the worst footballer I've ever seen. I get angry whenever I watch him play. His technique, positioning and his stupid hair – it's as though clubs keep signing him solely because he's Brazilian and therefore 'must be good'.

Let's continue on the world stage. What about Bulgaria's star of the USA World Cup in 1994, Trifon Ivanov? Despite starring in a side that entertained and excited by making it to the semi-final stages, nobody could stop looking at his shocking mullet.

And then, of course, there is Colombia's Carlos Valderrama. Despite his outrageous part-perm, part-afro do, which always drew attention, he was a player of sublime touch and elegance, who could control and pass in one fluid movement. Sure, his hair was ridiculous but it was his own and he carried it easily. His fellow countryman, René Higuita, on the other hand, had hair which almost defies description. A 'long perm' is about as good a description as any. 'El Loco', as he was known, scored forty-one goals in his career. Not a bad return for a goalkeeper. With stats like that and hair so iconic, how could he be anything other than a legend?

Closer to home, a brief glimpse at England over the years provides up the usual suspects: Barry Venison, Glen Hoddle and

Chris Waddle, for example. When he was starting out at Arsenal in the mid-2000s, meanwhile, Spanish midfield maestro Cesc Fabregas had an unforgivable barnet, a strange 1980s soft metal mullet effort.

But back to Scotland and our players' hair-raising exploits. Around the time of the 1978 World Cup in Argentina, goalkeeper Alan Rough was the poster boy for permagaddon.

Some can move on quickly when they realise the hillbilly hairdo is a mistake. Others, such as former Rangers midfielder Stuart McCall, cling to the mini mullet for dear life.

His Ibrox teammate Paul Gascoigne had several of his own moments of shocking follicular expression during his time in Scotland, whilst a young James McFadden could be found guilty of having three styles at once when he first appeared on the scene.

Bonus points for anyone who can remember Ramon Pereira who played in Scotland for two years, at Raith Rovers, Hearts and Livingston. He and his curious mullet lasted long enough to leave his mark on the follicular gallery of shame.

Of the current crop of players, Stevie May has the look of an Iron Maiden roadie. As for the top knot – a pony tail at the crown of the head – Welsh superstar Gareth Bale has to take some responsibility for popularising this look.

The fact is, it only takes one brave (or foolish) footballer to decide he wants a really stupid haircut for this new look to become a trend. To where all this might next lead, the mind truly boggles.

Exhibit 60
Mowsers

In 1872, Queens Park broke new ground for Scottish football as the first side to participate in an official competition: the FA Cup. They made it as far as the semi-finals, where they came up against Bolton Wanderers. The match ended in a goalless draw but Queens were so skint they couldn't afford to hang around for a replay and so had to withdraw.

Even then we were the poor relations to our English counterparts. Not much has changed. Even the daft, waxed, hipster 'tashes and beards have somehow managed to endure.

Before the 'grow a moustache for charity' initiative Movember launched in 2004, 'real men' would often be seen sporting humongous moustaches. Years before trendy types started to wax and sculpt their moustaches, footballers from the Victorian era sported Granpaw and Paw Broon mousers. Full, shimmering, hairy handlebars.

In the 1970s, there was a major trend in the growing of facial furniture and, suddenly, beards and lip foliage found themselves *de rigueur* again. At one point, even George Best, the most handsome and coolest footballing icon of the 1970s, decided to flirt with a 'tache. It says it all that even he found it too a difficult a look to carry off.

In many ways, the 1970s was a transitional decade. It acted as a bridge between the peace and love, anti-establishment protesting of the 1960s to the much harsher years of the 1980s, with The Specials singing 'Ghost Town', and Thatcherism, and the Falklands war. Around this time, the moustache quietly went out of fashion.

During this period, it was commonplace for a player's career to straddle three decades. Many careers would start at the end of the sixties and end at the start of the eighties. By this time, those willing to sport the lip brow stood out a mile. This made them a target for some serious verbals.

Some players could have a moustache and look alright with it. It always appeared that the team's hard man defenders were the chief proponents of the mouth brow. Likewise, there were some players who you'd look at and think, 'No, mate, that's not working for you.' Of course, when you saw how ferocious they were in the tackle, you wouldn't dare say it out loud. Some players seemed to draw a special rage and anger from their facial foliage and wore an expression so crazed that you'd be scared to look directly at them for fear of a mugging.

In the 1970s, we had über-cool curly-haired stars like West Germany's Paul Breitner. Trends are born when players go to the cinema, see Burt Reynolds and think, 'You know what, I'm having some of that action.' They see Brazilian superstar Rivelino and think, 'I'd suit one of those. Maybe I'll look more Brazilian and improve my first touch.' They watch Tom Sellick and think, 'I'm a ride with this lady-tickler.'

Scotland has produced a number of footballing 'tache masters. First up is Hamish McAlpine, the legendary Dundee

United goalkeeper. Hamish was a consistently proud-wearer of a tidy, well-trimmed moustache. In fact, let's line-up our snot-catcher eleven in a 3–5–2. Formation. We'll have Willie Miller (Aberdeen), Tony Higgins (Hibernian), and Stewart Kennedy (Aberdeen); Billy Hughes (Sunderland), Graeme Souness (Liverpool), and John Wark (Ipswich); Arthur Duncan (Hibernian) and Tony Fitzpatrick (St Mirren); and Davie Cooper (Clydebank) and Dixie Deans (Celtic).

My favourite among the crop of fuzzy-lipped superstars is Billy Hughes. He moved from his hometown of Coatbridge to Sunderland where he became something of a cult hero before later moving to Leicester. He is the brother of former Celtic player John Hughes, and was an integral part of the famous Sunderland side that won the 1973 FA Cup.

Hughes looked as if he could have taken Souness, Wark and Miller in a square-go. His moustache was as intimidating as his barrel chest. Truly, he looked like a cross between a hard man from *The Sweeney* and a Mexican drug enforcer. However, he suited the moustache and when you were up against him (or even in his own side) you weren't going to say otherwise. He played 332 times for Sunderland scoring 82 goals but only earned one cap for Scotland, which is far less than he (and his 'tache) deserved.

Exhibit 61
Tattoos

It only used to be your club's centre-half – the grizzled, no-nonsense enforcer who was not to messed with – who sported a tattoo. The combative hard man might have used his inking to declare his undying love for his mum, or demonstrating his patriotism with a Saltire, or be in possession of one those 'drunken sailor' anchor tattoos or dubious-looking thistles acquired in backstreet parlours in Hong Kong.

Football is a community and the actions of those at the top often filter down to players in lower leagues and Sunday pub teams. Now, it seems the modern player feels the need to show people just much of a footballer he is by having 'The Sleeve' – a full arm's worth of elaborate tats. It started with Beckham and has trickled all the way down to Brechin. Even the subs at Forres Mechanics now have them.

I wonder if it would be possible for a Scottish university to undertake a scientific paper to investigate my theory that the decline in our game correlates with the number of tattoos our players now have. In fact, if I were to spearhead a future think-tank after an inevitable World Cup or European Championship campaign failure, I would seriously look into it. Maybe there's something of a slow, negative, metabolic reaction to the ink being pricked into the bloodstream?

When players used to make haste for the snooker halls, bookmakers or nearest pub, the game thrived. Now, they can't wait to get home to play football games on their games consoles and, when they get fed up of that, they venture out to tattoo parlours. When players should be working on their crosses or first touch, they're adding to their body art; when they should be practicing free-kicks, they're designing their latest outrageous tattoo.

Fact is, the modern footballer is now a commodity. He's like his own PLC, with agents, accountants, lawyers, advisers and, of course, a tattooist. It is getting to the point that if a club's worldwide scouting network is alerted to a player who is the new Messi or Ronaldo with a bit of Pelé and Johan Cruyff thrown in, questions are asked. Temperament? Perfect. Can they take a pounding get up, dust themselves off, and be brave as a lion? Hundred per cent. Goals? Yes, a thousand: left-foot, right-foot, headers, free kicks, corners, penalties, the lot. Can they see a pass? Like a radar station. Can they read the game? They can work out moves like a chess player. What about physique? Statuesque, the perfect athlete, a remarkable engine. Tattoos? No. Sod that, then. We can't sign a footballer without tattoos. What's that? He's only ten? Doesn't matter. Dump the loser.

Players are social animals who love running with the pack. They look around, see someone else have something and copy. In advertising, they call it social proofing. Crowd behaviour. Seven billion of us in the world and, by and large, we're suckers for the herd. We seek validation from our peers. Social groups follow other social groups. When animals are unsure of what to do, they copy those around them. Marketing psychology tells us we are reassured by the concept of being in it together. When David Beckham started wearing glasses he didn't need to wear in an attempt to look more intelligent, loads of footballers copied him. When he started to copy US sportsmen, especially NFL and NBA players, who are adorned with tattoos, he became one of the first high-profile footballers to embrace the ink – and millions copied him.

One of the first inked-up sportsmen lavishly adorned with tattoos was a US basketball player called Allen Iverson. It caused no end of controversy and he was forever getting into trouble, mainly for refusing to cover up. Now, you'd be hard-pressed to find a basketball player – or, in our case, a footballer – without a tattoo.

Anthropologists advise that humans have tattooed their bodies since Neolithic times. The process and application may have changed but the rationale and intent hasn't. The derivation of the word comes from the Tahiti expression meaning 'to mark'. Their use varies, too. For some cultures they are a mark of a punishment, for others a status symbol. They might be a sign of dedication to a gang or faction, a map of key moments in a lifetime, or a simple declaration of love. Either way, it makes you wonder why and how they ever found their way into the world of football alongside fluorescent pink boots and other such blights on the game.

How long before we get the first player fully tattooed from head to toe? They are almost there, with legs, necks, backs and torsos all inked up. Total coverage is surely only matter of time.

Exhibit 62
Weaves

It's difficult to criticise a highly-paid man who is balding prematurely for turning his dome into a quiffed-up rockabilly look. We'd do the same . . . if we were daft enough and had the money. Imagine being able to do that? Leaving at the end of the season looking like *Kojak* and coming back in the pre-season with a quiff like Elvis?

Most footballers who have undergone a hair transplant have made no attempt to hide it. It's one of those situations where you've got to suck it up and take the flak – a small price to pay for a decent head of hair.

Football, as we know, is a world of trends and fads. A coach from ten years ago would view wearing glasses as an act of weakness, even off the park. Wearing specs would be to give the opposition a slight advantage. Wearing the same glasses now means you're studious and intelligent. If someone cool in football does something, others do it, too. Tattoo sleeves, glasses . . . and now hair weaves.

The first high-profile football-related weave I remember belonged to the English referee, Mark Clattenburg. He's subsequently had a few top-ups, but its first incarnation was a strange 'plastic-wiggy' thing. Then there was Wayne Rooney, who in fact has had two goes and, unfortunately, his hair appears to be falling out for a third time. If I were him, I'd be looking for a refund; at the very least, a coupon for a free fourth transplant. Rooney's took place at London's Harley Street Hair Clinic and cost thirty-grand. You'd expect better.

However, we have our own share up in Scotland. Guys like Anthony Stokes, when he was at Hibs and Celtic, and Leigh Griffiths, at Hibs and Celtic, and Kris Boyd, definitely not at Hibs or Celtic, and Steven Whittaker at Hibs, then Norwich, then back at Hibs – fair play to all those lads. So, too, James McFadden and Steven Fletcher.

If I was an average footballer on forty grand a week, I'd be sneakier. I'd spend a few grand getting one but I'd cheat at it, getting it done in instalments. Maybe make nosy people ask the question and suggest that, instead, I was just 'wearing it short and cropped'. Some have tried to do it more subtly, like Ryan Giggs. His fellow former Manchester United man Dimitar Berbatov started out subtly but has gone for a lush look now and has a cracker of a weave.

It's not only the players and the odd referee. Managers are at it, too. Antonio Conte and Jürgen Klopp, for example. Conte's is quite spectacular. Klopp's is a subtler weave. Still, it seems to be the way now for football: get a weave and success will surely follow.

In the future, football will be devoid of baldy players and that's sad. Imagine no baldy people playing football? Then one brave young new striker, who is thinning will say, 'No, I'm not having it, I'm going full Yul Bryner.' He'll ask his barber for a skinhead and women will find him attractive because he looks so unusual. 'Who's the hot, bald, guy?' they'll ask. Then, a few others will have one and before you know it, footballers will have their hair cut into the wood. Because where one man goes, others will surely follow.

COURTYARD

FOOD
&
DRINK

Exhibit 63
Argentina 1978

Scots have never been famous for having wonderful, sparkling teeth. That goes some way towards explaining why we have produced a number of brilliant toothless footballers, emanating from an era when the centre-half and centre-forward were allowed at least one assault, usually resulting in the loss of teeth, before the referee intervened.

Who can forget Joe Jordan's toothless, mischievous smile? And what about arguably our best ever player? Kenny Dalglish had lovely teeth and a beaming smile when he scored, then he didn't have teeth, and then he did. Ronnie Simpson, Celtic's 'Lisbon Lion' goalkeeper, had a hat with sets of his teammates' false teeth. It was his job to keep them safe and return them to their owners at full time before the victorious team photos were taken.

The tradition of a sweet tooth and the innocent bribery of sweeties off the van, as a treat if you behaved, started with the glorious blue and white striped sweets known as Argentina

Chews. They were like confectionery crack cocaine. Once you started, you were hooked.

The late kick-offs on school nights and being allowed to stay up to watch the World Cup seemed so much easier in 1978. The 'E' numbers in those chews must have made it possible. There's no way we would've passed a mandatory urine sample, never mind a mandatory blood test, for sugar levels. It's strange, though. When you gorged on the sweets, you had clarity of thought. They also made you think Argentina's military was doing everything in its power to make sure the hosts won the trophy – and they didn't disappoint.

On one memorable night, while chewing through the mandatory bag of ten chews, Argentina needed to beat Peru by at least four goals. As it turned out, they slotted six past an erratic (Argentinean-born) Peruvian goalkeeper.

It could be argued that the most lucrative business sectors after Scotland's performance at the 1978 World Cup in Argentina would have been in psychology, dentistry or litter collecting. Another notable craze from this time was 'doing an Argentina', which amounted to ripping anything made of paper into confetti.

The sweets helped ease my pain when I realised my hero, Johan Cruyff, would not be playing at the '78 World Cup either. Many of his countrymen subsequently blamed him for the Dutch not winning the tournament. To them, it was unforgivable that one of the greatest-ever footballers had refused to represent his county in their hour of need. The fact the Dutch made it to the final only exacerbated their frustrations.

Some years later, in 2008, Cruyff spoke candidly about his reasons for not attending the tournament in an interview with Catalunya Radio. 'You should know that I had problems at the end of my career as a player here,' said the Dutch icon. 'Someone put a rifle at my head and tied me up and tied up my wife in front of the children at our flat in Barcelona. The children were going to school accompanied by the police. The police slept in our house for three or four months. I was going to matches with a bodyguard. All these things change your point of view. There are moments in life in which there are other values. We wanted to stop this and be a little more sensible. It was the moment to leave football and I couldn't play in the World Cup after this.' The Dutch Master had clearly grown sick of the game – and, in those circumstances, who could blame him?

On a more tangential point, there was a story published not that long ago about an Argentinean dinosaur's last meal. Researchers had discovered the remains of its gut, which had somehow been preserved for 180 million years. When I got wind of this, I prayed his final munch included Argentina Chews. At best, I thought it would be a brilliant way to relaunch one of my favourite football-related pieces of confectionery. One of those nostalgic sweets takes you slap-bang back to the time of Archie Gemmill, Joe Jordan, Kenny Dalglish and Mario Kempes, but sadly no Johan Cruyff. If only we worked in advertising, we could tie Argentina Chews to a rampaging dinosaur which roamed across Patagonia.

Exhibit 64
Bovril

They say you never forget your first. I certainly won't. The time I popped my Bovril cherry, I was standing in a busy queue and, as I received it, a drunken fan bumped into me and the Bovril scolded my thigh. A bad situation was compounded when I drank it and burned the roof of my mouth.

In its own way, Bovril is an icon of Scottish football. Quite an achievement for something that is, basically, 'beef tea'. Its very existence begets some serious questions.

And yet, in the context of football (particularly Scottish football) it works. Once this cheap beef substitute was equivalented with the 'Beautiful Game', advertising execs could have been forgiven for thinking all of their Christmases had come at once.

Picture the scene. Mad Men's Don Draper is in a tense boardroom with the directors of Bovril. 'This is impossible. It's a beef cappuccino?' Don looks into the distance, calling to mind his troubled childhood. He thinks of his coldest moment. He's watching a football game – the sport with a rugby ball and men in helmets bumping into each other, not that other game Americans call soccer. He's ten years old. It's a cold winter's afternoon and he's freezing. He dreams of a hot cup of soup. Right then, Don has his Eureka! moment. 'Football, kid watching from sidelines, frozen pitch. He's cold. Can't feel his toes. Then, he has a hot Bovril and is warm, refreshed, enriched. Make it healthy. Tie it to a top team or player. That'll make the fans fall for it. This elixir of life, this winter warmer. Only a winter's tale . . .'

From the start, Bovril was sharp and clear with its narrative, using a former employee, HS Benson, who had left to become an advertising agent in 1889. The product was about strength: Bovril is good for you. By shifting the focus to the players, the message would pack more punch. It was genius. 'Drink Bovril, stay fit'. The fans wanted it immediately. Like all of the best advertising campaigns, Bovril's captured the imagination of the public.

But what about the product itself? Bovril was actually invented by a Canadian-based Scot, John Lawson Johnston. Born in 1839 in the Midlothian village of Roslin, Johnston was interested in food science and preservation. His uncle was a butcher, so he joined him as an apprentice, eventually taking over the shop in the Canongate. He made a success of it, too, establishing the business as one of the best of its kind in Edinburgh. It was here he began boiling up off-cuts and beef trimmings to create a beef stock which soon became immensely popular. This enabled him to open a second shop and a small factory. In 1871, he emigrated to Canada and set up the business there.

Johnston subsequently won a contract to provide canned beef to the French army. The French were rattled after the starvation and eventual surrender of Paris during the Franco-Prussian War in 1871 and decided to stock their fortresses with tinned beef which, they figured, would last until the next big battle. The French army, under Napoleon III's instruction, placed an order for one million cans of beef from Johnston. Due to the problems linked to the transportation and storage of so many cattle, however, Johnston suggested a cheaper, more versatile alternative: a good quality beef extract. This product, originally called Johnston's Fluid Beef, was just the ticket and met Napoleon's order.

From this, Johnston was able to scale up product development for a meat extract paste. He returned to London and focused on launching Bovril in the UK in 1886. The actual name is derived from the word '*bovinus*', of or relating to cows, and '*vril*' from the Vril-ya who were a superior race in an 1871 science fiction novel by Sir Edward Bulwer-Lytton, called *The Coming Race*. The 'vril,' is the electromagnetic substance from which they derive their powers. Scary stuff.

With Johnston's entrepreneurial skill and marketing savvy, Bovril started to take off, helped in no small part by Christmas Day in 1902, when Captain Scott and Ernest Shackleton had a comforting Bovril after a chilling four-hour trek across the South Pole – a shooty-in compared to a trip to a Baltic Brechin for a Scottish Cup tie. Advertising of the product, especially in the 19th and early 20th century focused on the healing and beneficial qualities found in Bovril with slogans such as 'For health and strength!'

So, now we know how the product was marketed and who created it, we must ask how it, along with the pie became a staple at most football grounds and firmly established as part of the 'big game' experience? There's photographic evidence online of what used to be known as 'The Bovril Stand' at Ibrox, from around 1910. The North Stand was nicknamed this due to the large Bovril advertisement on it. Interestingly, one of the more bizarre product placements for Bovril, around 1900, saw Pope Leo XIII drinking the product with the tagline 'Two Infallible Powers: The Pope and Bovril'.

Apart from John Lawson Johnston's instinct for marketing the hot beef flavoured drink and connecting it to strength, power and health and the most popular past time of the day, football, why did it connect? It may be more practical and go back to the French fortresses, and the long life nature of the product which would allow it to stay fresh in a rickety old stand warehouse or catering hut. It might also be that it's a natural match with the pie, far better than coffee or tea. The concept of a hot Bovril at the game could be also be a nostalgia trip, a yearning, something abundant in the football fan's psyche, to hold on to something dear, to reminisce and along with the pie, it's now a great double act at the game. Plus, if you're eating a pie and drinking Bovril, its one less person on their iPhone.

Bovril has pervaded our game so completely that there are even fanzines named after it. In the modern era, full of catering and hospitality suites, there's something unique about Bovril's place in Scottish football. So, when anyone asks a question like what links food and drink, Scottish football, the Pope and the Franco-Prussian war? Now you can tell them.

Exhibit 65
Buckfast

The Basques, who live in the region spanning the western Pyrenees at the border of France and Spain on the Atlantic coast, have the highest concentration of blood type O, the lowest frequency of group B and the highest in the world of Rh negative. It is said this blood type makes the Basque a ferocious warrior, one fiercely proud of his language, his tradition and his customs. In Scotland, there is a similarly high concentration of a substance pumping through the veins, mostly among the young male natives of a mysterious region known as 'the Buckfast Triangle'.

It could be argued that, after a half bottle of Buckfast, the vast majority of males across west central Scotland display a similar collective grouping. It's less genetic and more social. When they drink the tonic, their inner bampot is awakened, making them believe they can take on the world (or at least rival fans) and start a full-scale street riot.

Buckfast is a fortified wine and, while it may only be fifteen per cent alcohol, one bottle contains more caffeine than eight cans of coke. Its moreish, syrupy, Vimto-meets-Benylin taste is down to the colossal amount of sugar it contains and its array of mouth-watering chemicals.

The ease with which the half bottle slips into a raincoat pocket made it the perfect aperitif for our father, his father and their forefathers. The drink itself is seasonal. It's most prominent during the football season, marching season, festival season, Christmas season and any the reason-for-a-season season.

The 'Buckfast Triangle' is really a scabrous term concocted by the intelligentsia, the turncoats and avocado toast-loving sophisticates. It provides them with an excuse to turn their noses up at the proletariat.

Much like the humble pie, the Buckfast bottle has always been versatile, acting, for example, as an effective weapon. It was also far safer to pee into than a can. Before body searches and the banning of alcohol from the game, most people had been rattled full on the napper by its dark green bottle. If you think a bottle of Buckfast tastes bad, you should taste it after it has journeyed through the customer's urinary system and cracked you on the cranium.

Buckfast and its inextricable link with anti-social behaviour has slightly moved away from football to become something of a broader societal issue. It's one of the few upsides to come from all-seated stadia, an alcohol ban, better policing and stewarding. It still has its moments, though, causing the odd scuffle, minor riot and arrest for affray around those parts of the stadium where they sell questionable burgers which are unlikely to have ever been part of a cow. Curiously, any time politicians and campaigners highlight Buckfast as the scourge of their community, there's a huge spike in sales.

Buckfast is another example of social proofing. If you're heading to Aberdeen to see your team play on the Wednesday night between Christmas and New Year, usually through a blizzard, and you're worried the bus is going to slide off the road, that's when the Buckie is passed around. It's almost an affront to turn down a swig and, for some reason, its magical qualities make a three-hour journey take ninety minutes.

Equally, if it's a big game against your oldest rivals and it's been shoved to high noon to accommodate TV, then early drinking laws require that the half bottle is imbibed.

You have never truly been fully associated with any level of Scottish football and been a bona fide fan unless you've been acquainted with Buckfast. You've either tasted it, enjoyed its special fortification, faced a ned who was under the influence of it, or been hit in the head by a bottle (preferably an empty one). It deservedly earns a place in the alternative football museum. It is part of the fabric of the game. Football and the caffeine-fortified, anti-social-behaviour-inducing 'medicinal' wine are as one.

Exhibit 66
The Postmodern Fish Supper

The fish supper is central to the story of Scottish football's most successful era. When the players were rewarded with a post-match fish supper, they won European titles and the national side reached major competitions. It was, in its own way, a bonus for an away win. Now, the snack has reached post-modern status.

Throughout his playing career, the well-travelled forward Owen Coyle claimed it was superstition that forced him to eat a fish supper, washed down with a bottle of Irn Bru, every Friday. Somehow, he stayed as thin as a rake. Nobody ran off a chippy better (although the fact he was tee-total no doubt helped).

During Alex Ferguson's reign when Aberdeen won away games, legend has it the team bus would stop at a chippy on the way home for a well-deserved treat. When Inverness came down to the central belt and won, they pulled over for a fish supper in Auchterarder.

In the same way, every Scottish football fan going on their first away trip should always ensure they include the obligatory fish supper as part of the experience. It's a rite of passage, something you will always remember. There's something about growing up in west central Scotland which makes a fish supper a rare treat. In times gone by, it typically happened when someone in your house had a win, or some good fortune. Maybe they received a bonus or even a promotion, which allowed their fortunes to change. The first thing your parents did to celebrate was treat you to a fish supper.

We are always reminded of the fine margins in the game. We know players and managers will do anything to gain a psychological edge. Perhaps the opportunity to go off the rails and, as a team, tuck in to something that isn't too good for you makes all the difference.

The fish supper has become such an intrinsic part of the game that it has even become a trademark punchline to a poor football joke.

Sir Alex Ferguson presumably knew a fine fish supper when he tried one, having sampled his fair share on the way home after a big win. So, when he was asked his opinion of Eric Cantona, Ferguson would marvel at the Frenchman's dedication, his vision and his precision with a pass. Cantona, Sir Alex enthused, was like an orchestra conductor – but he was a terrible tackler, so bad Sir Alex famously said he 'couldn't tackle a fish supper'.

For all the chatter of deep fried Mars Bars in the context of Scottish cultural phenomena, I don't think I've ever actually seen one or know anyone who has tasted one. The fish supper? A different story altogether, and that's why it takes its plaice [sic] in the alternative museum.

It is through trips to away grounds like Tynecastle that you learn about The Gorgie Fish Bar. When traipsing to Maryhill to see a Partick Thistle game, you hear from other supporters that Jaconellis is a decent chippy. At Aberdeen games, it's the Bluebird. Coming from Airdrie or Albion Rovers games back to Glasgow, there's a wonderful chippie in Coatbridge called Porta Vila.

There are many who mock the Scottish diet. However, the fish supper wasn't our doing. The first reference to it was, in fact, in *Oliver Twist*, in 1838, when Charles Dickens wrote of a 'fried fish warehouse'. Some famous chip shops in England also claim they are the first in the UK. The first to sell fish and chips in Scotland was in Dundee, started by a Belgian immigrant.

When Graeme Souness arrived home in Scotland after a spell in Italy, he was scathing about Scottish players and their diet. He clearly didn't know it was Italian immigrants, from Barga in the north of the country, who helped popularise the fish and chip trade by opening shops across Scotland. Barga, a hilltop town described as the most Scottish town in Italy, holds the *Sagra del Pessce and Patate*, the festival of fish and chips, for three weeks, between July and August. So, if anything, we're being incredibly continental and cultured when we feast ourselves at the chippy.

Take that, Souness.

Exhibit 67
A Pie

To some people, the Humble Pie was a 1960s supergroup formed by Steve Marriot and Peter Frampton. For Scottish football, however, the advent of the humble pie was a pivotal moment and it soon became an integral part of the essence of our game. Some dodgy mutton held together by fat, encased in a damp, stodgy cardboard box-styled pastry. Delicious. The pie has always been a part of the match-day experience and, unlike the players on the pitch, you could depend on it never letting you down.

Again, it's a matter of versatility. The pie is a wonderfully multi-purpose food item. Part-sustenance, part-stomach-lining, it's mainly used to soak up alcohol.

As an artefact, the pie itself obviously long pre-dates Scottish football. It has something of an uncertain and strange origin. It has been around since ancient Egyptian times. Any Scottish football fan who has braved a pie stall at the back of a rickety stand will confirm that there still appear to be some around from those ancient days.

To earn a decent crust, some clubs have started catering to the more discerning, middle-class broadsheet reader who knows how to construct a sentence. 'Chicken, ham and leek, please, when you have a second, dear chap,' comes the posh cry from the back of the queue, accompanied by sarcastic whoops and imaginary handbags held to the chin. Suddenly, pies have become *cordon bleu*, with the braised steak and gravy particularly delicious. Scottish football has even started to cater for vegetarians, with the introduction of the macaroni pie.

The power of the pie is such that one particular Scottish club, based in Ayrshire, was even in danger of becoming more famous for its food than its football team.

Scottish football has remained quite straightforward when it comes to its pie position. However, all it will take is for a trendy bearded chef from Cliftonhill or Ochilview to visit and taste a pie in grounds like Brighton, which include Chicken Balti or steak with blue cheese, and they could take off here. It's imperative we don't allow complacency to set in. In a world where restaurants serve meals on slates from a roof and craft beer is served in a jam jar, we could be perilously close to losing the 'traditional' football pie.

I'm reminded of excellent advice given to the Beach Boys when they started writing more abstract stuff and less in the way of songs about girls and surfing. Their dad, Murry Wilson, and cousin, Mike Love, allegedly told them, 'Don't f**k with the formula.' That's how I feel about the pie. Don't mess with its simplicity. It's amazing what can happen when you keep things simple.

Exhibit 68
The Wagon Wheel (Macaroon Bar, Chewing Gum)

In the days before gourmet meals, canapés for posh fans and pizzas and burgers for the plebs, the Wagon Wheel, macaroon bar and ten-pence chewing gum were the height of football snack sophistication.

To some, mostly rich kids and future club fat-cats, the Wagon Wheel was considered the perfect dessert to follow a pie and Bovril. Like a classic centre-half, it's big, no-nonsense and reliable.

Why did the Wagon Wheel become a ubiquitous confectionery at most Scottish football grounds? Perhaps it was some official at the SFA who demanded that it be stocked everywhere. Maybe it was one of those products you could store for years and it always tasted the same: rank rotten. Whatever the reason, the Wagon Wheel has become a staple at most football grounds in Scotland. The marshmallow centre, with jam and chocolate covered crunchy biscuit provided the perfect sugar rush and hangover cure. Take it with a cup of tea and you had something close to heaven. The biscuit itself was launched some sixty years ago when Spaghetti Westerns were all the rage at the cinema. You couldn't put the TV on without *The High Chaparral, The Virginian* or *Bonanza* blasting out. The biscuit's branding was firmly aimed at the concept of cowboys on a wagon.

The Wagon Wheel is famously part of an ongoing conversation piece about its size. Are they getting smaller? Maybe my belly and eyes have become bigger? According to the makers, the biscuit has stayed the same size but our first experience was usually when we were kids, so our hands have grown. That sounds logical enough but I'm naturally cynical and remain unconvinced.

The mention of macaroon bars and ten-pence chewing gum will probably sound idiotic to anyone under the age of forty. To those over forty, it will evoke nostalgia and emotions that catapult us back in time. There were guys who walked around the grounds, back when they were mainly terracing, selling such treats. You rarely saw anyone ever buy them. There was also a guy who sold freshly-made cheese rolls but, every time he placed his wares on the terracing to complete a sale, the bottom of his cardboard box would get drenched in urine. Ah, memories!

These salesmen were extraordinary characters, particularly as they advertised their wares in the most unintelligible ways. In Scotland, and Glasgow and Lanarkshire in particular, the more obscure and unclear the shout, the more they sold. The *Evening Times* newspaper street vendors set the benchmark for this, incidentally. It's not clear what they were shouting but it couldn't possibly have been 'Evening Times'.

The Wagon Wheel, macaroon bar and ten-pence chewing gum have endured through it all. They have witnessed the despair of last-minute goals to relegate your team. They have looked on in stoic indifference as grounds erupted in euphoria at promotion. They were there for the first game under floodlights and for the first live TV broadcast. They were sitting in the kiosk when births were announced and when rock stars had the photo op for a snack to show they, too, were men of the people. The Wagon Wheel, macaroon bar and ten-pence chewing gum were there when the original terracing was ripped up for seats. They have survived fan insurrection, takeovers and more.

These three pieces of confectionery are football's equivalent of the cockroach capable of surviving a nuclear apocalypse. They can withstand everything, even Kasabian, The Killers and Oasis banging out via the PA system at half-time. Maybe it's because the game – at the top at least – is drowning in sponsorship, big money and questionable deals but these sweet-tooth stalwarts are a reminder that, while Scottish football might have its problems, there's a decency and simplicity at its heart – a reminder that football is for the many, not the few.

Either way, for their role in providing some sort of sweet sustenance to generations of football fans, Wagon Wheels, macaroon bars and ten-pence chewing gum, thanks for being there and, please, take a bow . . .

WING

VICE

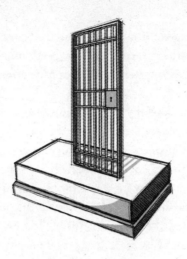

Exhibit 69
FIFA

In 2015, as his colleagues were falling like flies, arrests were being made in Zurich's Baur au Lac Hotel, and the organisation he was overseeing was being plunged into unruliness, then FIFA president, Sepp Blatter, awarded himself a $3million per year wage rise and a performance bonus of $12million. Such was the corruption pervading football's governing, HBO and Netflix could have moved to make a Mafioso melodrama about the organisation.

FIFA was formed in 1904, to arrange, organise and manage games between a handful of European countries. England initially refused the invite, feeling it was too established and a tad above it all. However, by the 1970s when FIFA was firmly acknowledged as the international governing body, it was an Englishman, a decent old bean, Sir Stanley Rous, who sat in the president's chair; he didn't take a salary. The controversies only really began at FIFA when João Havelange, a successful Brazilian businessman, ousted Rous and became president. Suddenly, the game changed. Rous had refused a continual barrage of approaches from interested parties, preferring to keep FIFA a closed shop. Havelange chose the opposite approach. And it was showtime.

Havelange successfully pitched himself as a man of the people, delivering on his promise to bring the game to the masses. He brought in big business and sponsorship and was also fond of the odd dictator or two. The fact he spread the wealth to many of the world's far flung corners won him unstinting support in those territories, enabling him to remain in post from 1974 to 1998. He devised the blueprint for his successors to follow. He also remained as FIFA honorary president until 2003, when he was finally exposed for bribery and corruption, at the tender age of ninety-six.

However, nothing Havelange ever did comes close to the egregious behaviour of Sepp Blatter. The Swiss presented himself as FIFA's Santa Claus, distributing gifts and bungs in return for votes. He looked after the football associations. They, in turn, showed their appreciation by keeping 'Don Blatter' in power year after year after year.

For most of my generation, you learned the acronyms of FIFA and UEFA way before UNICEF or OPEC. There was always a sense of fair play and equality, community and hierarchy. You had your own national football association; for us, the SFA. Then there was the European body, UEFA. Then, of course, you had the august world association, FIFA: The Fédération Internationale de Football Association. It organised international matches and the World Cup. There was always a familiarity and a sense of symmetry, a definite feeling of deference and respect for the governing bodies. FIFA's history and its foundations, its core values, were originally based around fairness and egality. What it stands for now? Anybody's guess.

When you look under the bonnet, you come to realise

FIFA was far from the upstanding organisation it should have been. With Blatter at the helm, it was routinely portrayed as a caricature of an organisation, a *Carry On* comedy caper. This suited it. While the world laughed at the perceived bungling idiocy, it was handling everything beneath the counter in a far more sinister fashion. I always looked upon Sepp Blatter as a cheerful, avuncular character, straight out of central casting for a European farce based on a randy politician. At first, I was disheartened by the allegations made against him but then it all began to make sense. UEFA and FIFA made the beaks and blazers of the SFA look like saints, a confused allotment society deciding who gains membership and who doesn't.

What happened to the organisation with integrity and decency? Well, everything changed when money started flooding into the game. Then, loads of questionable situations came up. When they did, Sepp Blatter was always able to bat allegations away by keeping smaller associations on side and securing their vote. The person who blew the whole scandal open was a man called Chuck Blazer, the former general secretary of the Confederation of North, Central America and Caribbean Association Football (Concacaf). He fully co-operated with US prosecutors – after getting caught. Claims of widespread corruption forced the US Department of Justice to indict fourteen current and former associates of FIFA. I may not be a top lawyer but I know if the US Department of Justice is out to get me, I'm done for. The FBI stated charges of 'rampant, systemic and deep-rooted' corruption. For the first time in its history, FIFA wasn't in the news for football. Further charges and arrests took place at the previously mentioned luxurious Zurich hotel. In December 2015, another sixteen officials were charged. Two FIFA vice-presidents were arrested, as was the former Brazilian football federation chief Ricardo Teixeira, the former son-in-law of João Havelange. He was accused of being involved in criminal schemes involving more than £132million in bribes and kickbacks in connection with Word Cup rights.

It turned out the guys running FIFA really were like the mob, only more brazen, with charges of fraud, racketeering and money laundering levelled against them. There was a feeling of schadenfreude at their hypocrisy and how the high and mighty had fallen from grace.

As recently as October 2017, the PSG owner, Nasser al-Khelaifi, who also owns beIN Sports, was questioned over paying bribes for TV rights for the 2026 and 2030 World Cups to former FIFA general secretary Jérôme Valcke. According to Swiss prosecutors, he offered up his Sardinian villa to Valcke for his personal use.

In August 2018, FIFA claimed to have rid itself of corruption. But if you dug below the headlines you discovered it had simply re-written its ethics code and removed mentions of the word 'corruption'. More alarmingly, it had also added a defamation clause, preventing employees from becoming whistle-blowers.

Later the same month, in New York, the president of South America's governing body, Juan Ángel Napout of Paraguay, was sentenced to nine years in jail for bribery, racketeering and wire fraud charges based around schemes to accept millions in exchange from companies seeking marketing rights to tournaments. The former vice-president of FIFA was forced to forfeit $3.7million and pay a fine of $1million. Around the same time, the former boss of the Brazilian Football Confederation, José Maria Marin, eighty-six, was jailed for four months, fined $1.2million and made to forfeit $3.34million.

Scotland's only link to FIFA these days seems to be our continual plummet down the official rankings. Our women, though, with Shelley Kerr at the helm, reached a record high of nineteenth in the FIFA rankings in 2018 and qualified for the 2019 World Cup – a feat beyond their male counterparts for more than twenty years. For the record, I would have no qualms about installing Shelly Kerr as the men's national team boss and putting Hibernian chief executive Leeann Dempster in charge of Scottish football. Equally, FIFA would no doubt be in much better hands had it been run with more women in charge. Let's hope that the organisation sees grater gender balance in the coming years – it seems to be the only way to ensure it gets back to doing what it's supposed to be doing: running the game for the good of the game and for all those that play it around the world.

Exhibit 70
Barry's Bar Bill

It became known as 'Boozegate'. After flying home from a 3-0 World Cup qualifying deconstruction at the hands of the Dutch in Amsterdam, Barry Ferguson, Allan McGregor and four others (Scott Brown, Gary Teale, Alan Hutton and Steven Whittaker), their spirits clearly under siege, manfully trudged to the bar in Cameron House, Loch Lomond, to let off some steam. The session started at 4:00 a.m. The four other lightweights managed to sneak off before the appearance of Scotland's team management. Getting hammered is allowed but not while on duty with a game against Iceland a few days away.

Ferguson and McGregor were, according to reports, still going strong until lunchtime, much to the amazement of hotel guests and their manager, George Burley, who bumped into them as he was heading for lunch. When Burley confronted them, Ferguson and McGregor, according to the same 'onlookers', were struggling to stand, let alone construct a sentence.

You could sense the scale and significance of the 'Scotland

Boozegate' scandal by the speed an indignantly puritanical Scottish press corps elevated it to the status of 'gate'. Those clean-living, media men and women, as pure as the driven snow, those sober, abstemious, upstanding pillars of the community, were outraged, shocked and dismayed.

Despite this, a few days later, both players were included in the eighteen-man squad for the crucial Iceland game. The incident could have been dismissed with some persuasion, a heartfelt apology, some humility and some clever 'just-the-lads-letting-off-steam' spin. However, as punishment, both were left on the bench for the Iceland game and, as TV cameras panned and press photographers snapped, the two decided to give the 'V' sign.

The players let down their country and club by getting rat-arsed and getting caught, yet the media mainly focused on Burley. He was portrayed as something of a cross between Corporal Jones from *Dad's Army* and an out-of-his-depth trainee Modern Studies teacher, unable to handle rowdy pupils. Maybe the players sensed he was a soft touch or too gullible. Burley often gave the impression he could be easily manipulated and the players and the press soon sensed the opportunity for blood.

From his first press conference as Scotland coach – despite starting his tenure well by endearing himself to the Tartan Army with his clear passion and pride at being named Scotland coach – Burley was undermined by then SFA chief executive, Gordon Smith who chose to go off-topic and appeared to speak for him.

What should've been Burley's introduction turned into a chance for Smith to take a few pops at those who were criticising the selection process. Burley was left looking bewildered and weak, which quickly became part of the narrative of his time in the job. In hindsight, Burley may have wished he said something along the lines of: 'Thanks, Gordon, but I've got this.' For Scottish football and 'the game', first impressions are lasting impressions. If someone is seen as a hot-head, or is argumentative, or considered a troublemaker, or is quiet and introverted, their card is forever marked. Scottish football always judges and doesn't forget. Burley, it was decided, was weak. And that was that.

The bar bill for the eight-hour bender hit an impressive £1,500. It's often overlooked but they generously bought drinks for many hotel visitors, too. Probably the same 'onlookers' and 'insiders' who grassed on them later to the papers. McGregor paid £800 quid for his tab, leaving staff a £50 tip. Vodka Red Bulls were £7.50 each.

As well as costing Ferguson the Rangers captaincy and a lifetime ban from the national side when he was just five appearances away from qualifying for Scotland's 'Hall of Fame', he left Rangers under a cloud, heading to struggling Birmingham where he appeared to take the Cumulonimbus with him.

Despite the way they had insulted Burley, the Scottish media were more perturbed at the way Ferguson and McGregor had let Walter Smith and Rangers down. Their disrespect toward their teammates and the fans was overshadowed with the media focused instead on Smith's anger at their behaviour.

A few months later, Barry gave his side of events, venting his fury at the way the incident was handled by the SFA and how the 'Boozegate' shame brought down the curtain on his international career. He spoke in the language of tabloid cliché.

The shenanigans of both Ferguson and McGregor were actually a throwback to the classic debauchery we had loved in the past. It was only a story because Scottish football had become so boring.

Burley won three of his fourteen games in charge. Kris Boyd, the form striker, was on the bench when Chris Iwelemu wrote himself into Scottish football history by missing an open goal in the 0–0 game against Norway. Boyd announced afterwards that he would never again play for Scotland while Burley remained in charge.

The gaffer may have felt the fates were conspiring against him. In truth, poor results, 'Boozegate', Barry Ferguson, Allan McGregor, Kris Boyd and Chris Iwelemu conspired against him. It was a toxic combination.

He lasted less than two years in post.

Exhibit 71
Betting & Gambling

Everywhere competitive sport is played, gambling will surely follow. Horseracing, boxing, golf and, especially, football.

Gambling has hit football particularly hard of late, with high-profile cases of players betting on matches making headlines and the flood of advertising from betting companies around the game – be it TV, radio or podcast advertising to flashing billboards at stadiums and almost ubiquitous shirt sponsorship – reaching tsunami levels. None of this is new, though. Gambling on football, from card schools on bus journeys to players doing fixed-odds coupons, has been around for a long, long time.

Football was a working-class sport and working-class people lived for the bet and the chance of winning. The less you had, the more likely you were to take a chance, even though you knew it was a huge risk.

I was thirteen when I first clubbed together with pals to put a coupon on. Along with the outside chance of winning, I loved the idea of the form, the stats, the numbers, the odds and the fractions. Factor in the unpredictability of sport and you soon realised it was almost impossible to predict an outcome. Didn't stop us trying, though.

There were the usual warnings and apocryphal horror stories from our concerned parents, fearful that the first bet would be a big win. There was a certain validity to those concerns. They knew how seductive it would become if one of us won big and how easily we could become addicted. Fact was, we always lost, so common sense prevailed and it was kept at a level where it was never more than a bit of fun.

I think our parents knew what we were up to but it wasn't as if we were spending the whole day in the bookies. Someone, usually the tallest guy in the street or the one blessed with a smattering of facial hair, would go into the shop and put the bet on, a fixed-odds football coupon, and that was us well-behaved for the rest of the day, listening to the radio and checking the TV for scores to see how our lines had done.

Betting was so firmly ingrained in our culture, it never felt unusual to us. You would have the pools coupon, too; you could pick teams out and win the pools by putting a wee X beside each team and a man would come and collect the coupon and the money. The problem now is that gambling is everywhere and, most crucially, it's online 24/7. If you have a gambling problem, it must be horrendous. Adverts for bookies are on constantly, games on radio are sponsored with odds read out throughout live commentaries. Scottish football's three major competitions are sponsored by betting companies. Footballers, generally from the same working-class background, were making it into first teams who didn't see the harm in placing bets. Now, they are banned, charged and dumped out of football if they're caught.

On most occasions, players aren't betting on their own side to lose. Though, even if they do, influencing the result isn't as easy it sounds. Let's look at the case of one Joey Barton. The

FA banned him for eighteen months in 2017 after an in-depth investigation into his betting activities, during which he revealed the thirty bets made on his own team which showed he ended up losing more than £3,000. There's a blanket ban on players betting on any matches, yet not much is done to scratch beneath the surface.

In 2013, when playing for Rangers, Ian Black was given a ten-game ban and fined £7,500 after admitting to a breach of SFA regulations on football betting. The player had been accused of gambling on 160 matches over a seven-year period, including betting in games involving clubs he was registered for. Those who are caught generally remind us the problem is rife.

Following the independence referendum in Scotland in 2014, the Smith Commission into further devolution gave the Scottish Government greater power to intervene on fixed-odds terminals in bookmakers. These roulette machines were described as the 'crack cocaine of gambling'. Ironically, it wasn't until an unnamed footballer's addiction to the games became so bad that he pleaded with bookmakers to ban him from their shops that the campaign against the machines gathered momentum.

In some ways, the irony will not be lost on many of the foreign players, particularly the South Americans, who must wonder why there isn't widespread corruption and match-fixing. We haven't been blighted like most countries with a terrible match-fixing problem. Maybe that's because we're too inept to do it properly.

Exhibit 72
The Bung

Scottish football doesn't have the money swirling around it to encourage or harvest a bung culture but we shouldn't become complacent – the world game has a serious root-and-branch problem. The former England international manager, Sam Allardyce, was forced to leave his post after just sixty-seven days when he became embroiled in a *Daily Telegraph* exposé in 2016. It was alleged that he offered advice on how to get round the FA's rules on transferring players and, more specifically, third-party ownership.

Allardyce was guilty of saying something while drunk and showing off in an undercover investigation. Of that, there's little doubt. What there is a lack of, however, is any concrete proof that he took illegal payments. He inadvertently became the lightning rod for a discussion on bribery and corruption and, in truth, with better guidance, he might have been able to weather the storm. Instead, he took the honourable way out and quit.

Investigations into football's underbelly have become more

about the dark arts, with journalists behaving more like Cold War spies than story-gatherers. Could there be a John Le Carré *Tinker Tailor Soldier Spy*-type book waiting to be written in the underbelly of Scottish football?

So, what is a bung? In layman's terms, it's an undisclosed, financial incentive to make a move happen. Why are they wrong? Simple: they are illegal and against the rules. They give an opponent an unfair advantage. The biggest problem with bungs and back-handers is they take money out of the game. Money which could be used for grassroots coaching is frittered away, paying off middle men in a deceit.

The range of the problem in Scottish football extends to the enticement of a fish supper with a pickled onion but it's something which can't be taken for granted.

Scottish football, these days, is run hand to mouth. Here's a simple, cold, hard fact which highlights the difference between the SPL and the EFL. Bournemouth finished ninth in the Premiership in 2018 and earned £123.8m. They tabled an offer of £120,000 per week to Jermaine Defoe who was relegated with Sunderland, a club who earned £99.9m for finishing last. Each team gets £84.4m at the start of the season, and then prize money depending on where they finish. Celtic won the SPL and earned £2.8m.

With regards to bungs, Scottish football has the untamed exuberance of the most predictable sitcom ever created. The bleakness and astounding banality make it funny. The fact it doesn't have any impropriety makes it sweet and charming in its own way. It's the stress of the mundane life, like *The Fall and Rise of Reginald Perrin*, or Ronnie Corbett in *Sorry*. Yet the satire, sarcasm, and acerbic social criticism come through in a tidal wave of dullness and a constant flow of tedium. I love it.

Exhibit 73
The Copenhagen Five

Infamy, infamy, they've all got it: infamy.

It's hardly hold-the-front-page stuff: five Scottish footballers getting wellied and starting a minor kerfuffle in an empty club in Denmark. The 'Copenhagen Five' sound like a 1960s Beatles-era beat combo or a Danish far-left militant group; less West Germany's Baader-Meinhof, more Bladdered, Mine's a Hoff.

In 1975, while representing their nation in Denmark, Billy Bremner, Joe Harper, Pat McCluskey, Arthur Graham and Willie Young wrote their names into Scottish football folklore by becoming involved in a fracas.

Bremner and Harper, playing for the full men's side, and the others for Scotland Under-23s, allegedly ended up getting drunk and starting a rammy in a club called Bonapartes.

Scotland may have been unpredictable when it came to qualifying for major competitions but, when it came to getting pissed and starting a riot in an empty disco and no end of disorder, we blew everyone else out of the water. Sometimes

Scotland players didn't need coaches or trainers; they needed a tour manager and a road crew.

The evening started out well for Willie Ormond's charges. His side had beaten Denmark in a European Championship qualifier, with Harper scoring in a 1–0 win. The previous evening, the Under-23s won by the same score. Young was in the Under-23s and was itching to hit the town but was advised to wait until the following evening and see if anyone from the senior side was going out.

The libations started in the hotel where the troops launched into the bevvy. None of your vodka and Red Bull here; they were straight on the Bacardi. The nightclub was quiet but staff took exception to the players, especially Graham. It went a bit Pete Tong after Young started fiddling with the lights at the bar and the police were called.

But none of this is what nudged them towards a ban. Rather, it was their behaviour when they returned to the Marina Hotel. Instead of being repentant and full of remorse, Bremner went 'Double Keith', all Richards and Moon, encouraging the others to help him trash a hotel room. Unfortunately, the room they wrecked belonged to Jock McDonald, an SFA committee man.

Much has been written about the ferocity of Bremner's temper. Few sentences exist about the fiery redhead, which don't refer to his usefulness with his fists. So, you can imagine how hard Jock McDonald must have been when he launched a right-hook that rocked Bremner into next week.

The then SFA secretary Willie Allan, was outraged at their behaviour and, wherever possible, delighted in calling the five 'the hooligan element'. He wanted them thrown out. The even bigger blazers, the international committee, convened a meeting where it was agreed the five wouldn't represent their nation again. Harper and Graham always maintained their innocence and had their bans rescinded a year later.

Young was treated badly. He, along with McCluskey, never played for Scotland again. Harper gained one more cap, against Iran in 1978, and Graham moved to Leeds, going on to win a further eleven caps. For Bremner, too, life really did mean life – it proved to be his last performance for Scotland. The draconian five-year ban infiltrated and eroded his illustrious career at Leeds United and, after repeated warnings about his conduct, he left the Elland Road club to sign for Hull City the following year.

Exhibit 74
UEFA

My brother-in-law shared many internal French flights from Paris to Nice with Michel Platini. Whenever Platini came on, the rest of the plane stood up to applaud him. Apparently, it happened everywhere he visited in France, in every room he entered. He was held in such high esteem, being on the same aircraft as him was tantamount to an audience with the Pope. In fact, Platini's nickname in France was *Le Roi* (the King). Malcolm, my brother-in-law, didn't stand and applaud. Maybe he could already sense the hubris that was coming Platini's way.

Platini was one of the finest French footballers ever to grace the game and is in exquisite company: Just Fontaine, Didier Deschamps, Thierry Henry, Laurent Blanc, Eric Cantona and Zinedine Zidane. Yet Platini is arguably the best of all. He is most fondly remembered for his time at Juventus and for steering France to victory on home soil in the 1984 European Championships.

Platini played seventy-two times for his country, scoring forty-one goals. He was an awe-inspiring midfielder, a magnificent playmaker and skilled dribbler, who was devastating from free kicks. He was the type of player who rarely lost the ball. Turns out, he was almost as adept at holding on to power at UEFA. Almost.

Like most football fans, I'm a hypocrite. When Platini started to show interest in and a flare for football administration in 1998, helping organise the French World Cup that year, I was delighted. He appeared to be the type of guy with integrity, who would wipe football clean of bribery, corruption and scandal. When he became the UEFA president in January 2007, I was genuinely delighted. To see where he is now, both hurts and dismays.

The SFA backed Platini in 2015, when it was announced he was running for toppermost of the soccermost: head of FIFA. The then SFA gaffer, Stewart Regan, couldn't get behind him quick enough. 'He will ensure every country, irrespective of size will have a voice,' boomed Regan. Within a few months, the former French captain and three-time 'European Footballer of the Year' was kicked out of the sport when the FIFA ethics committee threw the book at him over an odd £1.3million payment he allegedly received. They accused him and Sepp Blatter of abusive execution of office. He was banned for eight years and fined £54,000 (this was later reduced, on appeal, to six years and then four).

The key issue was the 2m Swiss franc (£1.35m then) payment made by Blatter to Platini. When asked to show any written proof of a contract, they couldn't provide one. More tellingly, they couldn't give a definitive explanation of why the sum was paid, conveniently, a few weeks before a presidential election when Blatter was facing a fight from Mohamed bin Hammam (the Qatari was eventually banned from football over bribery claims). The closest to an explanation was that it was payment for services by Platini for acting as a special adviser to Blatter between 1998 and 2002. According to Platini, despite FIFA earning £78m over the same four years couldn't afford to pay him. Blatter and

Platini believed their verbal contract was legal under Swiss law. The other breaches were mismanagement, conflict of interest, false accounting and non-cooperation with the ethics committee. What's French for everyone smelt a rat but couldn't find it?

In June of 2019, Platini was arrested and questioned over the awarding of the 2022 World Cup to Qatar

The most galling part of the scandal is that their outrageous behaviour has been pushed sideways and moved on in the hope it will be forgotten. What about Willie Johnston who took a hay fever pill, unaware that it contained a banned substance, and had both his reputation and character smeared by FIFA? He makes an innocent mistake and is hung out to dry. They, meanwhile, make countless misjudged or deliberate decisions, get caught and toddle off into the shadows. It's a scandal as big as the crimes they allegedly committed.

A new UEFA president, Slovenian Aleksander Čeferin, was elected in September 2016. He's certainly been busy and thus far appears a perfect fit.

In 2017, Platini appealed against his four-year ban in the top Swiss court. The court upheld the original decision, stating they didn't think the punishment appeared manifestly excessive. The charge of being found guilty of ethical breaches remained.

In May 2018, Platini admitted the 1998 World Cup draw was fixed. He told *France Bleu Sport*: 'Group A was France, Group F or Group L was Brazil, so if they both finished first, they couldn't meet until the final. That's all – it was simple.' In other words, the organising committee used 'a little trickery' to do everything in their power to make 'the dream final'.

'We did not spend six years organising the World Cup to not do some little shenanigans,' said a seemingly unrepentant Platini. 'Do you think other World Cup hosts did not?'

Mon Dieu!

WING

MODERN LIFE
IS RUBBISH

Exhibit 75
Aberdeen's Seagulls

Forget a place in the alternative football museum – Aberdeen's seagulls are worthy of their own docudrama.

This would be no cosy, Sunday night David Attenborough show either. More of a hard-hitting, controversial, groundbreaking show. Think vultures let loose on *Big Brother*, *Love Island* or *Strictly Come Dancing*.

The major problem with seagulls is that they are intelligent. They demonstrate ruthless efficiency, organisation and tactical awareness (quite unlike the Aberdeen defence). They are egomaniacs, fearless and love a big crowd. They circle around huge groups because they know wherever people congregate there's usually discarded food. They are far more intelligent than those trying to eradicate them – not to mention those running Scottish football.

These seagulls can sniff an ice-cream twelve miles away. They are the sneakiest, cockiest and cheekiest birds in Europe. You should see the way they squawk and fly above those in the stands.

They are like the Luftwaffe. They are more ferocious and fearless than any football casual.

It has become so bad that club execs have had to bring in a company capable of removing nests. They have even employed a hawk to scare off the crazed gulls.

The seagulls at Pittodrie are like highly-trained assassins, desperate to wage war on any fan eating a fish supper. You'll know how ruthless they are if you've ever tried to nick a chip off an Aberdeen fan.

I suggest we utilise them more effectively. If Hannibal was able to mobilise elephants across the Alps in 218BC in one of the most celebrated military achievements in the history of warfare, surely Aberdeen can train their seagulls in a similar way? If Police Scotland want a crackdown on rioting crowds, then look no further than recruiting the Aberdeen gulls. They would be cheap, too. Throw a fish supper into a crowd and watch them go to work.

Exhibit 76
After-Dinner Speakers

Scottish football has committed many heinous crimes over the years. Perhaps the worst, however, was the decision to give retired footballers a platform to tell cobbled together anecdotes and try and pass them off as a stand-up routine – one pulled straight out of a 1970s sitcom. There's always the joke about getting pulled off at half-time when they'd 'only received an orange' at other clubs. There's only so long you pretend that line's funny before your false smile turns to stone.

Footballers grow used to money and adulation during their careers and, when it stops, some find it difficult to readjust. Some, in fact many (far too many), get over this by choosing a path which enables them to regale us with their tales. Luckily for them, there are thousands of willing (gullible) football fans who will pay to hear ex-players' tales of dressing room bust-ups, fall-outs with their manager and the like. What happens in the dressing room stays in the dressing room – until you've no longer got a dressing room to change in, seemingly.

Go to enough of these dinners and you will start to notice a formula. Speak for twenty minutes, index cards as prompts, and don't go off topic and ramble. Open strongly and grab your audience with as much casual misogyny and sexism as you can fit into sixty seconds.

Our collective hearts do bleed for these former stars. It must have been both painful and difficult to spend the first part of your life running around playing outside, having fun, keeping fit and drinking and shagging for Scotland, all the while being handsomely rewarded at payday. This afforded them a lavish lifestyle – the extravagance, the modern detached and, of course, the expensive, impractical car to go with it. Who can blame them for trying to scratch out a sizeable wedge as an after-dinner speaker when that first career is all over?

However, let's imagine you're an established after-dinner speaker who isn't a famous ex-footballer. You've carved a niche in the market but are usurped by a tsunami of ex-pros who want a piece of your pie. Now you're squeezed out, most likely from guys you paid to watch for years.

Originally, there were a few eloquent speakers on the circuit and they were in high demand because they had the right style and tone. They covered a broad range of backgrounds from across society; not only sports broadcasters and journalists, but stand-up comedians, solicitors, prison governors and church ministers. People who knew how to hold a crowd and were far more nuanced in the tone of their set.

The best after-dinner events have an MC or comedian who compères and introduces a mix of ex-footballers – preferably one who retired within the last ten years, a senior pro from an earlier era, a football journalist or commentator of some esteem and, if you can, a referee. They are always a winning addition, providing fresh insight and stories you'll not have heard before.

I have nothing against anyone willing to go out and earn,

especially if people are prepared to pay £1,500 for your company. If it was me, I'd be doing three a night.

If you are a footballer coming to the end of your career and fancy yourself as a bit of a comedian, don't watch ex-pros do after-dinner speaking to get tips. Instead, watch politicians. They are now seriously cashing in on their profile. Barack Obama and David Cameron earn six-figure sums for such turns.

The most entertaining public speakers are usually those who tell us something we don't already know about someone they know well. It's also a good idea to make fun of one of your clangers: that infamous red card, the sitter you missed, that fourth (or was it fifth?) court appearance. The crowd might not support your team, so if you can show a more human side, it will endear you to them. Fake it if you have to.

In summation, politicians and footballers are quite sociable, so the idea of moving into public speaking is probably quite an astute, if somewhat obvious, career move. But, if you really must go ahead with it, please stay clear of the 'old favourites'. They were never really that much in favour to begin with.

Exhibit 77
Virtual Football

It's hard to believe, but gaming has become so popular that it's reached the point where TV channels are broadcasting console football. After lengthy discussions, BT Sport started broadcasting competitive e-sports, in February 2017. Now, fans can watch other fans playing their PlayStations. What a time to be alive…

It's surreal to think, no matter how authentic, that the beautiful game has been bounced down to an artificial dystopia. As EA Sports gleefully squeal in their marketing blurb: 'Infused with all the passion and excitement of the real-life sport, get closer to the action than ever before. Now is the chance to live out all your footballing dreams'. Or, alternatively, go outside, kick a ball and see if you can control and pass it with your weaker foot. Kick it off a wall, or a lock-up door, left foot and right foot. We are already crap at football in this country and we're not going to get any better if all our kids just play a virtual version.

It's unquestionably a commercial boon for companies such as EA Sports and BT Sport to get on board a popular, rapidly growing industry but football is about the team. It's about interaction and socialising. I was annoyed when Subbuteo and Super Striker appeared. Football was downgraded to a board game. If you were football mad, these games were ideal for a rainy day when you were told to stay indoors, and the FIFA and Pro Evolution Soccer games became a natural extension of this. But I never grasped the concept of playing football this way. And if I couldn't get my head around that, the concept of people paying to watch someone playing a computer game on TV is even more bizarre. Am I missing something? Have we become so far removed from reality and real competitive football that this passes the litmus test? How does the commentary work? 'And Davie there, sitting on his chair moving his thumbs like mad. Oh, he's injured his thumb… A blister injury? No… Look at the concentration on the man's face there as he twiddles away.'

Being efficient on games like FIFA19 doesn't mean you can play. I'm no stranger to the games console. When my pal upgraded to a PlayStation, I got his Sega Mega Drive and was a mean player of Tiger Woods Golf, more than capable of breaking seventy round TPC Sawgrass. In reality, I'd probably take seventy to do the front nine.

These consoles are one of the reasons why we'll probably never reach a World Cup again. I'd ban them, or at least ration their use. There's a severe shortage of kids kicking a ball in the streets and a dwindling hunger or desire to get out of poverty and play football for the team they support. Why work hard when you can vicariously enjoy the experience through a virtual simulation?

The counter argument is always the same – they have the same computer games in Spain and Germany and the homes of all the football superpowers, yet they still manage to qualify for World Cups, European Championships and win the Champions League. I don't know what's going on. It could simply be down to the Scottish psyche. We always look for fault and someone to blame. One of the excuses offered up for Scotland plummeting down the FIFA rankings was blamed on the teachers strike of March 1985. The EIS – the Educational Institute of Scotland, the main Scottish teaching union – encouraged its members to work-to-rule. In other words, teachers were doing exactly what they were contracted to do and no more. This meant any voluntary work, like taking the school football team, stopped. There was a full generational cycle, as teachers started to enjoy having their weekends to themselves and, once the strikes and work-to-rule had finished, continued to do so. It also meant many promising Scottish football stars of the future were watching *Swap Shop* and *Saturday Superstore* instead of going out to learn their craft on a Saturday morning. There's no doubt the teacher strikes and the deployment of work-to-rule had a disastrous effect on Scottish sport but the excuse has been well and truly clobbered to death.

The games console is definitely one of my new favourite excuses and I'm sticking with it for now. It's far easier to find something like this to blame than actually have a complete rethink as to why we are so crap at our beautiful and, at least for now, national game. Sometimes, we see the odd crop of great young Scottish players coming through, and so we continue to live in hope. But how many more are squandering their talent sitting in doors playing a virtual game instead of the real thing?

Exhibit 78
Crying Fan

You must have spotted them – those irritating fans in floods of tears, who appear utterly devastated as their team fall to defeat. They really like to go for it. We're aren't talking mild upset. Rather, full-on heartbreak, despair and tears. They go for dramatic effect because they know, on a darkening winter afternoon, as the floodlights come close to switching off, the TV cameras will have one last pan across the stands and they'll stand out. Oh, the angst and pain. They have this peculiar need to show the world how much they are hurting at the result. If I was one of the stewards, I'd be in the stands manhandling crying idiots out of the ground and switching the lights off.

Have you no sense of perspective? You're not a kid. You're an adult at a game (emphasis on the word '*game*') of football. Suck it up. Celebrate victory, shrug off defeat. Show some decorum.

From the first game to be broadcast live on Sky Sports in 1992, when Nottingham Forest faced Liverpool, these charlatans have been around and I'm having none of it. I always felt and hoped, like Morris Dancing and rolling cheese down a hill, it would stay in England. But fans in Scotland have started doing it, too.

Suddenly despondent Hamilton Accies and Hearts fans are crying for the benefit of the television cameras. But if you look closely, you can tell they are faking it. Crying at the football? Get a grip.

Exhibit 79
European Coefficient

Along with baseball's World Series, the Champions League is one of the biggest misnomers in sport. The competition has become a staid and predictable money-maker for the big clubs, which ultimately rewards mediocrity.

At present, the four top teams from the four top leagues in Spain, Germany, England and Italy qualify straight into the Champions League. From these sixteen, only four are actually champions. Then we have champions from smaller countries, like Scotland for example, who have to endure treacherous qualifiers just to make it to the group stages.

These games are tough for a number of reasons – sides from the middle of nowhere, on dodgy pitches, who, even though part-time, have been playing since February. Our teams tend to have been on the beach the week before the opening rounds. If they were breathalysed, they'd probably fail. They have to play in July before their season starts, when they haven't remotely found their match fitness or touch.

The UEFA coefficient system was brought in to seed and rank teams in international and club football. I preferred it when football administration was easier to understand. The principle is quite basic. It's set up to protect big teams and keep smaller teams in check. This being a UEFA idea – and since they're basically civil servants – they've taken something relatively straightforward and made it barely comprehensible. You only have to watch the way they drag out the Champions League draw to understand how skilled they are at making the simplest things complex and protracted. All they have to do is pull names out of a hat but, somehow, they've found a way to make sure the whole process lasts an eternity.

The coefficient is based on team performances in the Champions League and Europa League for the previous five years. The clubs receive two points for a win, one point for a draw and nothing for a defeat. It's like Brexit: overcomplicated, difficult and ultimately useless.

However, there's no point in criticising something if you don't have a solution, so here's my proposal.

If I carried any sway at UEFA, I'd encourage a special anniversary competition where only champions from each country are invited. The names go in into an Alpine shepherd's hat if it's over in Switzerland. And here's the really genius part: the champions of every country in UEFA play each other home and away. There's no seedings and coefficients don't come into play. Two legs, then on to the next round. We could fund it with the stacks of cash UEFA has squirreled away.

Of course, I'm well aware that UEFA, television companies and sponsors would crumble and die like the Wicked Witch of the West in the *Wizard of Oz* if they so much as read this simple proposal.

Exhibit 80
Gardening Leave

Gardening leave, as a concept, has existed for years in the corporate world. The term has now permeated Scottish football and has become a familiar news splash across the back – and sometimes front – pages.

In big business, it's used to describe an employee's suspension from work on full pay during a notice period. It's done for a number of reasons, usually to prevent their former employees from seeing anything confidential and using this information in their new job. Its move into football shows how far big money and the importance of fiscal responsibility has infiltrated the game. Now, top football coaches at major clubs are treated like the CEOs of huge corporations, those whose work is based on building up relationships and trust and, if they leave, are paid not take those secrets with them. The best at their job will be part of an elite group and coveted by other companies or, in this case, football clubs.

To some, mainly employment lawyers, it's the way forward – the correct, fitting and appropriate way to treat employees who trigger a notice period. To the fans, it's a sure-fire sign that their club is run by idiots who are wasting much-needed cash which should be reinvested in the team. Scottish football fans, in the main, simply view gardening leave as rewarding a losing manager for not doing his job well enough.

Scotland's most high-profile recipient of gardening leave is Ally McCoist. He was in the fortunate position, or was for a while, of having a more manicured lawn than the pitch at his beloved Ibrox. When McCoist's three-and-a-half-year spell as manager of Rangers ended in 2014, it was announced he was being put on gardening leave. McCoist claimed he was triggering his twelve-month notice period. His wage was reported to be around £750,000 a year, so why wouldn't he?

Despite what seemed like the perfect job, the club's record goal-scorer had a dismal run of luck behind the scenes. Imagine you're McCoist and finally, after years of waiting, you get offered your dream gig. You've served your apprenticeship and know you're ready to take it on. Then the club is sold. Craig Whyte comes in, then Charles Green, then the Easdales and Mike Ashley. Hardly strong and stable is it? While his former colleagues perhaps hoped Ally's beautifully tended garden would be blighted by an outbreak of Japanese Knotweed, he remained resolute and content to receive money to stay away.

Where did it go wrong for the club's legendary marksman? McCoist had taken over at one of the most traumatic times in the club's history on and off the park. He had to deal with liquidation, an administration and having to start from the bottom tier. What irked many Rangers fans was McCoist had a significantly superior wage budget than everyone else in the Championship and should've been miles ahead. The crowds were up as fans followed the side through the leagues, but they had grown tired and many disgruntled fans vented their anger toward the manager. When McCoist finally left his post, he was nine points behind Hearts in the Championship, with Rangers having played one more game. The defeat in the 2014 Petrofac Training Cup semi-final at the hands of part-timers Alloa Athletic. McCoist stated his concerns were due to a number of lifelong club staff being made redundant. So the cheeky chap decided to take £750K from the club, in protest. McCoist showed some generosity by reneging on the last three months of his salary and reached a settlement with Rangers in 2015, allowing him to take up a lucrative post with BT Sport as a football pundit.

Another high-profile gardening leave story centres around the months leading up to Brendan Rodgers's May 2016 appointment by Celtic. Having been removed from his post as head coach of Liverpool in October the previous year, Rodgers was on gardening leave and supposedly on track to earn £10 million over two years for weeding and mowing his lawn – £100,000 a week not to work.

In truth, it shows how amazing these guys are that they manage to get paid for doing nothing. Celtic stumped up £3m to bring Rodgers to Parkhead and reportedly paid him a salary of £2.3m a year for the privilege.

Gardening leave makes it sound like a sweet, relaxing euphemism. 'Oh, he's on *gardening leave*?' So nice and colourful and harmless. But at senior management level, it can be brutal and unforgiving. In effect, it's about removing influence from talented, once-powerful people. Despite being lucrative, it must be so frustrating. Mind you, for £100,000 a week, you could probably learn to live with it.

Exhibit 81
Officious Stewards

It's safe to say football stewards have a thirst for power. They would no doubt have loved a career as a police officer or traffic warden. They might even have considered something more popular, like becoming a referee, but probably decided the job wasn't quite power-crazed enough, so chose to become an officious match steward instead.

Something happens to these people when they put on their high-viz yellow coats. Psychologists might suggest it's about power and control, but there seems to be something deeper at play, something that sees them change from mild-mannered civil servants to Joe Pesci's free-swearing, mildly-psychotic character from *Goodfellas*.

It seems they become enraged by the most trivial matters and take every opportunity to act with hostility, hiding behind the improbable defence of 'Don't blame us, we're carrying out orders.'

What most sensible people object to is being asked at

European games to throw away small, innocent bottles of water, which are deemed to be potentially dangerous missiles. While this is happening, you can look across at the away section and watch as fire, flares and smoke bombs are set off every few minutes. The humble bottle of water is treated like a ballistic missile, while opposition fans are allowed to get ready for war with no questions asked.

Most stewards are answerable to a security officer who is usually a cynical, Sudoku-loving, *Daily Mail* reader who'd rather be playing bowls, on the golf course, or down the pub. They are brought in to preserve order. And yet most of the disorder I've experienced at football hasn't come from opposition fans but from the stewards themselves. Of course, it's important to recognise that they have a job to do, often in difficult circumstances, but there is always a sense that, as one of my friends observed perfectly, 'It's like the teacher's pet has been left in charge to put the names of those talking on the blackboard and they can't help but lap up the power.'

Exhibit 82
Snoods (and gloves)

Even the most rational and calm of football fans can be sent into an apoplectic rage by the sight of a player in a snood and gloves.

The fans want to see their star players sweat and toil for the cause; not look all snug and comfortable with a cosy snood and woolly gloves on. They should be driving forward, fighting for three points, sweating profusely. How can any footballer honestly turn around and say they left everything out on the park, when they're wearing a snood and gloves? If your heartrate isn't keeping the blood pumping around your body and your extremities warm, then you're not trying hard enough. If you notice the cold, you're not concentrating enough on the game.

At the height of their popularity, it was always over-indulged, entitled types, like Mario Balotelli, Marouane Chamakh, Carlos Tevez and Samir Nasri, who wore snoods. Sir Alex Ferguson and Roy Keane, hard men hued from the same rock formation, weren't fans. Sir Alex Ferguson's view of these neck-warmers was characteristically unequivocal. 'They're for powder puffs,' said the Manchester United legend. I wonder if anyone from the diversity department took him to task over the statement? Either way, he banned players from wearing them. Roy Keane agreed. 'They've all gone soft. I don't know how they do it and focus on the game. It's weird. That's the way the game has gone.'

Not everyone is as ruthless. Having spent years playing and managing in Milan, and therefore becoming a fashion guru, the then Chelsea manager Carlo Ancelotti said: 'Ban them? No, it's cold.' The then Bolton boss, Owen Coyle – born in Paisley, raised in the Gorbals – echoed Ancelotti's sentiment. 'I don't have a problem with players wearing them, if that's what they want to do.' The former Arsenal manager, Arsene Wenger, claimed snoods served an important purpose. He claimed they helped prevent injury to his players. How, I wonder? Neck injury from the weight of the brass neck from wearing one?

Snoods really are more of a reflection of the modern footballer's bad taste and shocking fashion sense, than anything else. In the end, they were banned back in March 2011 when FIFA (weirdly) cited health and safety fears – perhaps fearing that a centre-half might grab an opposing (or just 'posing') striker by the snood and accidentally choke him.

Sometimes the football authorities can move quickly and decisively to ban items they deem to be in violation of the rules, yet they seem to have greater difficulties dealing with racists, homophobes, misogynists, violent ultras and other toxic problems. The dastardly snood was so dodgy it was kicked into touch by none other than former FIFA president Sepp Blatter. The International FA Board unanimously agreed, at their meeting in Celtic Manor in Wales, that the snood was dangerous.

Here's Blatter's truly bizarre statement on the ruling.

'A snood is not part of the equipment and it can be dangerous, even like hanging somebody. The decision was unanimous. There was not even a discussion because this is not part of the uniform.

I was a player in both winter and summer weather and I never wore a snood. We must pay attention to the laws of the game. It was rejected unanimously not only by the board today but, before, by all the technical staff and by the secretary-generals. It's a non-issue.'

The ban was greeted with great approval in Scotland, where shivering in sub-zero temperatures is considered a sign of weakness. Hypothermia? Run it off, mate. Up here, the idea of wearing a snood to keep you warm meant you were beaten before you got on the park, a white flag of surrender before the game had even kicked-off.

Snoods are thankfully resigned to history . . . but we still have gloves. Gloves? What is the point of footballers wearing gloves? Unless you're a goalkeeper, they have no place in football. Yes, players and coaches say, 'But it's cold out there.' So get warm! You're paid to run about like an idiot. You don't need gloves. What about the idiots wearing short-sleeved jerseys and gloves? What sort of logic is applied when you say, 'It's cold, I need gloves,' then decide to wear a short-sleeved shirt? Gloves haven't yet suffered the ignominy of a FIFA ban as, evidently, the game's power-brokers can't muster up a legitimate reason to ban them. Seemingly, 'but he looks like a tool' isn't a good enough reason.

Exhibit 83
Hand Over Mouth

Neymar and Lionel Messi were the first footballers I saw putting their hands up to their mouths to cover what they were saying.

One lazy Sunday, I happened to catch a re-run of a Barcelona game. I knew it was a re-run because Neymar was playing and, by that stage, the world and its dog knew the Brazilian superstar had become the most expensive footballer in history, having completed his record move to Paris Saint-Germain for 222million Euros (roughly £198 million).

Messi and Neymar continued their confab with covered mouths as they chatted about something they didn't want us to know. To most, this would be a trivial and insignificant action – they were sharing a secret. To me they were being bad mannered. They were excluding me. I wasn't party to their every thought or deed. They'd decided their conversation was private. How dare they? Look at the two of them. The two best players in the world covering their mouths so we're not able to make out what they're saying? Why? *Why?*

Messi and Neymar are two modern kings of the social networking era. Theirs is a world of vast wealth and enormity; they are CEOs of a strange and wonderful business, which involves kicking a ball around a grassy field on one hand and, on the other, posting about their off-field lives on Twitter and Instagram (or having their minions do it for them). Both hold significant sway, with hundreds of millions of impressionable fans. Companies love them because they are ripe for advertising. But they have also learned that nothing they say to one another while playing goes unnoticed.

When the Brazilian national side was preparing for the 2014 World Cup, film crews were pitchside for every game and training session. The most watched Brazilian TV show on a Sunday night, *Fantástico*, then went to the bizarre, if quite cunning, length of bringing in deaf teenagers to help them lip-read anything coaches and players were saying. This led to the Brazilian team, including Neymar, starting to cover their mouths with their hands to stop the TV crews from catching any of their discussions on strategies, tactics or the stunning model in the main stand. The players were unhappy with the intrusion. However, in Neymar's case, when speaking to opponents, his eyes don't lie. He isn't discussing the weather or the death of the novel when he's seething and clearly saying something offensive.

I understand Messi and Neymar must get annoyed with cameras on them constantly but I also think their frustration is more about losing control of the narrative. They love the cameras when they are selling themselves (or being paid to sell something else).

We know that in professional sport, especially football, it can come down to fine margins in terms of gaining an advantage but this takes the Wagon Wheel. These days, even managers and coaches are at it, too. This is understandable, I suppose, at the very highest level, but it gets ridiculous when you see it happen at games between Cowdenbeath and Stenhousemuir. When you get six-year-old kids doing it in class, you know the hand over the mouth has reached critical mass. Is what they have to say really that important and secretive?

Exhibit 84
Headphones

We have become accustomed to seeing moody football stars leave the team coach and entering the stadium wearing outrageously large headphones. So big, it's often a wonder how they make it through the tiny framed doors of some of the more antiquated Scottish grounds.

Footballers like to copy people they think are cool. So when they see NFL players copying Dr. Dre, P Diddy and Snoop Dog they follow suit because they're cool, professional sportsmen, too, and they have an eye for what's hip and fashionable. The trouble is, NBA and NFL superstars look cool when they take to a fashion trend, especially if it's more street and urban. When you see Stevie MacTavish from Clyde – who is Scottish, white and works in the bank during the week – mimic the act, you realise good taste can quickly turn bad as it churns down the sporting cludgie to Scottish football.

We might ask why the footballer is actually wearing headphones? They say it blocks out peripheral sound and helps them to focus on the ninety minutes ahead. But we know the real reason – they're trying to look cool while also ignoring autograph or selfie hunters. I say they should, instead, be actively trying to soak up those peripheral sounds, the noise of the crowds, the fans, the excitement and atmosphere of the game. I say tune into the abuse and hatred from away fans as you approach the ground. It'll add fuel to your fire.

I often watch and think, 'Yeah, but what are you really listening to?' NFL players would be listening to something cool. The players here are probably listening to Coldplay or Ed Sheeran but pretending it's some sick beats.

I'm prepared to accept it could be my age. I remember when headphones were practical. I preferred them when they were small and discreet, like the headphones from my Sony Walkman (Google it, kids). Then there was the quantum leap when we evolved from the sonic cool of the thin Walkman black leads to white iPod headphones.

That's the downside of the headphone as a fashion statement and a status symbol. The more ludicrously expensive, the better. The big daft headphones used by footballers are acceptable in this rarefied world of tacky taste and too much money. My gripe is with the trickle-down effect, when it reaches guys who walk onto the 201 bus like gangster rappers. Mate, you're a bored civil servant who thinks he's a footballer; but everyone knows footballers haven't used public transport since the 1970s.

I'm not alone in being cynical about headphones, by the way. Some coaches – usually of an older vintage – don't like them either. The team should be chatting and communicating before a game. It's about the team, not individuals living in their own world. To some, they are another reason why we are shite at football and are presented as an example of the steady erosion of team spirit.

Football is a slave to fashion. If one NFL legend or 50 Cent or Kendrick Lamar decided to wear 1970s headphones, with their rubber inners and plastic-leather surroundings with a long, black, curly phone cable lead, every footballer across the globe would soon be jumping off the team bus like a roller disco king from 1978. If Ronaldo, Neymar and Messi wore trendy, big daft headphones, then Gavin McGinty of Forfar and Shane Ross of Peterhead would follow suit. They're footballers too, right? But just because you copy how these guys look, it doesn't mean you'll ever play like them. I'd love Ronaldo, Neymar and Messi to jump off the team bus playing 1980s cassette mixes on their Walkmans and watch them fly off the shelf.

(If you're reading, Sony, I'll accept a one per cent royalty for the idea).

Exhibit 85
The Academy Player

In principle, the humble football academy is a praiseworthy idea. It's also an expensive system which provides an education for kids, along with some football, to prepare them for the inevitable heartache and rejection life will throw at them. In reality, the numbers don't stack up. When you consider how few of these players succeed and manage to establish themselves in the first team, they would be better served saving millions, canning the whole project and farming out their players to a call centre.

Forgive my cynicism. At least the academy system is far better and less cruel than the apprentice set-up. You hear older professionals explain that kids need a challenge, that they need toughened up. Well no, they don't. Society has moved on. When these older guys were coming through, they were pushed to see if they were strong enough to handle the pressure through a mix of public-school bullying and national service. In the olden days (cue the Hovis ad music) young players were taught the football basics, like cleaning boots, sweeping up stadiums and painting stands. They were subjugated, bullied and given horrible tasks designed to break them. What about the football? When did they get to hone their football skills? Rarely, is the answer. Yet, perversely, who would've thought that the cleaning, sweeping and painting would see the national side regularly get to major competitions and club sides excel in European competition? That kind of treatment of young people is no longer acceptable – but there must be a link between the popularity of the football education system (the academy) and the fact we have become worse. The academy generation, thus far, has yet to see the Scotland men's team qualify for a World Cup.

The academy system is to football what the living room carpet is to my golf game. I'm unbelievable at putting on the lovely, level surface of the living room pile; there are no swales or undulations. I'm also relaxed and my technique is near-perfect. On a real course, as a professional, playing for glory and money, it's so much more difficult. In the same way, most academy players will have had ten years of drilling and repetition in a highly sophisticated yet sheltered environment, but do they have the confidence to take their skills into an actual game? It takes a special kind of player to do it under pressure, with a huge centre-half trying to break their leg on a surface like a poorly-ploughed field, in December, in a cup tie, at Peterhead. They may be able to control, pass and dribble like Puskás, Pele, Cruyff or Messi in the pressure-free environment of the academy but, with a crowd, filthy conditions and hardened opponents, the real game can often offer a brutal reality-check.

Perhaps if we could bring in the previously discussed elements of the draconian apprentice system, made to toughen the spirit and harden the resolve. If we brought back the reserve league set-up, there would be a more natural progression. As it currently stands, with the under-21 league, clubs are allowed to field a certain number of players over twenty-one; in fact, this is where

Marvin Compper played almost exclusively across his time with Celtic. But with the under-21 team changed to a reserve side, game-time with hardened, experienced professionals, returning from injury or trying to regain form and fighting their way back into the first team would be more beneficial. The teams they would face would also accelerate the learning process. Players struggling to break through are currently farmed out to get more games under their belts. If we could mix it up a bit with the old set-up and new system and have the future starlets roughed up a bit (not too much; we don't want police and social services called) then surely that is the ideal way forward?

Despite the wonderful and detailed analysis of their careers, serial trophy-winning managers such as Brian Clough, Bill Shankly and Bob Paisley found enormous success by keeping it simple with a basic set-up. A hard man to win the ball; a clever man in the middle to shoot or pass the ball into the correct space; a quick and tricky winger to cross it; and loads of fit bodies willing to run to get on the end of the cross to score. By the time the modern academy player had thought about 'tiki-taka' and controlling the ball, the opposition hard man had mugged him and passed it to his winger who then sent in a searing cross that was met at the back post.

Scottish football has changed beyond recognition. It now copies those across the globe with successful youth policies, such as Schalke, Santos, Sporting Lisbon, Ajax and Barcelona. These days, most top clubs have a well-oiled youth policy. Clubs like Ajax and, particularly, Barcelona are lauded for their academies and youth set-ups. Players are scouted from the age of ten and they all play the same way as the first team. Uniformity is key.

When it comes to Scottish football – when directors and fans are breathing down your neck – normal service, despite the drilling and training, is never far from a resumption: the big lad at the back blooters it long for the bigger but skinnier lad up front to wallop it goal-wards.

During his time in charge of Celtic, Brendan Rodgers bought-in to the academy system. The mantra he instilled was all about technique, passing and possession in order to create players who could deal with playing for the first team in the Champions League. In the last few years, the Parkhead side's academy has brought through players like James Forrest, Callum McGregor, Kieran Tierney, Mikey Johnstone and Anthony Ralston. It remains to be seen if this will be Rodgers' most profound legacy at the club.

Across the city at Rangers, despite having a six-star academy with top facilities at his disposal, former manager Mark Warburton overlooked the system when he was in charge. He claimed players such as David Bates and Ross McCrorie weren't ready for first team football and looked instead toward the lower leagues in England to augment his team. He didn't make it to his second anniversary in charge.

The big two will always have players coming through despite dips and peaks on the conveyor belt. A decent coach will always recognise and nurture talent. Interestingly, Rangers' current head coach, Steven Gerrard, seems to have a willingness to develop from within. That, of course, is how his storied Liverpool career began.

Most Scottish football fans love to see 'one of our own' come through at the club he supported as a boy and played for at every level on his way to the first team. But it happens rarely these days. If clubs were judged by their youth system, few would be able to hold a candle to Hamilton Academical. More should follow their lead.

At international level, the men's side hasn't qualified for a major tournament since France 1998. The Scottish FA set up a performance strategy and, in 2012, the SFA selected seven performance schools to nurture talent. Each school was provided with coaches and, over a four-year period, the most talented young footballers throughout the country were to receive an extra 800 hours of coaching to play football within an educational environment. In March 2016, they started 'Project Brave', a more streamlined, elite version of 'Club Academy Scotland'. In January 2017, the then SFA chief executive, Stewart Regan, explained the change: 'Project Brave was a refresh of the SFA performance strategy, so back in 2011, when the performance strategy was initiated, there were a series of focus-areas and all of those initiatives were put in place and led by the performance department. Five years on, we're refreshing that strategy and reviewing what's worked, where things need to change and we've had a working group making a series of recommendations so that Scotland can perform much better on the international stage.'

A fabulous lesson in how to speak at relative length without saying anything at all.

How difficult can it be to improve the nation's relationship with a football? There was no mention of kids getting a touch on the ball until it's second nature. No understanding of knowing what to do with the ball when under pressure and playing games. The word 'strategy' was mentioned four times but Scotland still fails to qualify for major tournaments.

And yet the dream persists. One day, we'll be back.

Won't we?

Exhibit 86
Smoke Bombs & Flares

Smoke bombs and flares are something you regularly see ignited at tasty European fixtures, usually in Turkey, Croatia, Italy or Poland, or in big South American games. Anywhere in the football world where you find any self-respecting ultras, they simply must have a vast array of pyrotechnics.

Flares add a certain piquancy to the game. As well as being visually dramatic, cinematic and theatrical, any time they're set off, watch the cameramen ignore the game and quickly focus on the offending pyrotechnics. They film well, are colourful and add to the occasion.

Their recent emergence in Scottish football has been met with scorn by the Scottish Chief of Police. They are an undoubted statement, a cry from the attention-seeking fan. But most importantly, they are now cheap and easy to buy. The downside? It's illegal to carry fireworks or pyrotechnics into a ground and if you get caught by the law, it's at least three months in jail. I wonder how parachute display teams, rocketing onto the centre circle to deliver a trophy, with canisters of smoke snaking out from their boots, will react to the news?

What is our fascination with flares? Are we summoning our inner caveman? Man has always looked for fire. Why are we so mesmerised? Part respect, part fear?

More to the point, they are dangerous and beg the question: why are they actually called a 'safety flare', if they burn at 3,000 degrees – and what are they doing anywhere near a football stadium? And why are stewards so bad at spotting them yet are experts when it comes to finding my wee bottle of water?

The concern is perfectly understandable. In this age of ultras, who aren't immune to waving the odd banner, unrolling a statement of intent which takes up the whole home section, made of highly flammable polythene, and flags which melt like a cheap nightie, what could possibly go wrong?

The fans want the authorities to keep out of it, believing the game is already too sanitised and will become boring if further bans are imposed. If it adds a bit of atmosphere, what's the problem? The consequences of it going wrong, though, don't bear thinking about.

Exhibit 87
International Breaks/Winter Breaks

International breaks, these days, are like a long week in jail. The gaps between club games and international fixtures are a ridiculous, infernal wait.

It wasn't always this bad. There was a time before UEFA enforced tight scheduling of international matches, when it was crash, bang, wallop, back to normal.

Now, the clubs say goodbye to their players and when they return they're sporting long hair and beards. They come back another shape, caused by too much work in the gym, and have lost their spark, edge and, in some cases, their first touch. It takes them a few games to return to the levels they were at before going off to represent their country.

The players leave their clubs after the weekend fixture and report at Cameron House (or wherever the SFA bean-counters have found a great Groupon deal) for Monday at 10.00 a.m. They train during the week, play a game on a Saturday, then another on a Tuesday. That then sets in motion a wait until the following weekend for the next club fixture. Two weeks, fourteen never-ending days.

Before there were two games to negotiate, international games were played on a Wednesday. If you were a faithful international player and were an unused substitute, you would be expected to report to your club side the following morning for training, which usually involved a long drive through the night.

It's the staggered scheduling that annoys me. If you don't have a game on the Friday, you have to wait until the Tuesday for the second group fixture. If this is the timetable (and it's the same for everyone), we need to accept it's necessary for TV revenue. However, what I can't forgive is a fourteen-day break for international friendlies as well. Seriously? A fortnight?

If the national side was qualifying through flair and exciting football, the gaps between games would be more bearable. However, the team has become so bad that the wait only serves to agitate as we await the inevitable disappointing result.

International breaks are in this museum because I don't like them, and I don't think I'm alone. As for the winter break? What a waste of time. 'Let's have a rest and go to Dubai.' It's also difficult to gauge when the winter starts and ends in Scotland. Sometimes, it snows heavily in March and April and is mild in December and January. Sides come back from winter breaks and look like they've lost their flow.

But back to international breaks.

I'm not sure how the coaches fill the hours and days. Double training sessions? Quiz nights? There's no drinking anymore, so there can't be any karaoke. Is sober karaoke a thing? International managers love having players to prepare for games. The clubs are left nervously praying that their star players don't come back crocked.

The Home Internationals was a competition held at the end of every season. Scotland played Northern Ireland, Wales and the Auld Enemy at Hampden or Wembley. This would take place over a week: Saturday, Tuesday, Saturday. Three games, one week. And each country would field their top players. It was exciting, well attended and the fans loved it.

So, it should be down to the clubs to put pressure on the authorities if their players return injured but, short of boycotting the international timetable, we have no option but to tolerate these lulls. Feel free to look scornfully at this exhibit – it's one of the banes of the modern game.

Exhibit 88
Mascots

The mascot, as a concept, is a strange phenomenon. Grown-ups inside daft outfits, whose modus operandi is to entertain the kids and run around like clowns on the sidelines during major games of football.

I mean, what the hell?

I'm not keen on mascots at the best of times but when you see them arm-in-arm with the team around the centre-circle during a minute's silence, you know the game has fallen down the rabbit hole.

Perhaps it's because mascots don't behave like they're in a football stadium at all. To them, this isn't a football park; it's a stage, a catwalk. They can't get enough of the attention. Then, when the team score, they become part of the celebrations.

When it comes to mascots, there's a definite pecking order. It's not quite the Hollywood star system, where mascots have impossible demands placed on them, but there's a definite hierarchy. You have the absolute major superstars – Celtic's

'Hoopy the Huddle Hound' and 'Broxi Bear' at Rangers. Then you have the classic bad boy – Dunfermline's legendary 'Sammy the Tammy'. Sammy's entertaining, with a bit of edge, prone to violent outbursts or pretending he's Evel Knievel as he performs the odd stunt and employs counterattacking tactics, like getting into a cardboard tank and firing at opposition fans.

Then we have the new kid on the block, who has strolled into town like he owns the place – Partick Thistle's 'Kingsley'. He was dreamt up by former Glasgow School of Art alumni and Turner Prize nominee, David Shrigley. I knew of Shrigley's work with the San Francisco punk band Deerhoof. This being Maryhill, the previous mascot, Jaggy MacBee – Pete Best to Kingsley's Ringo – was unceremoniously ousted to make way for the new man.

Despite myself, I've grown to like Kingsley because he does what art should do – terrify and intrigue in equal measure. Some called him a perfect artistic statement; others wondered what a nightmarish, Kafkaesque, dystopian mono-browed three-toothed, ugly, glue-sniffing vision of a sun God had to with the 'Harry Wraggs'?

Honourable mentions should also go to 'Paisley Panda', who merges both gallusness with a mischievous sense of fun at St Mirren Park.

Overall, though, the mascot as an initiative is part of the improved, family-friendly version of football and proof of the increasing 'Yankiefication' of the game.

At times, I get so bored I crave for the day when there's some sporadic violence. Forget about mascots racing each other; why not have Sammy the Tammy taking on Kingsley in an anything-goes fight?

Mascots don't belong in football, they are best left in places like American football, an athletics meet or, better still, a rugby game.

Exhibit 89
Synthetic Surface

Plastic pitches find their way into the museum because they are an aberration. Few issues get my dander up like plastic pitches. Games played on them are, more often than not, absolutely shocking – the ball bounces awkwardly and the pitches look terrible on TV. We keep being told football is a product and 'this is showbiz', part of the entertainment industry, and blah blah blah. It's professional football . . . yet we allow teams to play on *this*?

If you'd paid a fortune to go to the theatre to see a play but, when you got there, found it being performed on a bouncy castle, would you not feel short-changed? Actually, maybe not. Bouncy Castle Shakespeare Company presents *Othello*? That might be hilarious. Get me the application for *Dragon's Den*...

The plastic pitch is hardly a modern concept in Scottish football. The first synthetic pitch to host a senior Scottish match was at Stirling Albion's ground back in 1987, when they played Ayr United. But they're commonplace now. Of the current teams in the top tier, Kilmarnock, Livingston and Hamilton Accies all have them. What upsets me about this, especially in Killie's case, is they once had one of the most beautiful surfaces in Scottish football. The Scottish national side used Rugby Park for training because the pitch was so pristine, like a bowling green, throughout the season.

The Hamilton hierarchy maintains that, when the club moved to New Douglas Park from its charming if slightly fading and dilapidated old ground, it laid a synthetic surface for financial purposes, to serve the public and generate revenue for the club.

Airdrie has one that it rents out to locals wanting to play five-a-sides. It's understandable down the leagues but I'm not sure if they should be allowed in the top flight when top players are visiting and the game is televised. As we embrace the future, who remembers the casualties? What about the groundsmen? Are there any left, and, if so, where do they keep their hoovers?

When sides play against Hamilton, Livingston and Kilmarnock, they're at a huge disadvantage. In the four Scottish Leagues there are twelve clubs with synthetic surfaces. You can understand why many have them: fear of insolvency is the constant sword of Damocles that hangs over the Scottish game. When you have a business and it costs more to run than the money coming in, it's either time to find a gullible Lottery winner who's daft enough to part with their cash, or lay a plastic pitch. But why should the national side play Lithuania in Vilnius on an Astroturf pitch in a World Cup qualifier? Why do Celtic have to play a Champions League qualifier on a plastic pitch against Astana in Kazakhstan? It's a ridiculous situation in terms of fairness, yet we deal with it and get on.

The upsides? Games are rarely cancelled due to bad weather and the parks can be leased out to generate income. The downsides? People aren't coming through the turnstiles because the surface renders the quality of product on the park so insufferably poor.

Meanwhile, back at Stirling Albion, they moved to Forthbank Stadium in 1994 and their pitch, of natural grass, was voted the best playing surface in Scotland in 2018. Its own Graeme Glen was voted 'Groundsman of the Year'. Hamilton, meanwhile, was judged to have the worst playing surface.

Now, about *Othello* and the Bouncy Castle Shakespeare Company . . .

Exhibit 90
The Play-Offs

I know the play-off concept is popular with TV companies. Why wouldn't it be? A high-stakes shoot-out? Loads of excitement and drama? It's absolutely tailor-made for a television audience. But I'm not a fan. In fact, I think they're a terrible idea. They're extremely unfair and, in the same way as an earlier exhibit, 'Gardening Leave', they often represent a reward for failure.

Under the current Scottish system, a team could be terrible for a season, finish second-bottom in the league, yet avoid going down. I believe the second-bottom side should always go down. Equally, if you've played well for a whole season and finish second in the league below, you should be promoted. The play-off system rewards mediocrity. You may counter that it keeps a league alive, especially if you support a team who finds form in the run-in, but it doesn't reward teams who win the most games – and that's not right.

In May 2017, Brechin City, a team best known for its hedge row and bush, finished fourth in League One but gained promotion to the championship at the expense of Raith Rovers. Brechin finished fourth on fifty points; Livingston won the league on eighty-one points. Brechin had to play Alloa, who had finished twelve points above them, in the semi-final play-off and got through, beating Raith Rovers to go up. They then went on to finish the 2017/18 season without winning a game, amassing just four points. Played thirty-six, won zero, drew four, lost thirty-two.

A better case in point might be the struggle of East Kilbride. They won the Central Lowland League in 2017 and had to play against the winners of the Highland League to gain entry to the Scottish League . . . or so you'd think. Not in Scotland. Having won their tie against Buckie, they faced the side coming out of the league, Cowdenbeath, losing in a penalty shoot-out. I understand teams know the rules before they enter but you have to admit that's cruel.

I would stop the play-offs. I understand their popularity but I truly believe they are having a detrimental long-term effect on the game. They aren't for genuine fans and their clubs. They're probably more for the armchair fan. The play-off concept has undoubtedly filtered down from the English Championship to gain entry into the 'Promised Land' of the Premier League.

It reached crazy proportions in 2010 when the Premiership considered introducing a play-off between the fourth, fifth, sixth and seventh placed teams for access to the final Champions League place. Again, I understand the logic. It makes the league constantly competitive. If you started the season poorly, changed coach and went on a winning run, you could effectively go from being in the relegation places to a play-off spot.

I'm glad it was shelved, though. For any club side to play thirty-eight games, finish fourth and then have to go into a Lottery to retain that place is grossly unfair. Think about it. Why should any team that finishes outside the top four have any right to play in the Champions League? If you believe football is about evolution not revolution, and that you reap what you sow, you should be against the play-off concept.

It has had an adverse effect on the Premier League and, when the madness filters down to Scottish football, through the ridiculous trickle-down effect which football loves to embrace, the decisions hit everyone. When it reaches sides such as East Kilbride, a well-run club, playing in the fifth tier of Scottish football and formed in 2010 with the ambition of gaining membership to Scottish League Two, it becomes ridiculously unfair.

Exhibit 91
The Season Book

The season book, as it's now called, was once called the season ticket. But it isn't a book or a ticket anymore. Instead, it is best described as a credit card shaped item.

The season ticket was for fans with money, or at least a dad who had some. Only the most affluent fans had them in the 1970s. By the mid-to-late 1980s and early 1990s, when stadiums became all-seated and more anaemic, it was season ticket bonanza time. Clubs got wise to the idea that they could sell and allocate individual seats and provide a match experience.

The true fans pay up for their season ticket/book/card. Like most offers, it's not really a bargain. More a way of demonstrating loyalty to your club. They work on a number of levels but the basic idea is to entice and encourage fans to part with their money. They can do this by paying up front, in big instalments, or by monthly direct debit. The club are fond of any method which extracts cash from the fan and aren't too fussy how it comes in, mainly because they can then borrow against it.

For paying up front and supporting their club financially, the fan gets their seat at a slightly reduced price, the right to buy tickets for big cup ties and European games and, especially for the deluded fan, an air of superiority which makes them think their opinion carries some degree of authority. You know the type: 'Hello panel, first time caller and season ticket holder at [INSERT CLUB] . . .' Then they go on to make a dubious point based on the fact they contribute in some way to the running of their club. As a season ticket holder, they feel duty bound to prattle on in some nonsensical manner.

The upside to a season ticket? A guaranteed seat at every home game of the season. The downside? You can be stuck beside people who the late AA Gill would describe as 'always on broadcast, never receive'. The type of people who shout loudly so everyone can hear their opinion. And you're stuck with them *all season long*.

The deal used to be that you supported your team no matter what and didn't complain about the players. You showed up, bought a programme, got behind the team, took the good times with the bad, and tried to come through it all without too much psychological scarring. It's the 'support' part of the word 'supporter'. It would be great if we could get back to those simpler times.

Exhibit 92
Time Added On

Whenever the assistant referee holds up the electronic board with the substitute numbers or the amount of time to be added on, my eyes are always drawn to the big advert for the famous watch company that adorns the board. I suppose the fact the board is called the (add in luxury watch sponsor) Soccer Substitution Board will have something to do with it – the advertising is doing its job. But what doesn't seem to be doing its job is the actual timekeeping – and therefore we arrive at the point behind this exhibit piece being in the museum.

I would argue that, at least ninety per cent of the time, the machine the officials use is wrong and the amount of added time is inaccurate. It should be thirty seconds per substitution, plus injury time. It rarely is. If I had anything to do with football administration, I'd have a digital clock on the big screen and it would stop every time the ball goes out of play. During a break in play for an injury, for example, or for a free kick, or a corner, or a disputed decision. That, in turn, would therefore force the teams to play an actual ninety minutes.

Admittedly, it might mean games starting at 6:45 and running until midnight but who cares? Let's start the revolution here. If bands and comedians can play more than the allotted or expected time, why can't football? Fans across the globe pay for a ninety-minute performance but it has been worked out that the ball is actually in play for, on average, around fifty-five-and-a-half minutes.

I'd propose stopping substitutions from the eightieth minute – unless a player is injured – to prevent tactical, time-wasting switches. No substitutes to applaud the 'man of the match' performance. Any injury time or time-wasting which occurs in the four minutes of additional time would also be incorporated into the stopping of the clock. The fully allotted ninety minutes of play must be played. Imagine the howls if your team needs a late goal and the assistant referee holds up a sign suggesting at least eighteen minutes at the end of the game. Even then, we'd probably be short.

Another irritation with the time added on and substitutions board is the theatrical way the assistant referees hold it up and twist it around to let the crowd see. You just know they've been in front of the mirror rehearsing.

So, taking this new policy to its next logical step, if we're going to be there for days, we might as well have fun. Beer and food will be served direct to your seat, just like the American football experience. We know it's not going to happen, as we wheel in the classic 'excuse triumvirate': police concerns, traffic and TV schedules. But let's flip this on its head with a scenario. Imagine you booked your two-week holiday some time ago and paid for it in advance. Well you're only getting 8.54 days now, I'm afraid. Yes, I know you paid for a ninety-minute experience and are only getting fifty-five-and-a-half minutes, approximately sixty-one per cent of the game. Sixty-one percent of the fortnight is 8.54 days. Yes, I know this movie lasts for three hours and you've paid for the full movie in advance but sadly you're only getting two-thirds of the experience now.

The game has to adapt, pay refunds or change its pricing structure accordingly. Otherwise, start midweek games at 7:00pm and those on Saturday at 2:00pm. Give some actual value for money. Oh, and here's another idea: keep the ball on the park. Use the clock. Stop the clock. It's a simple idea. But the game needs – and deserves – it. So do the fans.

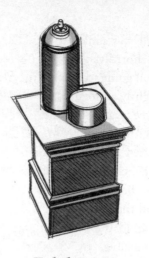

Exhibit 93
Vanishing Spray & Shocking Referees

I have always been intrigued by the fractured psyche of someone who dreams of becoming a referee. Is there a certain mentality required? What is it that makes a sensible, well-balanced individual ever want to become a referee, running around on a Saturday afternoon and having abuse hurled at them? There must be something in their personality, a need and desire to implement order. What makes them apply for the job? Are they officious? Fancy £800 for running about annoying thousands of people? No? Okay, what if we give you a holster with a canister of vanishing spray so you can act like a sheriff? Deal? Sign right here.

The vanishing spray, like Scotland's World Cup qualifying hopes, disappears after about a minute on the pitch. It contains butane, isobutylene and propane gas, a foaming agent, and was launched at the 2014 World Cup.

At the time, it was exciting and a talking point. Apart from seeing Germany batter the hosts Brazil in the semis, 2014's carnival of football was rank rotten. Like the spray itself, in the words of the short-lived post-punk Mancunian band Joy Division, 'What you going to do now the novelty is gone?' Now, it's just another slightly annoying part of the game.

When the referee's vanishing spray was launched, loads of footballers were growing their hipster beards, especially in Scotland. Refs missed a chance to foam up their plumage and shave it off. You get the feeling match officials would be annoyed by a beard. When did you ever see a ref with a big ZZ Top number growing off their chins?

The concept behind the spray, to stop players encroaching at free kicks, is laudable. However, the problem lies in the execution. The ref's idea of a yard is based on a stride of a 5'5' man. Seldom are the players back the correct distance. It's always around seven or eight yards. While this is going on and the ref's back is turned, players kick and disperse the foam. Distances should not be an issue, especially around the eighteen-yard box, where we have the six-yard box, the penalty spot at twelve yards, and, more often than not, the grass cut into six-yard sections.

Scotland has a proud and long tradition of producing terrible referees. From Les Mottram missing a goal at Firhill in 1993 – when Partick Thistle played Dundee United and Paddy Connolly scored – right up to any number of Willie Collum's mystifying decisions. I sometimes think the things he does are a cry for help.

Hugh Dallas? Well, his career was there for all to see, especially his questionable comedy content as a ref supervisor. Then there was 'Dougie Gate' when Dougie McDonald was 'economical with the truth' about his decision to reverse a penalty for Celtic when playing against Dundee United in 2010. After the game, Celtic manager Neil Lennon questioned McDonald about his penalty U-turn, which the referee claimed was on advice from his linesman. He later admitted that this wasn't true, the linesman had given no such instruction. McDonald was censured by the SFA Referee Committee for lying in his post-match report about the circumstances surrounding the penalty decision and, shortly afterward, announced his retirement from the game. The assistant referee, Steven Craven (what delicious nominative determinism), who corroborated McDonald's report, was given a lifetime ban.

Scottish refereeing incompetence isn't a new phenomenon. When West German goalkeeper Harald Schumacher collided with French striker Patrick Battiston in the 1982 World Cup in one of the most sickening pieces of foul play ever to take place on a football field, Dutch referee Charles Corver somehow failed to penalise the 'keeper. The referee later explained that he was watching the ball and so consulted his linesman, our very own Bob Valentine of Dundee, who advised Corver that nothing had happened. One of the most brutal assaults in football history matched with the worse decision ever and it was down to a Scottish linesman? Gives you a certain sense of pride, eh?

I suggest we forget the vanishing spray and get a drone out to the pitch and have it create an electrified beam. If the players cross the beam they get a shock. We've seen the way they roll about in agony after a tickle of a tackle, so let's see how they deal with a short burst of electricity through their system. And if the referee has a shocker, the drone could then give him a shocker. It would look dramatic on TV and the fans would love it. I realise that sounds like some kind of 1980s dystopian movie – but think of the fun we could have.

Exhibit 94
VAR Goal Line Technology

VAR (Video Assistant Referee) didn't appear until Sepp Blatter 'resigned' after his corruption scandal malarkey. Sepp was eventually removed from office by welders with a blowtorch in 2015. During his time in charge he was staunchly opposed to most forms of technology – apart from online bank transfers, one has to assume. To him, the game was about what you could get away with. Like Diego Maradona, it was all about the human touch.

Football, in comparison to other top sports (and by 'sports' we mean big money-making sports like American football, baseball or basketball), has been slow to adopt technology. VAR has been trialled and tested around the world for a few years yet, in Europe, UEFA continues to nudge it along only very slowly.

Trials started in 2016 and were implemented by IFAB (International Football Association Board), who overlook the legal side of the game. They stated VAR would focus on four key points: goal decisions, penalty decisions, direct red cards, and cases of mistaken identity.

Blatter was famous for fending off those trying to make the game fairer. Sepp still loved Betamax and presumably wondered why no one ever responded to his Myspace friend requests. Why would you ever want the correct decision given? He seemed to believe fans craved a level of idiocy or incompetence to complain about. But maybe there was something in his reluctance to embrace the white heat of technology and his wish to allow humans to make mistakes?

The downside to VAR is that it breaks up the flow of the game. It's also another kick in the teeth to paying fans in the stadium who believe live matches should remain unscathed by television interference. If they wanted the game to stop and start every ten seconds, they'd watch American football. Alternatively, they could cosy up and stay in the house like armchair fans and, allegedly for some, get more bang for their buck by stealing it from the internet and walking to the fridge every ten seconds for beer and cold pizza.

VAR will come to Scotland eventually. Its launch at the 2018 World Cup in Russia was well received. The number of penalties awarded increased. I suspect with a few tweaks, VAR will be accelerated and quickly rolled out. And yet, like most quantum leaps in football, there's a nervousness about change. Surely we are now only a few high profile errors away from a VAR re-think and the governing bodies fast-tracking it through. Former pros and pundits in Scotland were initially against it but, once they saw it in action, like the armchair fan, they loved the drama. By the time VAR comes to Scotland, it will be commonplace to watch referees draw an imaginary TV screen with their fingers, look blankly with a finger rammed in their ear, while some hapless incompetent at 'mission control' makes their decision for them.

Reports filtered through in March 2018 that the SFA bosses interrupted an urgent allotment application meeting to discuss the VAR system in Scotland. The SFA doesn't like ushering through major changes but, with the amount of flak heading the way of match officials, the quicker VAR is introduced the better. If the SPFL thinks it's too expensive, perhaps they should get someone like Domino's Pizza to sponsor it: 'VAR – we always deliver'.

Of course, this item has a sting in the tail. Typical of a tragic Scottish World Cup campaign, VAR rose up to bite us firmly in the national arse when Shelley Kerr's team were knocked out of the 2019 Women's World Cup. Having led Argentina 3–0 and needing a win to progress to the last sixteen, we conceded two second-half goals before a twice-taken VAR-awarded penalty made it 3–3 in stoppage time. The first penalty attempt had been brilliantly saved by Lee Alexander, only for VAR to rule (correctly, in fairness) that she had come off her line early. Second time around, Florencia Bonsegundo made no mistake. Once again, we were going home after the group stages – and, perhaps for the first time, we found ourselves wishing Sepp Blatter was still in office.

Exhibit 95
War Chest

Full disclosure: I have never seen an actual war chest. One can only assume it looks like a big treasure chest brimming with loot. If I was an incoming big-name coach at a Scottish club, I'd be checking to make sure the bank notes in the war chest weren't counterfeit and that there was real money underneath instead of bricks to weigh down the trunk. The war chest we speak of is the clichéd, ridiculously overused colloquialism adopted by a salivating press and media, which managers are said to 'demand' before taking up the impossible task of taking on an underperforming club.

This is sport, not war. This whole 'war chest' stuff is a bit over the top – but this is Scottish football and we love a melodrama.

The war chest can be promised by a desperate board determined to hold on to a manager, who is attracting attention from other clubs. The manager wants cash to buy big in the transfer market to improve his squad. The directors inform the press a war chest will be made available to launch a major campaign in the hope he stays.

The other thing about clubs with war chests is that they typically make offers that are dismissed as 'derisory'. The club subject to the offer knows it's a cheap shot because they've read in the press that the buying club has millions as its disposal.

On hearing that an incoming coach has been promised a sizeable war chest, the club's star player, who has had a dip in form and openly slated the incoming coach in an interview, issues a 'come-and-get-me plea' to other teams, as he knows he's otherwise destined to spend the next chapter of his career warming the bench.

Our game has never been awash with money but every now and then it shocks us with some top-drawer managerial appointments: Graeme Souness, Martin O'Neill, Brendan Rodgers, Steven Gerrard. These top names don't come cheap and they always come with the same rejoinder – a demand for a sizeable war chest to compete in the transfer market.

Scottish football can only dream of the huge bags of cash that are tossed around around the English Premier League. It is said that Arsenal's coach Unai Emery demanded a guarantee of at least £200 million before he took the job in 2018. It's difficult to work out where Scottish football clubs could compete. However, all is not lost for the Scottish game. Around the summer transfer window of 2019, there were some positives and green shoots of recovery.

In one possible transfer chain, Celtic could be sitting on a sizeable war chest. With a mix of good housekeeping buying 'projects' for development and selling on from their youth academy, they could be leading the way for Scottish football. If they sell Rogic to Zenit St Petersburg for £9m, Tierney to Arsenal for £25m and an unsettled Oliver Ntcham ready to move for £12m, the Glasgow giants would have generated £36m. This, when added to the £10m spent on both Boli Bolingoli-Mbombo (£3m) and Christopher Jullien (£7m) suddenly means you have

£46m transfer budget and a club getting close to competing despite the meagre TV money. There's no reason why Rangers, with Morelos or Aberdeen with McKenna can't start to sell, especially when the market, particularly the EPL, Europe and Asia, is awash with vast war chests. Don't stop believing.

GIFT SHOP

MERCHANDISE

Exhibit 96
Football Cards

These days, clubs are back in pre-season training before the sun block has even had a chance to dry. There's hardly any break from one season to the next. Clubs have so many commercial commitments, big glamour friendlies and, of course, our co-efficient is now so bad, that we spend most of July manfully trying to get our touch and fitness back while playing crucial European competition qualifiers against treacherous diddy teams. Unfortunately, those diddy teams have, more often than not, been playing for months and are in top shape.

In the 1970s, kids had to deal with a depressing, harrowing, long summer, interspersed with droughts or riots and countless days to fill with anything connected to football. The season ended in May, after the Scottish Cup final or the Home Internationals, and then didn't begin again until late August. By the end of July, you'd be so desperate to see a game that a pre-season friendly against Hartlepool or Scunthorpe caused no end of excitement. To fill those summers, in between going off for miles on walks, playing up the woods or taking on adventures in the country on our bikes, we would beg, borrow, or steal to buy football cards.

They came in packs of five with a strip of bubblegum. They amounted to nothing more than a photograph of a player on one side with information about him on the reverse. They were fun, interesting and, best of all, could be swapped with your pals. They were the forerunner to the more lucrative and glossier Panini sticker books. Football cards were like Betamax to Panini's VHS, providing wonderful memories for thousands of Scottish children crazy about football in the 1970s. If you got money, you bought cards and collected a big pile, trading with your mates if you ended up with 'doublers'.

I loved those football cards. I can still smell the printer dye, the feel of a fresh card, the excitement of opening the pack. No matter how hard we tried to collect a wide range of players and take the football cards and line them up in position on the floor, we always had loads of doublers. I seemed to be forever haunted by a player called Alex Rae, a Partick Thistle winger with a moustache. I never had any real collectables.

But still. Rank rotten bubble gum and cards of football players? These were humble times and we were so happy.

There was always one guy in the housing estate who had hundreds of cards and a pocket full of doublers. The same guy who had an Action Man with all the accessories, Subbuteo with Brazil team colours, stands and floodlights. To us, this particular guy was rich – and when I say rich, I mean his mum and dad both worked, they would holiday in Spain and they got a new car with a new registration at the start of every August. He was the first person I knew with a Barcelona strip. But I'm over it. I'm OK with it. I'm not damaged by the inequality of it all.

In the days before computer games, if it was pouring with rain, my friends and I might be allowed to play quietly indoors. We had a glorious imagination and laid teams on the floor. I always ended up with four Drew Jarvie cards and six of Drew Busby. I also remember Brian Heron of Dumbarton. This other guy, his doublers included Derek Johnstone and Kenny Dalglish. His *doublers*!

I remember the Kenny Dalglish card so well. At that time in my life, I don't think I wanted anything more. Kenny was wearing a Celtic away strip, all green. Imagine going into school on Monday with a Kenny Dalglish football card? When my pal set him up to play alongside Derek Johnstone, I had to tell him Kenny didn't play as an out-and-out striker so wouldn't be playing alongside him but slightly behind the striker, and I would nudge him into the correct position just behind Johnstone. As soon as I touched the card, I knew the game was over. The other kid gathered them up and left, outraged at my audacity for even thinking about touching his collection, let alone challenging his selected line-up.

Football cards became such a big thing they sometimes made the news. Collectors being robbed or some swaps and transactions turning ugly and ending in mass brawls. Such shocking behaviour for nine-year-olds. But there was a magic to the whole thing that remains permanently and perfectly lodged in my memory, a glorious golden nugget of childhood that I wouldn't swap for anything. Not even that Kenny Dalglish card.

Exhibit 97
Football Programme

In May 2018, there were worrying reports that the humble football programme was on the way out. Due to dwindling sales and fans finding more information online, their future appeared bleak. Oh, the young ones, wanting everything for free, eh? Let's hope this doesn't come to pass, as programmes have a long, wonderful, established tradition.

Initially, programmes were two-sided football cards, used as scorecards, featuring the team line-ups, and some local business adverts. By 1900, they evolved into a booklet with some editorial and more in-depth statistics. They helped the club as they served both as an additional revenue stream and a vehicle for getting the message out.

The programme really started to move towards becoming the publication we know and love today around the time of the 1920 FA Cup final, the first to be played at Wembley. Now, it's an intrinsic part of the matchday experience and a pillar of the football fan's world.

To some, the art, the history and the memorabilia factor makes collecting programmes something of an obsessive compulsion. What starts out as a hobby can quickly become an addiction. Some collectors buy to read and enjoy, others to complete a particular set – such as every game of a season – and others to sell. The dreaded line is always 'in good condition'. Spare us from rusty staples and tears and nicks. Whether they are kept in the loft or in a cupboard under the stairs, every real football fan has their own stash of football programmes.

Major collectors concentrate on three main elements: age, popularity and rarity. One surprising factor that contributes to the value of a programme is rain. Anything bought when it rained heavily can increase the value significantly because pages damaged by rain tended to stick together, smudging the ink. As a consequence, the programmes tended to be thrown away, making one in good condition rare and therefore more valuable.

If football cards were about relieving boredom in the early 1970s, collecting football programmes would get us through the close seasons by the end of the decade.

Looking through programmes with classic images of players, advertising hoardings and pictures of terracing where you once stood, makes them special. Then there are the lager adverts and pictures of closed shops and local businesses, and the buses. It's funny how buses have changed so much.

Programmes are also a reflection of society, a social history and a reminder of our past, a time when football clubs and stadiums were part of the local community, situated in the heart of the town, before the clubs sold out to supermarkets and moved to greenfield sites. You can't blame them for accepting the money, nor can you blame the authorities for wanting to keep riots between rival fans out of town centres.

Condition, value and price are crucial for collectors but no-one got rich collecting programmes. Maybe if you were related to someone who had collected league games furiously between the two World Wars then you might be on to something valuable. At that time, paper was scarce and programmes were sold as sheets of paper. Some of the sheets sold where British troops were stationed are highly collectable and sell for a decent price.

If you have a French or Spanish uncle who attended Real Madrid versus Stade de Reims-Champagne competing in the first-ever European Cup final, held in the Parc des Princes in Paris in 1956 (Madrid won 4–3), then you're in luck. Depending on its condition, it would fetch between three to four thousand pounds now.

For real value, the programme for the FA Cup final between Sheffield United and Spurs in 1901 sold for £19,000 in 2014. Man United's first FA Cup final, against Bristol City, was played at Crystal Palace and sold for £23,500 in 2012. (Interestingly, United played in what looks like an Airdrieonians strip.) The record, though, is for a programme from the 1882 FA Cup final between Old Etonians and Blackburn Rovers, which sold for £35,250 in 2013.

The golden ticket item? A programme from the 1966 World Cup final, which is probably the rarest of them all.

Scottish football has always produced quality programmes, from the lower leagues to the biggest teams in the country, to international games. Some clubs have developed their publications accordingly, with modern, slick, glossy productions. My favourite era had player profiles with the club's cult hero posing in flares and platforms beside his new Capri. You would have real, in-depth features on players in those days. There was a level of dedication and attention to detail that the 'fanorak' loved. Some of the graphic design and layout was also exceptional. Football was definitely more entertaining then. In fact, it was like a different sport. I love my Scotland vs Argentina programme from 1979, not least because it was the match where Diego Maradona scored his first senior international goal. The national side has produced superb programmes throughout the decades. Some are reasonably priced, loads can be picked up for a fiver while, for the more discerning, you can pick up a 1922 game against Wales for £199 or Scotland vs England game from 1937 for £95.

Whether it's as an enjoyable curio, something to saviour and enjoy (like a reminder of an old stadium where you were a regular visitor) or even as an investment, the football programme is deserving of its place in the museum. They are like time capsules that remind us life whizzes by and football, in particular, moves on with it.

Exhibit 98
The Overwrought Memoir

In the old days, footballers liked to keep their emotions firmly in check. Manic depression or bipolar disorder would have been diagnosed as being 'a bit fed up' and treated with a stiff drink, a brisk walk and the advice to 'give yourself a shake'. Everything had to be bottled up and kept in. What happened in the dressing room stayed in the dressing room. Now, it's gone the other way. Ex-players can't wait to spill the beans about bullying, bribery, gambling and addiction, some even claiming they were addicted to the old nookie.

They never seemed to think it was a problem until their career was over and they realised they had to face the real world. When they were living the high life, the money was mind-blowing and life was wonderful. They hardly parted with a penny because, everywhere they went, drink was bought for them.

If you grew up thinking the life of a professional footballer was the ultimate dream, well, it turns out it wasn't always brilliant. To the old guard, these books were the antithesis of what football was all about. These publications were an erosion of the game's soul. There was a real sense of betrayal. Amongst this generation, the sense of duty toward former teammates and the circle of trust at a club is a fixed, permanent bond.

But the audience has changed. The modern fan demands dirt. Society now encourages footballers to dispense of their baggage quicker than a backpacker at the Colombian border with Peru.

Once, the tales of a pre-season bonk with a local German lassie used to whet the appetite. Now, we require more. We want torment and regret, and as much of it as possible.

It is good that sportspeople now feel able to talk. It shows a human side. It also proves society, as a whole, has become more understanding when it comes to mental illness and addiction.

It amazes me players often end up so broke. If you consider the top players in the late 1990s were earning twenty grand a week in Scottish football, which is more than a million pounds a year, you'd think it would be enough to secure them for the rest of their lives. But now we've got to read about their heartache that they're skint because they weren't mature enough to handle it. Maybe this is why the better football books are actually about journeymen professionals and those fighting to compete to earn a living, as opposed to the famous players who blew it. Just please, spare us the memoir.

There are some excellent football memoirs out there: *What's It All About, Ralphie?* by the late Ralph Milne, *The Proper Charlie* by Charlie Miller and, somewhat surprisingly, *Full Time: The Secret Life of Tony Cascarino*. All are well worth a read.

Exhibit 99
The Panini Sticker Book

For kids of a certain age, growing up in Scotland, the World Cup didn't begin until you had your Panini sticker book. I never knew anyone who completed a whole book. Ever. It was the same for the Scottish league ones, too. My wife and her brother once shared a 1982 World Cup sticker book, coming up only one player shy of the whole set (a Belgian, who they couldn't find anywhere).

Initially, the top players from Scotland would be doubled up on one card, so you would have Strachan and Archibald of Aberdeen, and Jardine and Levein of Hearts. This changed in 1989 when Scotland got its own sticker book.

Collecting stickers, football cards and programmes was part of the magic of being a young football fan. If we couldn't get to the games or see a match on TV, they were an interesting way of idling away the hours. Then there was the desire to find a 'need': a sticker you required to complete a set. 'Got, got, got… NEED!' was a familiar refrain in classrooms up and down the land. There were also 'shinys', so called because they were, well, shiny and therefore extra special. Typically, these were reserved for the club crest.

Panini was formed by brothers Giuseppe and Benito Panini in Modena in 1961. Like most great ideas, it came to them by chance. While running a newspaper distribution office, the brothers found a collection of football stickers that a company based in Milan had been unable to sell. They bought the collection, repackaged it, charged ten lire for two stickers and eventually sold three million packets.

For the 2014 World Cup in Brazil, Panini published more than sixty-five million sticker books. Their South American base in São Paulo, printed nine million stickers PER DAY. Their Modena HQ was running off eleven million. Stickers, as it turns out, are big business.

It's a superb concept. With its sharp branding, Panini cleverly aligned itself with big tournaments and launched its first World Cup book in 1970.

By the time Spain 1982 came along, I was beginning to get into music and spent most of my money on vinyl. Big mistake. At the World Cup, with Rossi, Zico and Sócrates, the sticker book makers raised their game, debuting their improved, higher quality, shiny stickers. I still kept my hand in, reluctant to turn my back on one of the better World Cup traditions. Some of the more collectable wants from this World Cup for Scotland were Graeme Souness, Kenny Dalglish, Alan Hansen, Alan Brazil and John Robertson.

We can't mention the 1982 World Cup and not remind ourselves of a great Scottish link to the one of the most controversial games in the history of the World Cup. At the heart of it was that man again, Bob Valentine. He officiated 'The Scandal of Gijón' or what the Germans call 'Nichtangriffspakt von Gijón' the 'Non-aggression pact of Gijón' when West

Germany and Austria played out a game knowing what they needed to do for both sides to qualify. With the group's other final game, between Algeria and Chile, having taken place a day earlier, both West Germany and Austria knew that a West German win by one or two goals would see both sides qualify for the knock-out stages. What do you know, West Germany went 1–0 up after ten minutes and the two sides then played out a drab game with no further attempts on goal. It meant Austria knocked Algeria – who had beaten West Germany in their first game – out of the competition. The fiasco prompted FIFA to change the rules thereafter, making teams play their final group games simultaneously.

But back to the stickers. A completed sticker book from Mexico '70 now goes for more than five-thousand pounds. Yes, *five grand*. Even the worst World Cup – USA '94 – sells for £400. The wet World Cup from West Germany '74 and the ticker-tape World Cup from Argentina '78 now sell for around £700.

For most people, the sticker book experience begins with the best of intentions and no shortage of enthusiasm but ends when its completion becomes an almost impossible task.

Panini knew not only about the science of branding and selling but they were uniquely aware of the DNA of many of the football nations whose fans were fanatical about completing their own team first and then going all out to complete the catalogue. When you broke down the cost of the stickers and the number of boxes for each team, it revealed a genius business model. While I applaud their approach, I was also intrigued to work out the mathematics and probability to put a real cost on the completion of a Panini book.

For the 2016 European Championships, according to the *Daily Mirror*, Professor Paul Harper of Cardiff University's School of Mathematics, worked out the best and worst-case prices. He reckoned that, to fill the 680 player boxes, you would need 136 packets containing five stickers, costing £68. However, the actual 'real' price of completion meant having to buy 747 packs, costing £374.

The Panini sticker book takes pride of place in the museum, ideally with a few boxes left unfilled. Perhaps a kind benefactor will provide us with a completed copy as proof that such a thing actually exists.

Exhibit 100
The Replica Kit

Take a walk through any part of Scotland and you'll be lucky to see kids out kicking a ball. The world has changed. Kids aren't allowed out to play anymore. If you do see any of these elusive creatures, they will invariably be wearing a Barcelona strip or a Man City, Spurs or Arsenal shirt. Their iPad world is inward-looking, yet their connectivity is so much wider. Champions League, satellite TV and *Match of the Day* have given more coverage to football. The game consoles make them less of a team player. Their knowledge of the game is extensive, yet they have become more insular.

The football strip, as we know it, has been around since 'modern' football began in the 1850s. The branding and marketing of the replica kit, however, is a surprisingly recent concept. It was, in fact, Bert Patrick, the chairman of Leicester-based knitwear company Admiral, who, in 1974, saw an opportunity. He came up with the brilliant idea of producing replica team strips featuring the Admiral logo, which he had the exclusive rights to sell. Patrick paid the FA £15,000 a year for the privilege, charging a fiver for the top and nine pounds for the shorts and socks – extortionate at the time but it didn't stop them selling in their thousands. Not much has changed since.

Most fans understand it's a revenue generator for their club. Some of the world's biggest clubs sell more than two million replica shirts per year. If Bert Patrick was dealing with the FA to secure a deal for the England kit now, he would need to find in the region of £400 million, which is what Nike paid in 2016, securing the rights until 2030.

Historically, football began with public school boys or military teams and the team colours were flamboyant, usually from their schools or regiments. The kit has since come full circle. It has returned in some way to a more sensible look, more in keeping with the traditions of the club's history. However, there was a time in the 1980s when strips became flashy, garish and completely disconnected to anything the club stood for. Watching a big game at this time was like watching MTV on magic mushrooms.

There was a time when only the club badge was permitted on a top. I remember the hullaballoo when Hibs, in 1977, dared to emblazon 'Bukta', their shirt sponsors, across their chests. Bukta was the first sports manufacturer, dating back to 1879. Their major competitor was Umbro but they didn't come on the scene until 1924. After Hibs became the first side in the UK to use a sponsor across their jersey, Liverpool followed suit in 1977 and changed the way sponsorship was viewed in the English football league. Every replica shirt thereafter would also advertise the sponsor.

Now, clubs have strips like Formula 1 motor cars, with every inch treated like a place to earn cash. However, it's left to the loyal fan, the supposed lifeblood of the game, to foot the bill, shelling out for a new strip – or three – every season.

Nowadays, when clubs and manufacturers start work on a new kit, they typically try to find some kind of historic connection to reproduce. If the marketing departments at Nike, Umbro, New Balance, Under Armour or Adidas release a kit based on a strip worn in a significant game fifty years ago, fans seem even more willing to buy into it.

Most fans know the replica strip is a rip-off but they are still mysteriously willing to part with their money for one. It's tough to work out the more heinous crime – the price (close to a hundred quid for a full replica strip) or a middle-aged man with a beer belly squeezed into his team's top?

The Exit

Thank you for visiting the Alternative Football Museum. Do call again. On the way out, please see some of our gift ideas. We have the last-minute breakfast gift: The Kirk Broadfoot Exploding Egg. If you have a few thousand to spend, why not put a down-payment on a caravan from our Andy Goram Shoogily Statics range?

Do you support Dundee? Fed up with the current club's sensible fiscal direction and longing for the days when you attracted mob lawyers, war criminals and club legends like Claudio Caniggia and Fabrizio Ravanelli? Why not buy this Ravenelli replica shirt, pull it over your head and run about in celebration of his five appearances and zero league goals?

Does your boss or friend annoy you? Why not try these Simon Stainrod shoes and play 'Scottish Football Roulette': one is clean; the other contains a huge Raphael Schiedt.

Feeling creative? Thinking about learning a musical instrument? Well, why not learn on this guitar? It belongs to

Amy Maconald and, so long as it's with you, she won't be able to sing 'Flower of Scotland' before international matches at Hampden. Please, take it.

Kill time on those long winter nights by signing up to our YouTube channel and watch continual re-runs of Mark McGhee getting sent to the stand at Pittodrie before telling fans to go forth and multiply.

And don't forget your decapitated toy pigeon. This product is flying out of the shop, a fitting tribute to a bird that fell from the sky and landed on the Hampden pitch during a League Cup tie between Queens Park and St Mirren in July 2018. We contacted a student of augury – the ancient Roman study of looking at birds for omens – who claimed it was a protest at the SFA's referee appointments.

Like I say, do please call again.

ACKNOWLEDGMENTS

I'd like to thank the Scottish Football Museum at Hampden, the inspiration behind this book; Scottish football for its unparalleled and wonderful absurdity; and Peter Burns, my editor at Arena Sport.